6 Steps to Free Publicity

Marcia Yudkin

CAREER
PRESS
THE CAREER PRESS, INC.
Franklin Lakes, NJ

6 STEPS TO FREE PUBLICITY, THIRD EDITION
EDITED BY KATE HENCHES
TYPESET BY MICHAEL FITZGIBBON
Cover design by The DesignWorks Group
Printed in the U.S.A. by Book-mart Press

To order this title, please call toll-free 1-800-CAREER-1 (NJ and Canada: 201-848-0310) to order using VISA or MasterCard, or for further information on books from Career Press.

CAREER
PRESS

The Career Press, Inc., 3 Tice Road, PO Box 687,
Franklin Lakes, NJ 07417
www.careerpress.com

Library of Congress Cataloging-in-Publication Data

Yudkin, Marcia
    6 steps to free publicity / by Marcia Yudkin. —3rd ed.
        p. cm.
    Includes index.
    ISBN 978-1-60163-027-8
    1. Industrial publicity. 2. Press releases. 3. Small business—Public relations. 4. Small business—Management. I. Title. II. Title: Six steps to free publicity.

    HD59.Y83 2009
    659--dc22
                                                                2008027707

In memory of my mother, Florence Yudkin,
the best press agent a daughter could have.

Acknowledgments

Most of all, I'd like to thank the editors of *Bottom Line/Personal*, who printed an offer for the four-page version of *6 Steps to Free Publicity* that lay the groundwork for this book. Special thanks as well to Deb Brody, Diana Finch, Mike Lewis, and Marilyn Allen for their midwifing of the book; my sister JJ for ongoing legal advice; my sister Gila for helpful feedback on the first edition; and Anne Zononi for her help in shooting and editing my YouTube video. Thanks especially to all my interviewees for graciously sharing their stories.

Contents

PART IV: POLISHING YOUR PUBLICITY SKILLS

PART V: KEEPING THE PUBLICITY MOMENTUM GOING

Introduction to the Third Edition

Much has changed since the first edition of this book appeared in 1994. The Internet, which then consisted primarily of e-mail, was still the province of techies, college professors, and adventurous businesspeople. Although I had an e-mail account from a teaching position I had recently quit, I was not yet online in any serious or concerted fashion. At the last minute, Deb Brody, my editor at Plume/ Penguin, asked me to include something about online publicity and gave me the name of one of her other authors to interview. That discussion piqued my curiosity about promotional opportunities online, and very soon after I handed in the final manuscript of the first edition of *6 Steps to Free Publicity*, I dove into using the Internet for self-promotion.

What a fun immersion those early days were! Most people online then had accounts with America Online, CompuServe, or Prodigy. Only the truly intrepid or technologically adept ventured out to the Internet at large. Any business use of the fast-developing worldwide computer network was controversial and limited in effect, because the vast majority of anyone's market had not yet gone online. The lightning-fast spread of the World Wide Web and the explosion in popularity of e-mail accounts soon brought into being countless exciting new opportunities for promotion.

This front-to-back revision of *6 Steps to Free Publicity* takes into account everything I have learned since those pioneering years about using e-mail and the Web to earn media coverage, along with the time-tested, still-valid foundations of how to interest media gatekeepers in a story and capitalize on publicity opportunities to the fullest. It also includes the new publicity opportunities inherent in blogs, social media sites, online videos, podcasts, widgets, and more, as well as the increased visibility you can get on the Internet by optimizing your content for search engines.

Much has not changed a whit since the 1990s. You still need to come up with a snazzy, timely angle and understand the quirks of each major medium—newspapers or magazines, radio, TV, or the Web. Creativity and clarity still win attention, hands down, over routine, vague, or jargon-filled pitches, whether you're aiming at media gatekeepers or hoping to reach your target market directly online.

A few trends are worth noting. First, the public's appetite for interesting, relevant news continues unabated. Fast-breaking stories, though, move through the news cycle faster than ever before. This means that if you want to take advantage of what the media is talking about right now and tomorrow, you must get yourself in gear right away.

Second, be prepared for more skepticism than in the past about your bona fides. Because of several well-publicized PR hoaxes, you may be asked for more credentials and proof of claims in your releases when reporters get in touch than before.

Third, don't give in to the temptation to think that, because posting things online or sending messages by e-mail feels easy, cheap, and fast, those are always the logical or best ways to get out the word about you or your organization. In 2007, executive coach Jim Jenkins of Creative Visions Solutions in Frederick, Maryland, told me, "The Fortune 500 CEOs and top executives I am trying to reach do not search online much. Often they rely on print magazines, which they read on airplanes, to find consultants. When they read something in a magazine they trust that indicates a fit with their company's needs, they make it a point to get in touch." Accordingly, Jenkins made publishing articles in print magazines—not blogging or some other kind of online communication—a cornerstone of his publicity strategy.

Finally, although news releases rain on editors and producers as profusely as ever, realize that your competitors are not necessarily on the ball in this regard. I was surprised, while preparing this third edition, by how many friends of mine who had received extraordinary media coverage confessed that they haven't taken full advantage of the power of publicity in recent years.

As before, I'm eager to learn about your successes using the techniques you learned here. You might well end up in the fourth edition of the book!

Marcia Yudkin
Creative Ways
P.O. Box 305
Goshen, MA 01032
marcia@yudkin.com
www.yudkin.com or *www.pressreleasehelp.com*

Note: Unless otherwise indicated, all interviewee quotes in the book come from personal interviews with the author.

PART I

GETTING STARTED
WITH PUBLICITY

Chapter 1

Riches...Credibility...Prestige...Opportunity— What Publicity Can Do for You

On September 13, 1990, I settled into a middle seat onboard a USAir flight to San Francisco, trying to keep my excited glow from irking half-awake fellow passengers. A silver-haired woman arranged pillows on the aisle seat and started a conversation. Her third question punctured my restraint.

"I'm a writer and a writing consultant," I replied, and nodded toward a flight attendant who was passing out newspapers. "My partner and I have a company called WordRight. We're in *The Wall Street Journal* today."

She tilted her head sideways. Her eyes widened.

"Page one," I added, allowing myself a grin.

We got up to let by a well-scrubbed man who took off his shoes and introduced himself as a congressman from San Diego. As if to match that, my new acquaintance jerked a thumb at me. "This lady here is in today's *Wall Street Journal.*"

At his look of respect, a little more pride seeped into my smile, and, after our seatmate had closed her eyes, I traded stories and experiences with the congressman for most of the flight.

But media publicity can do a lot more for you than feed your ego and enable you to impress strangers on airplanes.

Publicity can sell your products or services without the burdensome expense of advertising. The makers of the game Trivial Pursuit had no advertising budget. Instead, by sending sample games or just the cards to game-industry buyers, celebrities who were mentioned in the game, and disk jockeys, they created a stir the media had to keep reporting. Consequently, sales reached $1.5 million the year the game was introduced. Around the same time, *The Wall Street Journal* ran a feature article about the "streetfighter marketing" ideas of Jeff Slutsky, who ran a one-man consulting business out of his home. "The day the article came out, my phone started ringing at 6 a.m.," he recalls. "It literally didn't stop until 10 p.m., and I got a steady flow of calls from that article for three years." Slutsky's free publicity translated into $50,000 of product sales in the first 90 days—"and big clients," he adds.

Publicity helps you rise above your competition. The more media appearances you rack up, the more *your* name comes to mind when people think "pediatrician" or "dating for nerds." The effect keeps building on itself in a three-stage cycle: You earn publicity by setting yourself apart from the competition; then it gives you a higher profile; then, feeling better about yourself, you easily make yourself still more visible. "It's a terrific confidence booster," says Steve Schiffman, a New York City sales trainer whose decades of publicity add up to his getting recognized on the street. "You develop poise and learn how to handle difficult questions. If you do radio and TV regularly, you can cope with anything."

Publicity bestows on you lucrative credibility. Media appearances greatly boost the perceived value of whatever you offer the public. When Boston actor Norman George sends out a full-page feature story from *People* magazine about him playing Edgar Allan Poe, theaters and cultural organizations take him seriously. Linda Barbanel, a New York City therapist who specializes in the psychology of money, says that the cumulative effect of 600-plus-and-rising media appearances was a quadrupling of her speaking fees.

Publicity can create profitable, unexpected opportunities. A question-and-answer feature about my work on creativity in the Sunday *Boston Globe* business section prompted Horizon Media in nearby Quincy to call and ask if I would be interested in collaborating on videos about creativity. "Yes!" I said to this proposal that I would not have thought up on my own. We worked on three training videos together and a pilot for a public TV series. Half a year after the *Globe* piece, a six-line notice that cost me nothing in the newsletter *Bottom Line/Personal* led to my contract for this book. (More about this later.)

Publicity can crown you as an expert. After Debbi Karpowicz promoted her humor book, *I Love Men in Tasseled Loafers*, on TV and radio stations, she was invited back as a dating expert. Because, as she puts it, her book chronicles dating disasters from the standpoint of a woman who loves shoes, the media also treated her as an expert on footwear. Similarly, when Claire McCarthy, a communication consultant in North Andover, Massachusetts, promoted a workshop she was offering called "How to Write a Love Letter," the *Lawrence Eagle Tribune* ran a three-quarters-of-a-page profile of her, and she received two write-ups in the *Boston Herald*. Even though the workshop never received enough registrants to run, the coverage prompted *North Shore Magazine* to interview McCarthy as a romance expert.

Publicity can give potential clients a long, close look at you. Merle Bombardieri, a clinical social worker in Lexington, Massachusetts, knows that her TV appearances have prompted people who needed counseling to call her. "Sometimes they had already heard of me, but people find it difficult to open their hearts to a perfect stranger," Bombardieri says. "They're afraid that a therapist might be judgmental or arrogant. But when they see someone on TV they get a sense of that person's personality and style. Several people who saw me on TV said that I seemed like an intelligent, approachable person with a sense of humor, and that made it much easier for them to call."

Publicity often rallies public support to your cause. Roughly 5,000 print articles and countless radio and TV stories contributed to 1 million people participating in the first annual Take Our Daughters to Work Day in 1993. Hundreds of millions more became aware of its goal of increasing the self-esteem and career awareness of adolescent girls. In 2003 and 2004, studies reported steep declines in women's use of hormone replacement therapy following negative findings on HRT discussed in more than 400 newspaper stories and 2,500 TV or radio stories. "It is hard to imagine another mechanism besides media influence that would explain how the message got out so quickly," two medical commentators wrote in the *Annals of Internal Medicine*. Quite likely, this publicity saved lives.

Publicity for good works earns you community good will. For 15 years after founding The Body Shop, Anita Roddick abstained from any advertising for her natural cosmetics. Instead she attracted mounds of media attention because of her environmental and social activism. One project of hers, "Trade, Not Aid," helped native cultures around the world to prosper by growing ingredients for her cosmetics. Roddick also organized a campaign to refurbish Romanian orphanages, and another for voter registration. At one point, The Body Shop estimated that it was receiving about $3.5 million worth of free publicity a year. People who admired the company's passionate stands "understand that purchases support a good cause," observed *Working Woman*, "and as a result are more likely to buy."

Publicity has the power to counteract stereotypes. When I visited Taos Pueblo in the early 1990s, I noticed and read a newspaper clipping framed on a shop wall about a Pueblo man making language videos for the tribe's young people. "Is this you?" I asked the shopkeeper, a silversmith. "My brother," he said. The conversation started by that clipping, during which I learned that the silversmith had studied dentistry at Harvard, opened my eyes about the sort of people who would choose to live and work in a traditional Native American setting. Similarly, articles in the Boston media about Empire Loan, a pawnshop, relieved me of the notion that only seedy, unshaven characters, thieves, and heiresses who had overspent their trust fund frequented pawnshops.

Publicity gets your message across in a seemingly objective manner. *Wall Street Journal* executive editor Frederick Taylor once admitted that as much as 90 percent of its daily news originates in self-interested news releases. Yet when the public reads what reporters have done with that information, it tends to trust and respect, as rarely happens with advertising. Breakthrough Software Corporation received dramatic proof of this credibility difference when it spent $6,000 to advertise one of its programs and received 100 responses. A free, favorable magazine review of the same program, however, generated 900 responses. The most influential media mentions, such as on the front page of the newspaper, aren't available at any price.

Publicity may make you eligible for professional recognition.
To earn the designation "Professional Member" in the Association of
Image Consultants International, among many other requirements,
you have to have received media publicity. In the classical music world,
organizations that award grants to community music groups take local
media coverage as an important sign of community impact and interest. Not only do the grants bestow prestige, but they also often spell
the difference between financial survival and failure. For scientists
and medical researchers, media coverage leads to more citations by
other scientists, sometimes used as a measure of influence in decisions on hiring and promotion. A 1991 study revealed that research
covered in *The New York Times* received 73 percent more scholarly citations the next year than research reported only in the *New England
Journal of Medicine.*

Publicity can greatly broaden your audience. A new biography of
Abraham Lincoln normally would have interest mainly for a limited
circle of historians and history buffs. However, Michael Burlingame, a
history professor at Connecticut College, sent a copy of his biography
of our Civil War president to a reporter in Springfield, Illinois, who
had been helpful to him. The reporter wrote a story about the book
that went out on the AP newswire and ended up not only in dozens of
newspapers across the country, but also in David Letterman's nightly
humorous take on current affairs.

Publicity increases traffic to your Website. The traffic boost occurs at four levels. First, even if the media doesn't include a direct
link to your Website or mention its address, people who read about
you will often search for you and end up at your Website through a
roundabout means. Second, when articles posted online include a
link to your site, readers click through, learn lots more about you, and
may wind up becoming customers, donors, or clients. Third, when
the media or others link to your site as part of or a result of your
publicity, the probability of your site coming up in a later Internet
search increases. And fourth, even if no media outlets pick up your
story, when your news announcement goes out online through
newsfeeds and news sites, interested people often find and read your
announcement or visit your site because the news release itself lifts
your profile in the search engines.

Publicity can provide the occasion for outrageous fun. Providence, Rhode Island entertainer Ron Bianco recalls sitting in his kitchen laughing out loud while he was planning a campaign to run his dog Bilbo, who was part of his folk-singing act, for president. In East Windsor, Connecticut, John Collins found a way to attract attention and have a blast with his otherwise unremarkable fledgling business of recycling toner cartridges from laser printers. A tongue-in-cheek article in his local paper, the *Journal Inquirer,* carried the headline, "It's a bird, it's a plane...no, it's Toner Man!" and showed him in a Superman-like costume. An employee said Collins's appearances as Toner Man helped relieve stress on the job.

❖❖ ❖❖

In today's economic climate, shooting for free media coverage makes especially good sense. Rochester, New York consultant and author Harvey Kaye says that 40 years ago, engineers were such a small percentage of the population that people who needed their services sought them out. His father, a professor at MIT, never had to do any marketing. Today, however, so many technical experts crowd the market that if they don't promote themselves, he says, it's career suicide. The same goes for therapists, restaurant owners, Web designers, hairdressers, accountants, and most others in business for themselves. The old saying, "Build a better mousetrap and the world will beat a path to your door," is not true today, if it ever was. People first need to know about your door from advertising or its cheaper and more credible alternative, publicity.

Publicity costs you nothing but time and energy, and, sometimes, money for distribution. Even better, you don't need a degree in public relations to receive the benefits enumerated in this chapter. *6 Steps to Free Publicity* takes you step by step through the process, including finding a hook that snags the interest of the media, writing or calling them, doing your best to ensure that your message gets through to the appropriate audience, and cementing relationships that enhance your opportunities for repeated media exposure, along with techniques that directly spread your message online to millions. In the coming chapters you learn:

- ❖ How to strategize about the appropriate goals, focus, and target audience for your publicity efforts.

- ❖ Why publicity doesn't necessarily involve hype and how to find the method of gaining publicity that feels most comfortable for you.

- ❖ How to write, format, and send a news release that has the best chance of resulting in media coverage.

- ❖ Other ways to attract the interest of the media, such as making a phone pitch, writing letters to reporters and editors, and staging unique events.

- ❖ How to spread word of mouth by neatly encapsulating your message, getting friendly with the media, and being memorable.

- ❖ The dos and don'ts of dealing with reporters, producers, bloggers, and other media folks.

- ❖ How to perform on radio, TV, video, or the Web like a pro.

- ❖ Ways to come up with creative publicity approaches and carve out the time to execute them.

- ❖ How to go beyond what Andy Warhol called everyone's "15 minutes of fame" to a lasting media presence for you, your business, or your cause.

Throughout the book you encounter examples of real people who used the methods I describe to get their word out. I've concentrated on low-cost, high-impact strategies that most reasonably motivated, ordinary mortals might be able to pull off. Don't worry if you sometimes have the reaction, while reading of other people's exploits, that "I could never do *that.*" I've included enough different approaches that you're bound to discover some that feel right for you. And because no one emerges from the womb knowing how to land media coverage, you get nitty-gritty advice for each aspect of the process.

Although publicity can launch you toward fame, influence, and fortune, it does not offer a magic carpet ride for everyone, every time. Its uncontrollability can be a problem, but also an advantage. I couldn't have known the afternoon I mailed hundreds of news releases about a catchy new business service that the Gulf War would break out overnight and drive all otherwise newsworthy stories out of reporters' minds. On the other hand, who would have guessed that a simple letter and sample copy of a newsletter would have led to a piece in the *Maine Sunday Telegram* about *The Tightwad Gazette*, through that to an article in *Parade*, and through that to a contract for a book by the same title that reached national best-seller lists?

Publicity-seeking might be called an adventure except that, unlike hunting elephants, it holds few dangers. Rarely does publicity backfire, and rarely does a series of intelligently conceived, knowledgeably executed publicity campaigns totally fail. And you won't have to practice for years before you reap rewards. By following the guidelines in this book, Barry Murray of Hallandale, Florida, wrangled his first TV interview, his second, and all the way up to his 500th and beyond, not to mention being promoted to marketing director of the company for which he worked, Truly Nolen Pest Control. So, let's get started now with the questions and perspectives that can get you thinking like a publicity hound.

Chapter 2

Thinking Like a Publicity Hound

Suppose you're opening a new branch of your hardware store in Cactus Junction, Texas, population 2,500, 158 miles southwest of Dallas. Cash flow is one-way so far, and you've heard that publicity is the low-cost alternative to advertising, so you contact every newspaper in Texas with your announcement, printed up in classy italic type at your local print shop. For good measure you throw in all the NBC, ABC, and CBS affiliate stations from El Paso to Texarkana, and National Public Radio in Austin.

For a prosaic local store opening, does that sound to you like a wise expenditure of effort? Because I deliberately chose an extreme example, you're probably shaking your head.

Effective publicity involves a match between your goals and the needs of the media. Without considering what you hope to achieve from publicity, you're unlikely to receive an optimal outcome. And, unless you take into account what the media wants to cover, you might as well have addressed your materials to a black hole. For the best outcome, begin your quest for publicity with a frank, dispassionate assessment of the results from which you would most benefit.

GETTING CLEAR ON YOUR GOALS

Use the following checklist to zero in on your specific needs and wants.

1. Which of the following do you want most: credibility and prestige; customers, clients, donors, or attendees; or changed or opened minds? It's alright to want it all, but the long-range aim of establishing your reputation as a trombone player may require you to target different media outlets and choose different tactics than the short-term goal of selling out the hall at your recital next month. A campaign to enhance your musical reputation can be sporadic and diffuse, as can a crusade to change the image of the trombone, but a push to sell tickets must reach the concert-going audience in the appropriate time and place with accurate information about the performance. Articulating your priorities lays a solid foundation for any successful publicity venture.

2. Where, geographically, does it make sense for you to aim: nationally, regionally, or locally? If you're opening a new hardware store, you need to recognize that few people will drive hundreds of miles, or even a dozen miles, to buy nails if alternatives exist. If your operation included a nails-by-mail program, on the other hand, regional and national publicity could yield customers. Don't let the glamour and glitter of famous media outlets and huge audiences blind you to your need to focus on where your prospects live—in this case, right in and around Cactus Junction.

3. Who, specifically, are you hoping to reach? A consultant friend of mine hired a public relations firm to get her media exposure. After some months they announced that they'd booked her on a national TV talk show. Instead of whooping for joy, my friend asked when the show ran. Because the show aired in the afternoon, she declined the opportunity. Her target audience was corporate executives, and how many of them watch the tube in the daytime? Once you know that you're trying to get your story to, say, sofa manufacturers east of the Mississippi, men who are self-conscious about going bald, or potential fur buyers with a social conscience, you can concentrate on the media outlets they read, listen to, and watch.

4. Are you hoping to sell a particular product? If so, then persuading, cajoling, and even begging the media to include contact information (your postal address, phone number, and/or Web address) is crucial. According to Cambridge, Massachusetts publisher Jeffrey Lant, most entrepreneurs greatly overestimate the willingness of consumers to go to a lot of trouble to order something. If getting in touch with you requires anything more complicated than the top entries in a Google search or a call to directory assistance, most people won't bother. Having her Website address listed in *American Way* magazine as the place to buy a copy of her booklet, "39 Secrets for Effective and Enjoyable Meetings," meant the difference between a nice ego boost and more than 1,000 orders at $6 each for professional meeting facilitator Peg Kelley.

Not everyone agrees with this reasoning, however. Greg Godek, who self-published *1001 Ways to Be Romantic* and *1001 More Ways to Be Romantic* under the imprint of Casablanca Press, says his main concern during media appearances is to build up his image as "America's Number-One Romantic." Godek believes that implanting that image in the public's mind results in more sales in the long run than would a short-term fixation on selling a certain number of books each time he goes on the air or shows up in print. Whether or not he's right, as part of your strategizing you ought to ask yourself how much maintaining a certain image matters to you. Your answer should affect your thinking on my next question as well.

5. Will you welcome any and all publicity opportunities, or will you want to pick and choose among opportunities to maintain a certain image and focus? Because of his image-building strategy, Greg Godek found himself in the unusual position of persuading a producer of the Oprah Winfrey show not to book him. When Oprah's producer invited him to appear on a show about sex, Godek carefully explained that anything he would have to say would come from the slant of romance, and, after a long discussion, the producer agreed that he was not right for that show. "I could tell she was impressed," Godek says, "because most people would do anything to get on Oprah. That puts me in a better position to get on when the topic is right for me. I'm convinced that if people don't see you as you really are, it won't help you."

Likewise, Tony Putman, a marketing consultant in Ann Arbor, Michigan, shies away from newspaper publicity because he's afraid they'll mistakenly position him as an advertising guru. "That would be damaging to my public image," says Putman, who, in fact, stresses other means of marketing besides advertising, for service businesses. Although I think there's much you can do to ensure that reporters get your point (see Chapter 14), I agree that it's a good idea to consider whether some media might be irrelevant to or inconsistent with your goals. For example, because my market tends to be better-educated people and I offer serious professional services and products, I wouldn't get excited about a chance to appear in the *National Enquirer* or on the *Jerry Springer Show*.

6. Do you have reason to lean more toward one medium than another? The tangibility and relative permanence of print make it ideal for many publicity-seekers, but if you were, say, a comic entertainer, your preferences might run in this way: most helpful, TV; next, radio; next, a widely read "what's up in entertainment" blog; next, a newspaper or magazine article with a photo; least helpful, an article without a photo. Or if you're a high-energy, high-personal-impact salesman, you might feel that the hotter electronic media capture your essence best.

THE KEY THAT UNLOCKS MEDIA DOORS

Once you settle your priorities, you can turn to the other half of the match that produces effective publicity: namely, what interests the media. Here the crux is understanding the fundamental question in the mind of any editor, reporter, or producer: Why would our readers (or listeners or viewers) be interested in this story now?

This fundamental question breaks down into three parts. If you present your case to the media in a way that speaks to all three concerns, you come as close to guaranteed coverage as any law-abiding citizen can. First comes "our readers/listeners/viewers." Every media outlet from *Business Week* or *CBS This Morning* to *Ski Area Management* or *The New Age News Hour* has an audience profile and an editorial mission that determine what does and doesn't fall within its scope of coverage. If the audience to which your media pitch appeals resembles the audience of that outlet, then so far so good. You meet this requirement partly by choosing your target media intelligently and partly by being explicit about what connects you or your business or organization with a particular audience. Send something to *Ski Area Management* headlined "Health Professionals Offer Free Seminars" and they'll toss your materials out, but change the headline to "Ski Resorts to Host Free, Entertaining Seminars on Preventive Back Care Courtesy of Vermont Chiropractor Group," and they pay close attention.

Second comes "this story." Yours had better be a short, focused story, not an endless saga. Stick to one main point each time you approach the media. Instead of saying, "Your readers might want to know how I rose from poverty, conquered cancer, recently sold my shoe repair shop, and patented an automatic bird feeder," talk about how you got off welfare while raising seven kids alone *or* how you recovered from your doctors' death sentence through experimental surgery *or* how you sold Sole Mate to an Italian chain *or* how your new device makes bird seed accessible to bluebirds but not blue jays and black bears. If you've got so much claim on public attention, spread out your stories over several campaigns.

Journalists call your choice of focus the "hook" or the "angle" of a story, and it does the job insofar as it addresses the third and paramount concern of media people: "now." What makes your story timely? Or how can you inject timeliness into your story? You can give yourself a crash course on newsworthiness by reading newspaper features or listening carefully to nonlead news items, asking yourself what makes each story relevant now. As America braced for the release of the film *Jurassic Park*, for instance, both National Public Radio and ABC News aired reports about a man named Donald Bean, who had created a theme park in Moscow, Texas, called Dinosaur Gardens. Bean had opened the park years before without any media taking notice, but the impending arrival of a blockbuster film on dinosaurs had elevated anything to do with dinosaurs to public relevance.

Devoting careful thought to the element of timeliness makes your publicity efforts pay off. In many cases, it's worth inventing a sideline service, event, or unusual characterization of what you do to entice the media to spread the word about you. To generate ideas, use the following checklist of ways to provide a compelling "now" for editors and producers.

10 Ways to Be Timely

1. What is new about your business or organization?

What's new might include anything from just opening shop to promoting someone within your organization. Consider any or all of the following "what's new" items as excuses for getting into print:

✦   Just opening. Kristopher Setchfield's attempt to launch a massage therapy practice in Northampton, Massachusetts, earned him two color photos and several paragraphs of ink in the context of a story about the training program at nearby Greenfield Community College from which he'd recently graduated. Cathryn Peters got five newspapers and one TV station to cover the fact that, after 26 years, she was closing down the only wicker repair business within driving distance of Zumbro Falls, Minnesota.

✦   Posting record quarterly profits, receiving a grant, capturing a more favorable market share, lowering prices, surpassing previous years' donations, hiring or promoting people, giving recognition awards, renaming the company, and/or relocating and other organizational news—these kinds of notices regularly run in business papers such as *The Wall Street Journal, Investor's Daily,* or *Business First of Louisville.*

✦   Offering new services or programs, or serving new areas or populations often sparks full-length feature stories. Here "new" also includes "been doing it for a while, but no one knows about it yet." For instance, a participant at one of my seminars was a patent agent who ran a class on patenting an invention for inmates at a state prison in Massachusetts. She wasn't certain she wanted this publicized, but I told her that any half-awake reporter would jump to do a story on her class.

✦   Releasing new products or new versions of products. Trade and special-interest consumer magazines usually have a section in the front of every issue where they highlight new products and services relevant to their readers. Using the headline "New 100-Percent

Natural Product Increases Plant Growth by Up to 300 Percent," entrepreneur Sue Valentine got nice placement in the new products column of *The Growing Edge* magazine for her Bountiful Garden formulation.

Contacting appropriate media three or four times a year with these kinds of announcements would not be too much. *The Wall Street Journal* isn't alone in relying on unsolicited information. Hometown newspapers and trade magazines couldn't fill their pages without receiving seemingly mundane notices from people like you. You get best results by combining this strategy with one of those that follow, but remember: If you don't tell the media what you're doing, who will?

2. WHAT IS DIFFERENT OR DISTINCTIVE ABOUT YOUR BUSINESS OR ORGANIZATION?

If your dry-cleaning establishment is Tibetan-owned and operated, that's news. If you use your PhD in sociology to study home cleanliness while you clean houses, that's news. If your counseling service specializes in helping people who get bad news from genetic screening tests, that's certainly media-worthy.

Kim Merritt of Cumberland, Maryland, was only 16 years old, though an experienced chocolate-maker, when she took on the project of producing 18,000 candy bars for her high school's annual fundraising drive. For fun, she wrote to editors at more than a dozen magazines she was familiar with, about what she was doing, such as *Teen*, *Cosmopolitan*, and *Good Housekeeping*. Both *People* and *Ms.* magazines bit, and the national publicity that continued to come her way for years helped her specialty chocolate business, Kim's Khocolate, thrive. When Merritt was 25 years old, she was still using her age as a hook. "Even when I'm 80, the story of how I got started will interest people," she laughs.

Here is where thinking like a publicity hound gives you the chance to set yourself apart from the competition and turn a ho-hum product or service into something newsworthy. Because my partner and I at WordRight knew that the editing services we offered had little publicity value, we added an extra attraction (overnight editing by fax), concocted a name (WordRight Express Editing), and started a promotional blitz. The material I wrote, headlined "New National Overnight Editing Service," not only earned us press from Massachusetts to Alaska, but it also caught the eye of business guru Tom Peters, who quoted from it and discussed it in his book, *Liberation Management.*

Some years later, I produced an audiotape on procrastination and then decided that the audiotape format had zero publicity potential. By mulling over what might be an innovative format, I invented what I called a "postcard seminar"—participants received 10 weekly oversized postcards, each containing food for thought and a brief exercise adapted from the audiotape. So far as I know, I was the first to deliver transformational material on a series of postcards—and that got me feature coverage in the *Chicago Tribune*, the *Los Angeles Daily News*, the *Tampa Tribune*, *Entrepreneur*, and dozens of other publications.

3. Do you have an event you could create or publicize?

As you'll learn in Chapter 10, occasions that tempt the media to cover you can be quite creative and require a lot of work to organize and pull off. However, events can also be as simple as giving away free samples Saturday from noon to 2 p.m. on Main Street, holding auditions for your company's Talent Show of the Century, or presenting a lecture at the public library. For the media, events transform business as usual into something that can be announced, witnessed, and reported on at a specific time and place. Remember that the more colorful or visual your event, the more you'll be able to draw photographers and TV cameras.

4. Can you make your products or expertise relevant by piggybacking on current news?

A smart career counselor in search of clients would keep one eye peeled for any change in unemployment statistics. If more people were finding jobs, the up-to-the-minute hook would be "How Not to

Be Left Behind in the Current Rehiring," whereas if joblessness stayed the same or worsened, the timely pitch might be "Micro-Targeted Resumes Win Jobs Despite Hiring Lull."

The connection can be much more distant or unexpected. When a hurricane devastates Louisiana, an insurance agent in Oregon can release a set of tips on how to make sure you're covered in case of a disaster. A systems integrator told me that poor IT management was a factor in the disastrous downfall of Enron Corporation—a perfect angle to publicize his expertise. A restaurant might use newly released statistics about an epidemic of high cholesterol levels as an occasion to tout its heart-healthy menus.

Some of the best opportunities exist when an event, such as a natural disaster or an economic problem, lingers on the front pages. Reporters become desperate for a fresh and sometimes oblique angle on the story. When the El Niño weather pattern lasted for ages, wreaking havoc in many areas of the United States, Barry Murray tied that into an expected increase in the prevalence of termites to publicize his company, Truly Nolen Pest Control. As the foreclosure crisis chugged along nonstop in 2008, National Public Radio interviewed certified financial planner Steven Rosenberg on whether homeowners in trouble should ever raid their 401(k) retirement accounts, while Illinois lawyer Josepth P. McCaggery announced a poll in his blog to determine whether the increase in foreclosures was causing more couples to divorce. Experienced publicity hounds are constantly sniffing out opportunities to tie what they do to the news.

5. HAVE YOU DONE OR COULD YOU DO SOME RESEARCH TO MERIT PRESS COVERAGE?

The American Association of University Women has landed on the front pages and in national news broadcasts numerous times by commissioning formal studies on the barriers girls and women experience in schools and colleges. Its findings reached millions more through humorous treatments in more than a dozen comic strips, including *Nancy*, *Peanuts*, and *Doonesbury*.

Yet you can receive media attention for informal polls or surveys that wouldn't meet scientific standards. Alan Weiss, president of Summit Consulting Group, Inc., in East Greenwich, Rhode Island, distributed brief questionnaires to newspaper employees about whether they felt underpaid and whether management was honest with them. The results appeared in *Editor and Publisher,* where key prospects for his consulting services read the story. You could simply ask for a show of hands while speaking at your Rotary Club and write up the tally as "Local Executives Reveal Their Biggest Daily Annoyance: Interrupters," and lead into advice from your booklets on time management.

6. Could you sponsor an interesting contest or award?

Any contest gives you two excuses for publicity: one to announce the contest and the other to reveal the winners. Try to make it more creative than a raffle. Pauline Bartel of Waterford, New York, launched a "*Gone With the Wind* Trivia Contest" at a nearby bookstore to promote her book, *The Complete Gone With the Wind Trivia Book.* When the contest was long over, she wrote about her experience in the *Freelance Writer's Report,* where I read about it.

Joe Killoran, who published a newsletter called *The Frugal Bugle* for Canadian tightwads, issued a public challenge to haggle a copy of the book *The Tightwad Gazette* from a bookseller for far less than list price. Another time he dared readers to come up with a way to buy postal stamps at a discount. In Canada, that's possible, and the contest earned him publicity in *The Financial Post.*

To give an award, you don't have to deal with entries; you can just select and announce a recipient. For years, Senator William Proxmire of Wisconsin made media hay out of his Golden Fleece Award, bestowed on a project that flagrantly (to his mind at least) wasted taxpayer money. Gary Blake of the Communication Workshop in New York City made up something called the Percy Award, named after the pompous phrase that clutters too many letters, "pursuant to your request." His comments on the worst examples of poor writing he could find appeared on radio stations and in newspapers across the country, including *USA Today.* "They helped my image as a crusader for good writing," he says.

7. Is there a holiday or anniversary you could hook onto?

Sure, you know about Father's Day and National Secretaries Week, but what about Humpback Whale Awareness Month? Carpet Care Improvement Week? National Cheer Up the Lonely Day? Made in America Month? The bible of special days, weeks, and months is a work called *Chase's Calendar of Events,* available in most public libraries. Until I took a close look at it, I didn't realize that many of its entries were sponsored—that is, invented—by individuals, companies, and organizations. For example, National Bathroom Reading Week originated with Red-Letter Press, which publishes 21 different books especially designed for bathroom reading. Relationship Renewal Day came into existence when therapist Peter Rosenzweig thought it up as a way to plug his book, *Married and Alone: The Way Back.*

All you need to do to get your catchy creation included in *Chase's* is to submit your information according to the instructions at the back of the volume. Even if you do no other promotion, you could still be deluged with media inquiries from around the world, says Ruth Roy, a sponsor of Stay Home Because You're Well Day.

Just a half hour with *Chase's* should spark plenty of ideas for taking advantage of existing occasions. Mental health and alcohol counselor Szifra Birke of Chelmsford, Massachusetts, organized and promoted a kids' poster contest for National Children of Alcoholics Week. The contest was covered three times by the *Lowell Sun,* as well as in the *Boston Globe* and two other area newspapers. One of my writing students brought to class a clipping from the *Globe* that started off, "Today is Tuesday of National Get Organized Week," and listed tips from Barbara Hemphill, a board member of the National Association of Professional Organizers.

Of course, don't overlook traditional holidays or well-known anniversaries. Many publications and shows eagerly embrace novel story

ideas in connection with, say, Veteran's Day or Martin Luther King
Day. If you provide legal advice for ex-servicepeople or founded a
racial harmony community program, those are the times to let the
media know. Greg Godek, author of the *1001 Ways to Be Romantic*
books, concentrates so intensely on publicity as the clock ticks down
to February 14 that on Valentine's Day he's giving interviews for practically 24 hours straight. Communication consultant Laurie Schloff
remembers that in 1964, she and her 13-year-old friends received
coverage in the *Elizabeth Daily Record* in New Jersey for their celebration of the first anniversary of the Beatles' arrival in America.

8. Is there a trend in the general population or some particular population to which your offerings can relate?

Here you borrow timeliness from general currents that drift through
society rather than from the headlines. According to Kim Merritt,
in the mid-1980s entrepreneurship was such a hot topic that the
Association of Collegiate Entrepreneurs was getting two to three unsolicited calls from the press every day. In the 1990s, "cocooning"
(staying home for entertainment), thriftiness, environmental awareness, and embarking on one's fourth career became trends that provided publicity opportunities for many people. In the 2000s,
publicity-seekers took advantage of trends such as tattooing and or-
ganic farming going mainstream, elders continuing to work at older
and older ages, and the growing concerns about the privacy of personal data.

9. Can you suggest a surprising twist on received opinion?

Actor Jim Cooke faced a challenge when he began to portray
Calvin Coolidge in a one-man show. "No one is out there holding a
meeting saying, 'Let's bring Calvin Coolidge in,'" he says. Because the
stereotype of "Silent Cal" is that he said nothing, Cooke drummed up
media interest by demonstrating that Coolidge had a sense of humor,
held more press conferences than any other president, and was one
of the last presidents who wrote his own speeches. "He's also the only
President with Native American blood, which interests people now,"

Cooke says. Another twist: the organization Murder Victim Families for Reconciliation, is inherently newsworthy because most people expect that the families of murder victims would be especially gung-ho for the death penalty.

10. Can you provide a pretext for a light, witty report?

Humor is always in demand. Dan Poynter, author of *The Self-Publishing Manual*, sent a tongue-in-cheek flyer to the media about what might otherwise have been just another seminar. After the headline "Boot Camp For Publishers," it ran for just eight sentences, beginning with, "If you've got the right stuff, Dan Poynter wants you for two days of training so rigorous you'll think you've joined the Marines! Join publishers from all over North America for this number-one, high-intensity, combat marketing drill.... Class space is limited to the first 18 recruits." *Publishers Weekly* and numerous other magazines picked up the story.

→→ ←←

As you may have gathered, you can lure the media with an angle that is not your central purpose or feature. If you have trouble figuring out what might interest masses of strangers about you or your business, ask a friend or colleague to help you answer that question. Fresh from her success in promoting *I Love Men in Tasseled Loafers*, Debbi Karpowicz helped her hairdresser get started in PR by getting him talking, and learning that he used coffee to get rid of red highlights in hair. Karpowicz sent out sample packets of coffee stapled to a news release that started off, "Discover How to Perk Up Your Hair With Coffee," and the hairdresser received a call from *Allure* a week later. Her hairdresser wasn't running a coffee-treatment salon, but being mentioned in a national fashion magazine stamped him as a somebody and lent him a valuable celebrity aura.

Although timeliness is paramount, a few other factors can heighten the appeal of your story to the media. Will your story push the public's emotional buttons, either with tragedy or uplift? Editors and producers like to leaven death, doom, and destruction with classic crowd-pleasers such as children, animals, and chocolate. Can you establish that your information impinges on huge numbers of people? If you've invented a device that helps people with bad backs, you've got better odds of wide press coverage than if your invention makes life easier for people who like to go snow camping. Or does your story resonate with some archetypal drama akin to "the big break" or "Joe Doe fights City Hall"? When retailer Rick Segel of Medford, Massachusetts, opened a men's clothing store, he twisted an advertising slogan made popular by a prominent competitor and got sued. "What happened to me was a 'David versus Goliath' story," he says, "irresistible to the media."

23 MORE WAYS TO BE NEWSWORTHY

1. At the library, look up the news of 50 or 100 years ago and tie that to your service or product.
2. Break a record. *The Guinness Book of World Records* sells one million copies per year, and even your staged attempt to break, say, the ice-eating record, can make the news.
3. Don't do something everyone else does—and have an interesting rationale. For instance, leave a message on your voicemail saying you won't return any calls and that people should call back during certain designated hours.
4. Make predictions, preferably outrageous and unexpected, with a credible explanation.
5. Invent a new use for your product—for instance, your hors d'oeuvres can also help catch fish.
6. Find an employee with an out-of-the-ordinary personal story, especially one that can tug at the heartstrings of readers or listeners.
7. Launch a community service project. When your local TV station learns you give free makeovers to the homeless, they'll rush to cover you.
8. Let the media know about an ordeal you survived, such as a real-estate developer profiled in *Entrepreneur* who'd been audited 32 times in one year.

9. Tie what you do to the season. Landscaper Mike McGroarty had been trying for years to get into his local paper, the *Lake County News-Herald* in Perry, Ohio. He finally succeeded one spring, perceived as the proper season for gardening stories.

10. Revive a tradition. Use chalk instead of the colored markers on white boards everyone else has now.

11. Play the local card. Even something as tenuous as the fact that you once vacationed in the area and loved it can create a connection that gets you covered in places where you do not live.

12. Offer a surprising guarantee. A urologist who offered a money-back guarantee on the physician's fee for his vasectomy reversals landed himself in the *National Enquirer*, where advertising would have been prohibitively expensive.

13. Investigate your marketing reach. Having subscribers in 59 countries or clients who drive 500 miles to see you impresses reporters, producers, and bloggers.

14. Highlight a comeback, such as recovering from bankruptcy or a medical death sentence.

15. Share your numbers. If you've been collecting data on the extent of lawsuits against cities and towns, lots of media outlets would like to peg a story on what you know.

16. Sound the alarm. Have you long had a dark what-if scenario, related to your expertise?

17. Reveal your hobby. A collection of china doll figurines isn't expected from a burly lumber company president.

18. Use cutting-edge technology. Be the first in your industry or locale to use some high-tech gizmo.

19. Offer surprising facts, such as about the history of toothbrushes if you're a dentist.

20. Turn your TV-watching to good use by making a serious point about an issue raised in this week's episode of a popular situation comedy.

21. Donate your product or a gift certificate to a good cause—for example, a new wallet for every high school graduate in your hometown.

22. Get offbeat endorsements. How about blurbs from a punk rocker, a bartender, or a has-been politician for your door stoppers?

23. Raise a question prompted by a blockbuster movie or book. A Woburn, Massachusetts real-estate agent was quoted in her local paper on the question of whether the movie *A Civil Action*, depicting a toxic waste case in her town, would affect local real estate values.

→→ ←←

I'll get to the "hows" of approaching the media soon. First I want to address the "yes, buts" that hold many professionals, entrepreneurs, and people passionate about a cause from seeking the publicity that would benefit them.

Chapter 3

The Comfort Factor: Exposure Without Feeling Exposed

In the fall of 1980, I learned that *The New York Times* had decided to buy a personal essay I had written about the challenges and frustrations of college teaching. Before I had more than two minutes to celebrate, the telephone rang again. Someone from the *Times'* photography department was on the line.

"We'd like to send out a photographer to take your picture," he said.

"You're kidding," I replied. So focused had I been on polishing the article to please the *Times* that this possibility hadn't occurred to me. It dampened my excitement. "Gee, I don't know if I want to have my picture in *The New York Times*."

"Whyever not?"

I wasn't sure how to explain the reluctance I felt. "I don't know. It seems so, so publicity-seeking." I spat out those words.

The man chuckled. "No more than writing the article in the first place." He paused. "Come on, we'd like a photo. It'll be fine."

He did talk me into setting up a shoot with their photographer, but most of me felt relieved when the *Times* ended up running an illustration instead. The photo felt like some sort of encroachment on my view of myself. I knew this wasn't rational, but though I'd written a rather personal statement, so long as only my name appeared along with it, I felt I was putting it out into the world invisibly.

The details of my story are unique. I'll bet, though, that somewhere in your psyche lurk fears or discomforts about publicity—anywhere from one or two shadowy hang-ups up to a whole truncheon-swinging gang of objections. Most people I've talked with, even those who appear to be born-with-a-horn self-promoters, get the creeps about at least some methods or circumstances of putting themselves forward.

One friend told me that the first time she received a promotional flyer from me in the mail, her first thought was, "What chutzpah!" Cold calls or mailings to strangers didn't faze her, she explained, but she could never see herself sending something that talked herself up or asked for business from people she knew. A book author and consultant told me, "People who get to know me tell me I'm so smart, I should be charging more and have more of a public image. They're right, and I know that the problem goes all the way back to my childhood. It's my Achilles heel."

According to Brookline, Massachusetts psychiatrist Michael Pearlman, resistances to promotion persist because of fears, unexamined beliefs, and deep confusions fostered by our culture, starting with the very term *self-promotion*. "That's a contradiction in terms," he says. "You can't promote your *self*, only what's of value in what you do, which is an entirely separate thing from your self." Unconfronted fears about publicity may have wide-ranging ramifications for your ability to reach other goals, adds Joy Schmidt, who teaches entrepreneurial skills in Southfield, Michigan. "The very thing that keeps you from talking to the media may be holding back your business in general. The problem may be that you don't feel great about what you're doing. And in that case you can't pull customers in, because you're likely to be always thinking about yourself rather than the customer."

I hate to see fears and misconceptions hold people back from receiving recognition that could be theirs. This chapter helps you distinguish the concerns that are reasonable from those that have insinuated themselves into your head without good grounding. I also provide plenty of ammunition in case you decide to fight fears that seem to represent lost legacies from long ago. Whether your reluctance comes from constant admonitions not to show off while you were growing up, from viewpoints you absorbed when you were already grown, or from explicit thinking you've done about different ways to reach your goals, you can learn to find—and respect—your unique comfort zone with publicity. You *can* enjoy free media coverage without performing major surgery on your personality or forcing yourself to compromise your dignity.

20 PREVALENT FEARS ABOUT AND OBJECTIONS TO PUBLICITY

1. PEOPLE WILL THINK I'M BRAGGING.

If you shrink from marketing in general or feel a vague "ick" at the thought of media coverage, this one, deeply ingrained, might be the culprit. "Kids naturally get excited about what they can do, but lots of parents tell them, 'don't brag,'" says Nancy Michaels, owner of Impression Impact, a public relations firm in Concord, Massachusetts. "So they learn not to talk about themselves. But seeking publicity isn't bragging. It's just letting people know what you do."

When marketing consultant Tony Putman works with professionals who appear ambivalent about spreading the word about themselves, he gives them this definition: "Fundamentally, marketing in any form is helping people see what difference you're signing up to make in their life and the value and cost of what you have to offer to them. Through marketing, you enable potential customers to make the most accurate and appropriate decision they can make." He adds, "Unless someone has a deep issue with authority, it usually takes them only 20 to 30 minutes to get it."

The dialogue, I imagine, might go this way:

Q: Do you think there's value in what you do?

A: Of course. I'm an excellent doctor (chef, accountant, contractor). I save people's lives (cook great food, keep track of people's finances, build fairly priced houses that last).

Q: Do you mind if people know how well you do that?

A: Of course not. I just don't think I should have to tell them.

Q: You just told me, though, and with total conviction.

A: Yes, but this wasn't for real. You weren't a reporter or a potential patient (client, customer).

Q: You mean to say you could be frank with me but not with the people in a position to have their lives saved (their tastes satisfied, their finances safeguarded, their housing needs filled), or with the people in a position to pass the word on to those people?

A: Uh...[mental light bulb goes on].

If you identify with this trepidation, you might try writing out your own dialogue similar to this, with one part played by the voice of reason, the other by the part of you that wants to appear selflessly absorbed in your work. Resolving the conflict isn't necessary for getting on with the business of publicity, however. If you feel it's too self-serving to tell or write the media about yourself, have someone else do it. Kenneth Palson of Worcester, Massachusetts, came in one day from feeding expired parking meters along Main Street in front of his hardware store and remarked to his brother Chuck, "Someday a reporter's going to come along and find out what I'm doing." Chuck Palson asked, "How about today?" He dialed the city desk of the *Worcester Telegram and Gazette* and said, "You should have seen what I saw today on Main Street...." Within hours, a reporter arrived at the store to get the story.

As did three other public relations professionals I spoke with, Nancy Michaels confessed that she has a hard time doing for herself what she does all the time for clients. She resolved the dilemma by deciding to start a newsletter directed toward her clients and putting the media on her subscription list. "That feels more comfortable for me than calling them up and talking about myself," she says.

2. I'd feel as though I was begging.

Linda Barbanel did have this thought at first when she graduated from her analytic training and needed to lure patients into her office. But she quickly changed her attitude. "I'm not hustling, I'm helping people, and in order to help them they need to know that I'm available," she says. "I always present myself as a resource, and that way, I feel both professional and empowered." Another therapist, Szifra Birke, recalls having a newspaper reporter in one of her weekly groups. "She was always asking for story leads, and sometimes she was desperate for ideas. One day she pointed a finger in my face and said, 'The newspaper is a hungry animal, and it needs to be fed!' I've never forgotten that. It shocked me to think that they need us rather than the other way around." The media does need you and, if you approach them off your knees, you're more likely to precipitate an exchange that gratifies both parties.

3. PEOPLE IN MY FIELD DON'T CHASE THE MEDIA. I'LL LOSE RESPECT AND CREDIBILITY.

Let me guess: You're middle-aged or older and work in law, medicine, or academia. Until 1976 and 1979, respectively, the American Bar Association and the American Medical Association forbade members to advertise, and disapproval of blatant promotional efforts lingers in those professions. Stephen Kling, who works in healthcare advertising, used to specialize in helping doctors design promotional campaigns. "Doctors would tell me, 'Look, I'm sorry to be calling you,' and insist on meeting at night. It was as if they felt they were meeting a loan shark." Kling recalls cases in which a doctor spent well into five figures and then pulled back, essentially throwing away the money, at the first whisper of criticism from colleagues.

Academia never had written rules against advertising or promotion, but becoming a media star might conflict with the ivory-tower obscurity and footnotes-in-place correctness deemed appropriate for professors. Yet whatever your profession, you'll find options in this book that wouldn't reek of sleaze to even the fussiest of your colleagues. You can discreetly chase the media with no loss of self-respect or credibility.

4. YOU HAVE TO HAVE A LOT OF NERVE TO APPROACH THE MEDIA.

Have you ever called Mr. or Ms. Unapproachable for a date? Or dared to write a letter applying for a job you were sure thousands of other people wanted? Then you've got the right stuff to woo the press.

5. The media just wants glitz, sex, and fluff.

Yet the public is also hungry for inspiration and information, and the media often rises to the occasion of fulfilling those needs, too. "There are plenty of shows that are looking for content," says Paul Edwards, co-host of "Home Office," which airs Sunday evenings on the non-glitz, non-fluff Business Radio Network. The media gladly spread the word about one of Joy Schmidt's clients, a children's clothing store that offers discounts to foster parents. Schmidt herself is blind and finds that practically anything she does makes an inspirational human interest story. "One reporter couldn't tear himself away from my talking computer," she laughs—again, no glitz, sex, or fluff.

6. If I seek out the media, they'll publicize my competitors, too.

So what? If your competitors are honest players, you'll look good in their company. It might be time to update your attitude about competition. "I don't have competitors, just allies," says Jay Conrad Levinson, author of the *Guerrilla Marketing* books. "When people ask me if there's anyone else who does what I do, I mention Jeff Slutsky. We recommend each other and I don't have any problem with that at all. I fervently believe that we're in the age of cooperation, not competition." If Levinson's philosophy seems far out to you, just remember that if an article profiles you along with five other accountants, some readers may resonate with your comments and become clients. If other readers resonate with the comments of the other accountants, aren't you still better off than without the publicity?

7. I'll end up looking like a fool.

Jeffrey Lant agrees with you here. "People are terrified of making a mistake," he says. "Don't worry—you will, and don't let that stop you." Lant recalls a lot of ridiculous situations he's landed in during his quest for publicity: radio stations that were broadcasting from closets, a TV host who interviewed him in a field, surrounded by cows. "Once I appeared on a show where the other guest was a woman who designed historical costumes for parrots. Just go with it," he advises. Early on Linda Barbanel swore during what she thought was a commercial break. To her mortification, the host informed her that they were on the air. The only consequence beyond the moment, though, was that it turned into a family joke. You'll make mistakes too. But is publicity-seeking really different in that respect from anything else you might do?

8. I'M NOT A BORN PUBLICITY HOUND, THE WAY DONALD TRUMP OR MADONNA IS.

Bad examples! Unlike most of us, real-estate mogul Donald Trump grew up with a role model in the house. When Donald was toddling around in his playpen, his father, real-estate developer Fred Trump, used a public relations firm to issue news releases commenting on the state of the economy. But you can learn to exploit the media even if you come from a family that never went so far as to supply obituaries to the local paper. And as for rock star Madonna, at least one psychoanalyst has commented that she is addicted to provoking outrage. Rest assured that normal people can keep their publicity-seeking from spiraling to ever more shocking heights.

9. PEOPLE WILL GET JEALOUS OF ME AND CUT ME DOWN.

Consultant Debra Benton recalls that when she began getting local publicity, people would say to her, "You're always in the newspaper," when she was written up just twice a year or so. This reminds me of a saying in China: "No pig wants to be the fattest; no tree wants to be the tallest in the forest." I'm not sure the thinnest pig or the shortest tree has a perfect life, either.

10. I'M TOO HONEST TO DO WELL WITH THE MEDIA.

Have you been watching too many political debates? In fact, if you want to become a regular source for the media, you must be honest and avoid self-serving exaggerations, says Charlotte Ryan, author of *Prime Time Activism*. Provide reporters with relevant facts they don't have to double-check, and you could become the environmentalist or missing-persons tracer they call to comment on breaking news.

11. Forget the glory. I want proof that time spent on publicity will show up on the bottom line.

You'll find publicity-seeking frustrating, says Stephen Kling, if you only feel comfortable in a world where spending $10 gets you $10's worth of results and spending a thousand dollars gets you 100 times those results. "You may get an avalanche of responses or nothing," says Paul Edwards. If you need indicators of what the possible avalanche might be worth to you, turn back to Chapter 1 and reread what happened with Trivial Pursuit and Jeff Slutsky.

12. My services are confidential. I'll lose cachet from publicity.

Wisely or not, this concern didn't deter Harry Freedman, a stand-up comedian who makes high fees putting on corporate audiences, from agreeing to a major feature and photo in the Sunday business section of *The New York Times*. Twice the article pointed out that if too many people knew he existed, or what he looked like, his ability to pretend to be a top bank regulator or whatever could collapse. He replied that people have a habit of believing what they're told and that he looked like "a generic executive," so he wasn't worried.

You may land in a more difficult bind if you guarantee confidentiality to those you serve and then can't provide the media with verifiable examples of what you've done. But don't worry about becoming uncool when you gain publicity. The prestige and payoff from being on the evening news more than outweigh being an in-group secret.

13. I'm not the sort of person the media would want to promote.

If you think you're not mediagenic, imagine someone who can't speak or walk and has only just enough movement in a few fingers to control his wheelchair and electronic voice synthesizer. That's Stephen Hawking, the award-winning theoretical physicist who wrote the best seller *A Brief History of Time*, who has appeared on *Late Night With Conan O'Brien*, *The Simpsons*, and *Futurama*, and has starred in a television documentary. As far as the media is concerned, the only flaw that disqualifies you from publicity is being boring—and even "The World's Most Boring Weatherman" could probably be made interesting on a slow news night.

14. How can I give away my secrets? That's how I make my living.

One marketing consultant refused to speak to me for this book, giving this as a reason. My experience indicates that she was mistaken. After I published *Freelance Writing for Magazines and Newspapers*, I began giving seminars, thinking that people who attended a seminar would want to buy a book to take home. Many did, but to my surprise people who had already bought the book showed up at the seminars, too, plunking down up to eight times the cost of the book to hear, in person, what I had written.

Grace Weinstein, who wrote *The Lifetime Book of Money Management* and has coordinated a conference on publicity and promotion for financial professionals, responds to this worry: "Readers may get some free advice when you're quoted but they'll never get enough to eliminate their need for professional help. Instead, they usually read what you said and say to themselves, 'Hey, this person knows something and might be able to help me solve my problem.'" As long as you have a depth of expertise, you'll find that media exposure increases rather than decreases the demand.

15. Too much publicity would be bad. I could get overexposed.

No, the media spotlight doesn't do to people what too much sunlight does to film. Since 1977, when Joel Goodman created The Humor Project, an organization in Saratoga Springs, New York, that helps people focus on the positive power of humor and creativity in everyday life, he has appeared in the media more than 4,000 times in more than 150 countries, and says it only keeps on building and benefiting his cause. "We were the first organization in the world to do what we do, and we've generated more media on the subject than anyone else. Reporters tell me they saw my name in four out of five or five out of five of the articles they looked up, and that motivated them to call." When your reputation rests on a solid foundation, you remain the one to quote and invite on the air.

16. I'M NOT SURE I CAN TALK COHERENTLY AND PERSUASIVELY TO THE MEDIA.

Do you mean that you're not a natural talker? Then read Chapters 11, 14, 15, and 16, and practice. Or do you mean that you know how to do what you do but not explain it? Michael Pearlman, who co-leads workshops for entrepreneurs in addition to his psychiatric practice, told me that he didn't feel ready to go to the *Boston Globe* about his program. If that's because your business offering hasn't completely gelled yet, fine, don't push it. But perhaps you just need practice—or a media coach, a professional like Susan Harrow or Rebecca Shafir (see Chapter 24), who helps you create sound bites and reel them off with pizzazz. The more you simply talk about your offering to sympathetic friends, colleagues, and customers, the more confident you feel about being able to articulate the significance of what you do to the media.

17. I'LL LOSE MY PRIVACY.

I confess to this one. Although I've had my photo on book jackets, in magazines and newspapers, and on the Web, I continue to feel a tug between the safety of anonymity and the pleasure of acclaim—not to mention the desire to make sure stalkers don't show up in my backyard. When I created a video of my home-business lifestyle and posted it to YouTube, I made sure we didn't show what my house looks like or anything like street signs that an outsider could easily look up to find its location.

But I may be exaggerating the threat. Jay Conrad Levinson, who has many more books in print than I do and has had his full-page photo in *Entrepreneur*, says that people do recognize him, "but not much. I enjoy it because it's low-level and nonintrusive." Perhaps you have to be a politician, entertainer, athlete, or a regular TV talking head before you need protection from "Hey, you're ____, aren't you?"

18. IT'S SO MANIPULATIVE.

Yes, publicity-seeking often involves calculated moves, but that doesn't necessarily make it deceptive, corrupt, or unscrupulous. On the contrary, most of those I spoke with who consistently get media coverage said that without whole-spirited enthusiasm, they wouldn't have been able to win over reporters and producers. Sheer manipulativeness, in other words, doesn't work. "You have to be excited *and* have some real substance to offer," says Ron Bianco, who has successfully courted the media. Saying that he has a singing dog usually gets him attention, but, he adds, "It's also always important that I have a bona fide show."

19. I DID IT ONCE AND THEY MISQUOTED ME.

And when you first tried to ride a bicycle, didn't you fall down once or twice and then keep on trying? Mistakes are inevitable in learning any new skill, and when it comes to media coverage, every attempt may not go smoothly. However, as you'll discover in Chapter 14, whether or not a reporter gets your story accurately is partly within your control. *Investor's Business Daily* once featured Janice Hoffman's company, Before & After, on its front page, noting that it's located in Waterville, Massachusetts. There is no such town, however. The paper's one-line correction, "Janice Hoffman, Professional Organizer, is located in Watertown, Massachusetts," was spotted by a Channel 4 reporter who had not seen the original article and in short order put her on the air. "That was definitely my favorite typo, ever," she notes.

20. I don't know how to do it.

Aha! That's the easiest of them all for me to respond to. Just read the remainder of this book!

→→ ←←

I may have missed your particular qualms, so to complete your self-assessment you may want to take a few minutes for the following exercise. It's simple enough that you should be able to read it and remember it without having to reread or tape-record the directions. Close your eyes and let yourself become deeply relaxed. Then imagine yourself having achieved flattering national publicity. Notice what that looks like, sounds like, and feels like. Also, notice all the consequences of publicity and what they look like, sound like, and feel like. All in all, is this what you want? Notice a signal that means yes, maybe, or no.

Exploring Your Comfort Zone

Let's say that you identified with several of the concerns listed in the previous section. Now what? The next step is to find the ways of seeking publicity that feel comfortable for you. Observe your reactions as you read or reread the dozens of examples sprinkled throughout this book. Which of the things that others have done can you see yourself doing? Which get you talking to yourself, walking around the house restlessly, or jotting down plans on scrap paper? Which provoke a warm, surprised feeling of inspiration? All these constitute clues to publicity methods to which you can wholeheartedly commit yourself.

Also take note of the possibilities that attract you but also somewhat scare you. Those probably lie at the border of your comfort zone. With a little imaginative reflection, you can include those in your repertoire, too. In my studies of creativity and procrastination, I've found that people have idiosyncratic, personal patterns of what enables them to painlessly accomplish something new. Use the following questions to tune into *your* tendencies.

1. Do you like to plunge right into new things or wade in gradually? If someone at the pool tells you the water's cold and you characteristically go ahead and dive in anyway, then you might want to start out with your first publicity blitz to the major media. That won't feel right to you, though, if you prefer to walk in up to your knees, splash water onto your arms and chest, and go ahead only when you feel acclimated. In that case, start out with local media or on professionally familiar territory, venturing further when you get used to the process.

2. Are you more comfortable with speaking or with writing? If you're naturally eloquent and persuasive when you talk and hate trying to get the same effect on paper, then take everything I say in Chapter 4 under advisement and concentrate on phone pitches and schmoozing instead. If, however, you start to stammer whenever you're on the spot, put your effort into written materials that are so terrific that they practically reduce the need for follow-up interviews.

3. Do you believe that modesty is next to godliness, or have you been your own best promoter since you ran for sixth-grade president? If you've always flinched at being asked to sell yourself at job interviews, no one says you have to shine the spotlight on yourself. Place the spotlight on your product, your service, or your customers. Think of yourself as the stagehand who pads around backstage in black to keep the set arranged. But if you love being under klieg lights, you've probably already invented creative publicity tactics of your own (and I'd love to hear about them!).

4. Would you rather lurk behind the scenes or sit in the glory seat out front? During the brief existence of WordRight, I wrote most of our news releases, and my partner talked to the reporters who called. Although that meant that her name got into the papers more than mine, I didn't care. I'd already seen my name in print a lot, and she got more of a kick out of gabbing with reporters than I did. You can always designate, and train, a contact person to speak for your organization if you find interviews bothersome. Your son or daughter, your summer intern, or your receptionist might have the enthusiasm that would make him or her a great spokesperson.

5. How concerned are you about the tackiness factor? Although some people with a substantial media presence appear to have sought the limelight, others come off as if acclaim and attention were thrust on them. You can seek publicity *and* maintain a dignified professional image by choosing your tactics carefully. Instead of firing out indiscriminate inquiries, contact a science reporter for the *Los Angeles Times* or someone else whose work you respect. Persuade an ambitious former student to develop an intellectually informed piece for *The Atlantic Monthly*. Write letters to the editor that correct mistakes in your area of expertise. Prepare fact sheets that remain true to the complexity of your views.

6. Are you a loner or someone who always gravitates to groups? Although I've addressed you throughout this book as if you were seeking publicity alone, if that doesn't appeal to you, why not form a publicity team or publicity club so that you can cheer and coach each other through the process? Or designate someone as your publicity buddy and keep each other on track. Critique one another's news releases over lunch, lick stamps together, and celebrate each other's triumphs.

7. Do you do best when the stakes are high or when it doesn't matter if you fail? I've heard people say, "I *had* to go all out. I'd have lost my house to the bank otherwise." If high stakes motivate you, plunk down a nonrefundable fee for a giant auditorium and then get busy generating the publicity that will sell out the hall. If the mere thought of losing it all paralyzes you with fear, time your first publicity push for an event that will come off well without any press at all.

✦✦ ✦✦

Overall, maximize what you enjoy and minimize what you dread. And to adapt a saying of George Orwell, ignore any advice in this book sooner than violate your educated sense of what's right for you. In other words, after reading and thinking about my suggestions, if you find yourself thinking, "I really ought to _____, but it gives me a headache," don't. Either modify my advice or hunt back through the book for an alternative that sits as well with you as a perfect-fitting pair of pants.

PART II

WRITING TO
GET PUBLICITY

Chapter 4

6 Steps to Free Publicity: Creating and Distributing a News Release

U p to now I've minimized use of the term *news release* (also called a *press release* or *media release*) so that I could orient you and help you get comfortable and focused with publicity. But now it's time to introduce you to a basic tool for gaining the attention of the media.

A news release is a brief document in a specific format that demonstrates to news people why you or your business merit media coverage now. It usually takes up just one page, or at most two, and doesn't require fancy typesetting or design. Hence, it fits any budget. Its power lies in its compact, scannable format and in the compelling way in which you answer that all-important media question dissected in Chapter 2: Why would our readers/listeners/viewers be interested in this story now?

Before I take you step by step through the process of writing your own release, I'd like you to take a look at one example of this miracle-working species of correspondence. Upon receiving the following news release, which I produced for a client, several boat magazine editors called immediately to say they would be featuring Gabison's product in an upcoming issue.

Sample News Release #1

For: Tarpaulin Drainage Systems, 14553 SW 77 St., Miami, FL 33183.

Contact: Daniel Gabison, (305) 256-0075.

FOR IMMEDIATE RELEASE

New Drainage System Saves Boat Owners Toil and Expense

Miami, February 11, 1993—Among those who dread rain most are boat owners. Until now, every one of them watching a downpour has known either that they'll have to get over to the boat soon and bail out the buckets of water accumulating on the boat cover, or, although they've installed a system to drain the water, it is endangering the longevity of their tarpaulin. Now, however, boat owners can buy peace of mind with a simple Punch-Drain that removes rainwater automatically, protecting the boat and prolonging the life of their boat cover.

"The Punch-Drain came to me out of necessity," says Miami-based boat owner Daniel Gabison, the inventor. "In the rainy season, my boat cover would fill with water, and I'm not talking about just a bucket or two. Although I drained the water every few days, after a short time the tarpaulin would start to sag, tear, and deteriorate under the great weight of the collected water."

Gabison tried the two available systems designed to prevent water from accumulating, both of which required the tarpaulin to be stretched tight, so that the device either broke or tore a hole in the tarpaulin. Instead of trying to keep the tarpaulin tight, Gabison designed a solution that got rid of the water while leaving the tarpaulin slack. His Punch-Drain, patented in 1991, drains rainwater straight to the bilge, from which it drains out through the boat's bilge hole.

The Punch-Drain, all American made, costs just $14.95 and is available through boat supply stores or direct from Tarpaulin Drainage Systems, 14553 SW 77 St., Miami, FL 33183. For more information, boat owners or dealers can call (305) 256-0075.

↦↦ ↤↤

Can you see how obvious it is on even a quick read how boat owners would benefit from learning about Gabison's invention? Now here's how to produce an effective news release of your own.

6 STEPS TO FREE PUBLICITY

STEP 1. FIND A NEWS ANGLE FOR YOUR HEADLINE.

Select one or more of the media hooks discussed in detail in Chapter 2: something new or distinctive about your business or organization, an upcoming event, a tie-in with the news, and so forth.

Then compose an eye-catching, informative headline using that hook. The headline can take up more than one line on the release, so go on as long as necessary to complete the idea. If possible, include the benefit to media audiences of your hook in the headline. Just as in newspaper headlines, you can use a compressed, telegraphic style. For example:

❖ Olympic Coach Recommends Anaerobics—No-Sweat Exercise—for Couch Potatoes

❖ February 17 Executive Panel to Proffer Strategies for Success in a Stagnant Economy

❖ Durango's Only Theme Park Opens Child-Care Center

STEP 2. PRESENT THE BASIC FACTS FOR THE ANGLE OF YOUR HEADLINE IN PARAGRAPH ONE.

Answer the journalist's "Five Ws": Who? What? When? Where? Why (or how)? Notice that I said the basic facts *for the angle of your headline,* not the basic facts about your product or service or you. In many cases, these are not the same. For instance, in the first paragraph of the sample news release you just read, I didn't include the who, what, when, where, and why about the invention of the Punch-Drain, but rather the five Ws about how it saves boat owners toil and expense—the angle stated in the headline.

Who: Boat owners.

What: They can buy a device called the Punch-Drain that removes rainwater automatically from boat tarpaulins.

When: Now.

Where: Implicitly, anywhere boats get rained on.

Why: To protect their boat and prolong the life of the boat cover.

Weave your who, what, when, where, and why together in an opening paragraph for your release. If you can make your pitch catchy, that's fine, but a straightforward, factual style does the job, too.

Step 3. Gather or create a lively quote that elaborates on the basic facts for paragraph two.

Here you quote someone who can back up the basic claim of the release—you, the company president, the originator of the event, product or service, a satisfied customer, or someone who carries special weight with your target audience. A quote brings the story to life, provides perspective, or adds star appeal. In a release I wrote for a conference linking large New England companies and potential small-business suppliers, I quoted Massachusetts senator John Kerry on why he had signed on as a sponsor of the conference. Chapter 19 tells you how to get useful quotes from others to use in publicity, but often you really will be the optimum person to quote, and you can have fun here putting words into your own mouth.

Step 4. Elaborate further on basic facts in paragraph three.

What else do you want to communicate to editors and producers? You can continue to quote yourself, quote someone besides whomever you quoted in paragraph two, or report additional facts that support your claims in straight prose. You might want to place biographical information about you or historical data about your subject here. I didn't include much about Daniel Gabison because he wasn't an expert in boat design, and his regular job had nothing to do with being a boat owner who had invented a better drainage solution that would help others like him. Don't distract; support your story!

STEP 5. END WITH THE NITTY-GRITTY DETAILS.

What are the practical details (prices, addresses, dates, phone numbers, URLs, how to register, and so on) that any media notice about your subject should include? Combine these details in a sentence or two. At this point you'll have drafted a four-paragraph news release. Congratulations! Polish it and format it similarly to the previous sample and the one that follows.

SAMPLE NEWS RELEASE #2

For: Creative Ways, P.O. Box 1310, Boston, MA 02117.
Contact: Marcia Yudkin 1-800-333-8376, marcia@yudkin.com.

FOR IMMEDIATE RELEASE

Marketing Upgrades: New Low-Cost Alternative to the High Fees of a Crack Copywriter

Boston, MA, July 8, 1996–"My last mailing cost me hundreds of dollars and I didn't get any response!" "I know that my brochure/ sales letter/ad/press release is terrible—help!" Until now, only two options existed to help business owners flummoxed by their marketing ineptitude: They could hire nationally known top copywriting talent, for thousands of dollars, plus, in many cases, a royalty on resulting sales; or they could tap a local penster for a reasonable flat fee, for serviceable but not sensational work. Finally, though, a national expert on persuasive writing has devised a way to provide business owners and professionals with potent, sparkling marketing materials at a cost that fits most budgets.

"I most enjoy improving copy, rather than writing it from scratch for others," says Marcia Yudkin, PhD, author of *Persuading on Paper: The Complete Guide to Writing Copy that Pulls in Business* (Plume/Penguin Books) and seven other books. "And after being asked again and again for help, I discovered that almost anyone could write a terrible sales letter, press release, ad, or brochure for me to upgrade. By asking questions to elicit missing background and details, I'd quickly have all the ingredients I needed to cook up a more lively, compelling sales presentation. By not having to start from scratch, I could perform my magic for a fraction of what I'd otherwise have to charge."

Upon receiving drafted material or an existing marketing piece by fax or mail, Yudkin quotes a flat fee for transforming it into a powerful profit generator. Most marketing upgrades cost between $125 and $395, and she's handled products and services as diverse as software, legal services, and a novel design of men's underwear. With the convenience of fax, e-mail, and the postal service, she serves many clients she never meets face to face, as far away as the Marshall Islands.

More information is available from Marcia Yudkin at (617) 555-1234; P.O. Box 1310, Boston, MA 02117; marcia@yudkin.com.

→→ ←←

This news release put a fresh spin on the editing-by-fax service that I had been carrying on for many years. Instead of emphasizing the technology I used, this time I pitched my service as a cost-effective solution for business owners in need of copywriting help. About six weeks after I sent this release to business magazines, *Business '96* called to tell me they'd be featuring my service in the sidebar for an upcoming article. Once they knew about me, they mentioned my services several times more in years that followed, bringing me interesting clients who came back to me again and again with regular assignments.

Here, as in the previous sample, using the standard news release format gives editors all the information they need exactly where they're accustomed to getting it. Keep your release to one page, if possible.

First line: Provide your business name and address on the top line.

Second line: Supply a name, phone number (plus cell phone number if that's different), and e-mail address that editors can use to get more information. Be sure that the contact person can speak knowledgeably and in detail about the subject of the news release. If you want to look as though you have a bigger operation than you do, and come off as if you're not blowing your own horn, make up a fictional person whose name you always use on news releases. Then when a call comes in for, say, "Trudy Einhorn," you know it's from the media and you can say, "Trudy's not here at the moment. This is Joe Business. May I help you?"

"For Immediate Release": This signals that editors can use the story immediately. If you've run a contest and don't want the winners' names released until October 15, 2009, you'd write instead, "For Release October 15, 2009."

Headline: Center this, and, where possible, use boldface and slightly larger type. Running on to three lines for the headline is perfectly okay.

Dateline: Write the city, state, and date for the story's origin. This imparts a nice journalistic flavor. Plan carefully so that you distribute your release on or a bit later than the date stated here. If you're using a news release distribution service, they usually insert the applicable date for you.

Step 6. Send it off.

To do this, you may need to make two procedural decisions: how you'll find the media addresses and which delivery mechanism you'll use. Here are your options:

1. Use a news release distribution service. You pay a fee, generally several hundred dollars, and the service takes care of getting your release out to the media world at large or to some geographical or topical segment of the media that you specify. With this option, you do not need to trouble yourself with finding the current contact information for the *Washington Post*, ABC News, or *Concrete Weekly*. The ease of having someone else efficiently dispatch your release is of course offset by the cost. Five release distribution services I recommend are:

   → PR Newswire: *www.prnewswire.com* (888-776-0942).
   → Business Wire: *www.businesswire.com* (800-221-2462).

> ✦　eReleases: *www.ereleases.com* (410-248-1408).
>
> ✦　Emailwire: *www.emailwire.com* (281-645-4086).
>
> ✦　Press Release Network: *www.pressreleasenetwork.com.*

(You'll find more detail on these and other publicity companies and resources in Chapter 24.)

2.　Buy a media database or targeted media list. You receive either a wide-ranging list of media contacts in a printed directory or digital database, or you get media contacts for a certain city or industry. This seems like a cost-effective solution because you pay once for something you can use again and again, but it has a pitfall. Any compiled database is out of date the day after it is created. When you purchase it and use it for, say, a year afterward (you'll feel tempted to use it even longer than that!), its information becomes less and less valid. The news release distribution services put considerable effort and expense into keeping their databases current, and that is part of what you pay for when you hire their service. On the other hand, if you're planning a big, one-time publicity push and you buy a database or list right before you need it, this option makes perfect sense. The databases usually include postal addresses, phone and fax numbers, e-mail addresses, Web URLs, and, if you're fortunate, editor/producer names. Inexpensive media databases or media list sources include:

> ✦　Easy Media List: *www.easymedialist.com* (720-565-8455).
>
> ✦　Gebbie Press All-In-One Media Directory: *www.gebbieinc.com* (845-255-7560).
>
> ✦　Online Press Releases: *www.onlinepressreleases.com* (617-249-0604).

3.　Subscribe to an online media database service. With this option, you buy access to an online database of media contacts that you can consult and use as much as you like as long as you continue to subscribe. These contacts tend to be significantly more up to date than lists you'd buy. Sometimes this type of service includes an easy-to-use submission interface, not just the data you need. Examples:

 ✦ Contacts on Tap: *www.cornerbarpr.com/cot/signup.cfm* (816-472-7727).

 ✦ Corporate News: *www.corporatenews.com* (208-939-2564).

4. Track down email addresses yourself on the Web. This costs nothing but requires a considerable amount of time. First, you can use online media directories, which provide well-organized links to media Websites. Once at the Websites, you need to poke around, often in "Contact Us" or "About Us," to find contact information for their editors, reporters, and producers. Or, if you know which media you want to target, type in their URL or track them down in a general search engine and go directly to those sites. Comprehensive online media directories (also known as media jump sites) include:

 ✦ MediaPost: *www.mediapost.com.*

 ✦ NewsDirectory: *www.ecola.com.*

 ✦ NewsLink: *newslink.org.*

5. Use resources at the public library. It probably has one or more media directories, and if you are targeting a narrow topical niche, this may be an important bit of research for you, because printed directories may contain magazines, newspapers, and newsletters that don't show up in an online search. When trying to reach, say, quilters, every publication for that market should be receiving your releases. Naturally, you can buy these tomes instead of consulting them at the library, but they cost several hundred dollars each. Some media directories, profiled in greater detail in Chapter 24 are:

 ✦ *Bacon's Newspaper and Magazine Directories.*

 ✦ *Bacon's Radio/TV/Cable Directories.*

 ✦ *Standard Periodical Directory.*

 ✦ *Gale Directory of Publications and Broadcast Media.*

 ✦ *Standard Rate and Data Service.*

 ✦ *Oxbridge Directory of Newsletters.*

My favorite resource in this category is *Bacon's*, because it indicates each media person's preferred medium of contact, whether phone, fax, e-mail, or snail mail. In fact, merely looking through the listings in *Bacon's* is educational, in demonstrating that it is nearly impossible to generalize about editors' and producers' preferences. Every permutation of the four contact possibilities (for example, prefer e-mail or snail mail, do not want phone or fax pitches) appears here. Hence, the best answer to one of the most frequent questions I'm asked from new and experienced publicity-seekers alike—"How should I transmit my release?"—is that it depends. Don't assume that e-mail ranks far above the other delivery methods simply because it's free and convenient for you. At some media operations, e-mail simply isn't part of the company culture, and the gatekeepers like to have something printed on paper that they can scribble on and route around the office.

IF YOU USE E-MAIL

E-mail contact with the media presents a multitude of pitfalls into which you can tumble and injure yourself if you don't take care. Through the years, I've collected rants from journalists who are nearly united in their condemnation of the following practices as clueless and rude:

✦ Sending attachments. Transmit your release cut and pasted within a regular old e-mail. Not only do attached files harbor a danger of viruses, so that some companies frown on opening attachments from unknown sources, but they also sometimes don't open properly at all. Because they take an extra step to read, they allow your recipient to pause and wonder, "Should I bother?" instead of simply reading. Attachments are also unmanageable when someone's reading e-mail on a smartphone while out and about.

➤ Sending PDF files. Although attached files are annoying enough, sending a release as an attached PDF (Adobe Acrobat) file makes no sense at all. The recipient can't cut and paste text from such a file into the story she's writing, only read it on screen or print it out. And because people often turn to PDF to prevent cutting and pasting, this format sends the counterproductive message that you are trying to protect rather than spread your news.

➤ Use of the "cc" function. Learn to use the "bcc" or "blind carbon copy" function on your e-mail program when sending something to multiple recipients, because this suppresses the list of to whom you're sending, whereas the "cc" function fills the beginning of each recipient's e-mail with your distribution list. Media people get peeved to see they're one of a crowd of recipients, with their e-mail address exposed.

➤ Forgetting a phone number. When working on deadline, media people usually reach for the phone rather than reply by e-mail. If you leave off the phone number from your e-mailed release, you may lose some publicity opportunities.

➤ Sending just a link to a release on the Web. "We in the media do not have limitless time to 'Websurf' and 'go fishing' for your press releases," a reporter just back from a massive computer expo sounded off. "The Web can be slow. Our time is limited. We have merciless deadlines. When we ask you for text by e-mail or fax, we need the information that way to get our copy in on time."

➤ Sloppy writing. Numerous editors—they're professional word people, remember!—complain that the informality of the e-mail medium makes many more people send a slapdash effort at communication than when setting out thoughts on paper. Proofread anything you're going to send by e-mail as rigorously as anything to be carved in stone.

➤ Stupid subject lines. "Press Release" as the subject of an e-mail doesn't tell the recipient anything useful about its contents. Instead, insert the headline of your release into the subject slot. Because e-mail programs often have limited space for the subject line, reword the headline with the most important words first, before the likely cutoff point.

✦ Unreadable text. If you have an advanced e-mail program that nicely renders colors and fonts, you might not realize that some recipients of an e-mail that looked attractive to you before you sent it get something not just ugly but close to indecipherable. You wrote "Microsoft's 'Achilles heel'— poor debugging" and this comes out in some e-mail programs as "Microsoft?s ^ÆAchilles heelúÇ ß¥ poor debugging." You didn't intend this, but it makes you look dumb. The cure: composing something to be sent as e-mail in an unforgivingly simple program such as Notepad that doesn't create curly quote marks or long hyphens.

✦ Wildly misdirected releases. Just because e-mail is free of per-recipient charges (at least for now), don't send your release on laser surgery improvements to a reporter who covers cars. The world is much smaller than you'd think, and it's not a good idea to annoy anyone.

✦ Multiple sends. A friend working for a large trade magazine once wrote me, "Over the weekend, some PR person apparently went through our Website and sent the same e-mail to everybody in the editorial department, all 50-plus people. Some got the same message five times. Because it was health-related, most of us forwarded it to the health-beat reporter, meaning he got dozens of copies of the same message. This doesn't make any of us feel too kindly toward the sender, to put it mildly."

✦ Subscribing the media to your e-mail newsletter. You shouldn't sign anyone up involuntarily for your e-mail news-letter, but doing this to a media person is a double no-no. You don't want to get selected as the clueless dummy of the month and get publicly skewered. Sending a pitch letter (see Chapter 6) by e-mail describing your publication in tantalizing terms is safer and wiser.

❖ Instant messages. Unless a reporter or producer is already a best buddy, forget instant messaging, sending a Twitter message, contacting a media person through their Facebook or LinkedIn profile, or sending event invitations or digital postcards that require the recipient to click to a Web page.

ADDITIONAL TIPS FOR GETTING THE GREATEST MILEAGE FROM YOUR NEWS RELEASES

1. Keep the tone objective, not promotional. Hype, unsubstantiated superlatives, or direct sales pitches ("VimVy Vitamins will make you stronger, sexier, and sassier") all kill interest in giving you free media space or time. Whenever you want to include an opinion or praise, attribute it to someone—a real person only!—and stick it within quotes. "'VimVy Vitamins will make you stronger, sexier, and sassier,' says Hypatia Hiram, a customer since 1988," is more likely to survive screening.

2. Proofread rigorously. Editors have told me that if they spot a single typo or misspelling in a release, they toss it out. Send your release through the checklist in Chapter 17 to eliminate common writing errors.

3. Produce different versions of your release for separate, distinct audiences. When Dan Poynter was issuing a new edition of his *The Parachute Manual*, he sent out three releases, one for each market to which his book appealed. For piloting and aviation magazines, he used the headline, "Skydiving = A New Way to Fly"; for sports magazines he talked about parachuting as the fastest non-mechanical sport; and for parachutists, most of whom were probably already familiar with his book, he offered a straightforward announcement that a new edition was available. "In talking about skydiving as a way to fly, I was using language to which pilots could relate, but that experienced skydivers would think was dumb," says Poynter.

Similarly, in connection with the publication of the original edition of this book, I prepared releases for legal magazines and papers that started off, "New Book Helps Lawyers Overcome Fear of Promotion," releases for dental publications that began, "New Book Helps Dentists Overcome Fear of Promotion," and so on. Likewise, I created versions of the last sample release in this chapter, on the next page, for authors and publishers, nonprofits, hotels and inns, the real estate industry, and more.

4. Plan to be available after you distribute your release. Just before you head off to Tahiti for three weeks is not a good time to send off news releases, unless you've prearranged to be accessible there. For daily newspapers, radio, or TV, distribute your stuff around two weeks before any date on which you'd like coverage; for weekly papers, a month ahead; for monthly magazines, three or four months ahead is wise. Allow even longer lead times for bimonthly or quarterly periodicals.

5. Take advantage of the option to send photos or audio/video files along with the release. Some of the news release distribution services allow you to post one or two photos or graphics or a short audio or video file for transmission along with the release, either for a small additional fee or no extra charge. This is a fantastic opportunity to add dimension to your story if you have or can create relevant photos or audio/video footage. According to publicity expert Joan Stewart, appropriate images can double your chances of getting media coverage.

If you've written a decent news release that appears complete, some media outlets run it word for word, condense it, or rewrite it, embellishing on the information you sent them. Others call you to get additional information, satisfy themselves that you are legitimate, or invite you to be a guest on their program. If you hear only a loud, resounding silence, this does not mean you've done anything wrong. Make sure you've followed all my guidelines and try again. Even Madonna's redoubtable press agent can't get her exposure everywhere, all the time.

There's one variant on these formulas that I'd like to share with you before we turn to supporting materials for your news releases. For magazines and for increased traffic from search engines, sometimes you'll want to issue a news release that isn't timely but instead offers useful, well-targeted information for a certain audience. The following release makes a faint stab at timeliness, but the substance has just as much relevance last year or next year as now. If you're hoping to spread the word about your expertise, I recommend releasing "evergreen" tips such as this on a regular basis.

SAMPLE NEWS RELEASE #3

For: Creative Ways, P.O. Box 305, Goshen MA 01032.
Contact: Marcia Yudkin, 1-800-333-8376, marcia@yudkin.com.

FOR IMMEDIATE RELEASE

In Today's Nervous Economy, Financial Planners Can Attract New Clients and Encourage Referrals Through Teleseminars

April 25, 2008, Goshen, Massachusetts—Despite all the buzz about social media, viral media, and blogging, an incredibly easy-to-use, precomputer medium can be a productive marketing tool for financial planners: the telephone. Teleclasses or teleseminars—which are essentially an extended telephone conference call—can be a cost-effective way for financial planners to appeal to mid-career professionals and other busy clients who would never attend a lunch or dinner seminar. A new self-study course from veteran teleclass presenter Marcia Yudkin (*www.yudkin.com/teleteach.htm*) enables teleseminar novices to get a fruitful program up and running within weeks.

"If you can keep an audience listening on a telephone call, you can run teleseminars as a marketing, retention and referral tool," says Yudkin, the author of 6 *Steps to Free Publicity* and 10 other books. "They don't require you to understand computers or to be Web savvy, and it's possible to run them at little or no cost."

Just a few of the countless ways financial planners can implement teleconferences:

- ✦ Free Q&A financial planning session for parents of college-bound teens.

- ❖ Joint appearance with a tax professional discussing for clients why and how planners and tax pros need to coordinate strategies.

- ❖ Paid four-part teleseminar on the basics of investing.

- ❖ "Question of the month" call, announced by postcard or voice broadcast to client list.

- ❖ Referral tool: no-sales-pitch retirement planning teleseminar that clients can invite four friends to attend.

Yudkin's comprehensive "Teleteach for Profit" course includes information on costs, teleclass structure, marketing, publicity, logistics, technologies needed and not needed for success with teleseminars; samples of pertinent e-mails, postcards, transcripts, and other people's teleseminars; one-on-one consulting or moderation of the participant's teleclass; free distribution of one teleseminar-related news release; and two months of access to a private member forum for feedback and answers to questions. Including every ingredient necessary for success in marketing through teleclasses, the program costs $795.

For more information on "Teleteach for Profit," go to *www.yudkin.com/teleteach.htm*.

❖❖ ❖❖

Although Chapter 16 discusses a way to get the attention of key media people without spending a cent on distribution, news releases remain the easiest, most cost-effective method. You never know in advance which media outlets will respond with interest, and, by distributing news releases, you can reach dozens or hundreds simultaneously. Many public relations professionals insist that you must call recipients of your news releases to follow up. But most of the individuals I spoke with for this book whose businesses get constant press never—never—make follow-up calls. Hence, I'd say that, although polite follow-up calls along the lines of "Did you receive my press release?" may sometimes provide an extra opportunity nudge, they're not necessary. Just write your most compelling, carefully targeted news release and, in Dan Poynter's words, "Lick it, stick it, and send it." Then watch the results pile up.

Chapter 5

Supporting the Story With a Media Kit or Online Media Room

Most of you, I'm assuming, don't have gargantuan publicity budgets at your disposal. Hence the common request, "Please send me your media kit," might provide you cause for alarm. It sounds fancy and intimidating, doesn't it? A media kit (also called a "press kit") is nothing more than a packet of materials that you send any member of the media when he or she asks for it, or that you send in advance when you are trying to appear on a major talk show. Its contents reinforce your claim to be worthy of publicity. Except for the photographs, you can prepare everything that you need to back up your story for the media by visiting any office supply store and a copy shop. If you have a Website, you can eliminate the media's wait time for a media kit to arrive by mail through a special area of your site devoted to the needs of the media.

COMPONENTS OF A MEDIA KIT

Of the following ingredients, those preceded by a star are standard and pretty much required; those preceded by a dash are optional.

* **A black-and-white or color glossy photo,** either 5×7 or 8×10. Include your name and contact information on the back. Instead of writing on the back of the photo with a pen, use a sticker or mailing label printed with the information, or write with a felt-tip marker. Generally the media prefers a head shot. In most cases, black and white will flatter you more than color, notes Rob Frankel, author of *The Revenge of Brand X.* "Very few people spend the time or money to get a color shot right. Lighting alone can turn Cinderella into the Wicked Witch of the West."

Most professional photo labs offer bulk rates for 12 or more copies of the same shot. If you think you'll need hundreds of photos, you can save hundreds of dollars by ordering lithographs instead. They look fine to the uneducated eye, and their quality is clear enough for publication in newspapers and most magazines. (See Chapter 24 for a wholesale source of publicity lithographs.)

You can also enclose a CD containing a selection of digital photos. Be sure these are high-resolution images—that is, 300 dpi or better. You can find more tips on taking and using photos at the end of this chapter.

* **A bio (biography)** of you or your business or both, in paragraph form. Do not enclose a résumé. You are not applying for a job! The bio should highlight your most important accomplishments, particularly recent ones, and should make you sound interesting. For a media kit you need a one-page biographical description about yourself or your organization—both, if the organization has a significantly different history from your personal history. A news release usually contains a condensed, one-paragraph version of your bio, as do your own marketing materials. A one-sentence version of the bio comes in handy as a blurb to accompany articles by you or in "coming attractions" notices about you.

Whatever the length or slant of the bio, begin with a catchy summary first sentence. Lead off with the most important thing or things you want the reader to know about you or the business. For example:

✦ "Helen Planetstein has been active in the save-the-whales movement since 1989, when she helped publicize the plight of a beached whale on Cape Cod."

✦ "A certified plumber and electrician for the past 15 years, Tom Reilly launched his inventing career in 2006 with a patented, nontoxic drain declogger."

✦ "Quintabulousness, Inc., an interior design firm for hardened individualists, is the creation of local socialite Beverly Monoppilino."

Then add supporting details in the following sentences.

Normally you should not arrange facts in strict chronological order. Instead, go in order of decreasing importance. Remember that the purpose of the bio is to present background information in an engaging way, not to be comprehensive. Accordingly, you need to select ruthlessly what needs to be included and what can be left out. Customarily, bios use third person (he/she/it/they) rather than first person (I). When you edit and polish a bio, think lively and think specific. Use complete sentences and paragraphs instead of the clipped style typical of résumés, and be sure your final version passes all the tests in Chapter 17.

Following are the dual bios I wrote in 1990 to accompany the book *Smart Speaking* by Laurie Schloff and myself. The condensed bios that appeared on the book jacket follow. In the longer version, I avoided the dry, flat tone of the average bio.

FULL-LENGTH SAMPLE BIOS

Laurie Schloff's speaking career began at the age of 4 when she sang 14 verses of "Davey Crockett" to 200 folks at a nursing home in Old Orchard Beach, Maine. She officially entered the field of speech with a masters of science degree in speech pathology from Columbia University and a certificate of clinical competence from the American Speech-Language-Hearing Association. Since 1980, Laurie has been a senior communication consultant with The Speech Improvement Company, a nationwide communication consulting firm based in the Boston area. She works with clients in all walks of life, from attorneys to zoologists, and from secretaries to executives at companies that include Polaroid, John Hancock Insurance, Hit or Miss, the Ritz Carlton Hotel, Digital Equipment Corporation, AT&T, Massachusetts General Hospital, and Harvard University.

→→ ←←

Although Marcia Yudkin played the Cowardly Lion in *The Wizard of Oz* at summer camp at age 12, she didn't become serious about public appearances until going on the lecture circuit after the 1988 publication of her third book, *Freelance Writing for Magazines and Newspapers.*

She has been a keynote speaker at numerous writers' conferences and presents workshops on creativity and getting published coast to coast. Marcia has a doctorate in philosophy from Cornell University and is vice president of WordRight, which provides writing seminars and consulting services to companies and individuals in Boston and throughout the Northeast.

CONDENSED SAMPLE BIOS

Laurie Schloff is a senior consultant with The Speech Improvement Company in Boston. She has taught at the university level, has consulted with major corporations, and conducts workshops nationwide. Marcia Yudkin is a founder of WordRight, a Boston writing consulting company, and the author of *Freelance Writing for Magazines and Newspapers*.

—**Articles by or about you.** These should be readably photocopied, with some indication of where and when the pieces appeared. Many people clip the masthead or logo of the publication (that is, the name of the publication in its distinctive type style) and paste it up together with the article. This can catch attention better than simply writing the publication's information in the margin by hand.

—**Tip sheets by you.** These are lists such as "10 Ways to Mouseproof Your Cellar" or "7 Reasons You're Probably Paying More Taxes Than You Should" that are equivalent to articles but haven't been published. (See Chapter 7 for more on why and how to put these together.) If you can't do desktop publishing yourself, take them to a place that can format and typeset them nicely for you.

—**News releases.** Include any that are relatively recent and still characterize you or your business.

—**Other marketing or publicity material.** If you have a brochure or printed newsletters, include them.

—**Media contact sheet.** If you've been featured in the press or on radio or TV several times before, include a list of the publications or shows.

—**Quote sheet.** If you have three or more testimonials from authoritative figures or from media reviews, print them up together on one page. Include complete attribution for all quotes: the person's full name, job title, and company (or other credential). Otherwise they are meaningless. (See Chapter 19 on how to obtain and edit testimonials.)

—**Fact sheet.** Whenever you can provide an easy-reference roster of facts about your subject, you position yourself as a credible information source. Because fact sheets are likely to be saved and quoted from in issue-oriented articles that do not focus on your business, print yours on a letterhead or include all your contact information so you'll receive credit if they're separated from your media kit. Offer statistics, explode myths, and recite research findings in your fact sheet.

—**Talking points.** If you're aiming for radio or TV, include a list of questions the host can ask. These should be intriguing questions designed to lead into what you want to talk about, such as, "What do you think is the biggest mistake most entrepreneurs make?" or "You've said that there are three situations in which people can do their own divorce. What are they?" The purpose is not to show journalists how to do their jobs, but to get them interested in finding out the answers from you—on air. Alternatively, you can provide a crisp, concise list of your major points if you think your answers will be more compelling than the questions designed to generate them.

—**Client list.** Consultants or seminar leaders who do business with famous corporations, organizations, or individuals may want simply to enumerate them, without any quotes. If your list begins, "AT&T; Bell Labs; CalTech Alumni Association; Boeing..." that's almost as strong as fantastic quotes.

—**Photo or sample of product.** Inventors or manufacturers will should consider enclosing a sample of what they make or information on how to obtain a sample. Jim Scott, maker of Great Scott! fudge, says that a scrumptious sample of his product along with a news release helped win him features in *Bon Appetit*, *Food & Wine*, *Chocolatier*, and the *Los Angeles Times*.

—**Creative packaging or enclosures.** If your service or product lends itself to humor or fantasy, sure, get creative. But try something cute to promote your blue-chip investment brokerage, and you'll usually be laughed right into the wastebasket. Debbi Karpowicz did get an excellent response when she sent out media kits for her book, *I Love Men in Tasseled Loafers*, in bona fide shoe boxes. Each contained a news release rolled up and tied with a leather loafer tassel that she had persuaded the Allen-Edmonds shoe company to donate. The kit also contained a photo showing her in a nearly backless gown, looking seductively over her shoulder while holding up a men's loafer. Just as appropriately, actor Norman George's promotional photo shows him dressed in period costume as Edgar Allan Poe, the focus of his show *Poe Alone*. George encloses a 12-inch black feather reminiscent of Poe's famous poem, "The Raven," along with the photo, copies of articles about him, playbills, flyers, and endorsements. "An inexpensive promotional item helps your release stick in the mind of the editor," he says.

Generally people place these materials in a 9×12 colored folder with pockets. Linda Barbanel makes a subtle statement with folders in green—the color of money, her theme. She hasn't found any other sort of customization necessary. But if you like, you can personalize generic folders by pasting your business card neatly on the front. Book authors can paste extra book covers, or a color copy of the book jacket, on the front of the folders. Remember to include your contact information on each item in the packet, because recipients may separate parts of the kit.

ONLINE MEDIA ROOMS

Setting aside an area of your Website specifically for the media brings you several advantages. It can eliminate the time your materials might otherwise spend in the mail getting to media folks, lightening the stress of reporters and editors on deadline and saving you the expense and trouble of sending materials by overnight mail. A comprehensive and well-executed online media room can also catch the attention of reporters, editors, and talk-show scouts who roam the Web looking for sources or guests. Just as usefully, this information can help impress members of your target audience poking around various corners of your Website.

In 2001, world-famous usability expert Jakob Nielsen sat 20 journalists in front of a computer and asked them to find specific company information, including how to contact the company's PR person, at the sites of large organizations. Only 60 percent of the time did the journalists manage to find what they were looking for—the equivalent of a grade of "D." Many participating journalists complained that they didn't trust a contact link such as "PR@companyX.com," but rather wanted the name of the person receiving the e-mail and another way to reach that person in case the e-mail received no reply.

You can do much better than the companies in Nielsen's study by using the following guidelines to make your Website media-friendly.

- ✦ **Make your online media room easy to find.** Too often, sites bury the kinds of information media people look for five levels down. Instead, provide a main link called "Press Room," "Media Room," "In the News" (this combines clips and links for past coverage with info for the media), or "About Us."

- ✦ **Post all media materials (except photo files) in HTML on regular Web pages.** Don't require the use of Flash. Don't put news releases in pop-up windows, which can't be printed out. Don't make visitors download documents that could very well be presented as straightforward text. Don't put media information in PDF format, which doesn't allow for cutting and pasting.

- ✦ **Include downloadable photo files for print and electronic use.** Glossy magazines require a resolution of at least 300 dots per inch. A photo that looks fantastic on your Website usually isn't suitable for reproduction in print. According to Hilary Kaye, a PR practitioner in Tustin, California, don't assume that your fancy-dancy digital camera or camera phone gets the job done well enough for newspapers or magazines. "Low-resolution photos taken with digital cameras may be fine for Websites but are not appropriate for print media. Less expensive digital cameras cannot provide high-resolution shots, so your usages will be confined to the Internet," Kaye says. Whereas print publications need a resolution of 300 dpi, Web-based media prefer images with a resolution of 72 dpi. So provide both high-solution and low-resolution downloads in your online media room.

→ **Offer accurate, specific contact information.** This means a name, a personal e-mail address, a phone number, and the location or time zone.

→ **Make past news releases available.** Include the date of each, and place the most recent release first.

→ **Support your credibility with links to previous media coverage.** Remember to respect copyright laws, which protect the complete text of articles, the layout of magazine or newspaper articles, and media company logos. I was once flabbergasted to see that a well-known Web guru had "edited" an article I wrote quoting him for a major business magazine by presenting on his Website just the portions of the article about him, under my byline. When I gently brought it to his attention that this was improper, he deleted this chopped-up version of my work and did what he should have done to begin with—that is, provided a link to the article on the business magazine's site.

→ **Facilitate last-minute fact-checking.** Try to anticipate the basic facts reporters, editors, or fact-checkers might need to confirm at the last minute, and make the answers easy to find. This includes your physical location, date of founding, the identity of key personnel, and the spelling of names that might appear in articles.

→ **Provide other elements that might belong in tangible media kits.** Tip sheets, fact sheets, quizzes, talking points, and a client list all make sense here as well. Audio or video clips make a nice addition online, when you have them.

→ **Include statements on current controversies.** It's peculiar for a journalist to go to the media room of a company that's had recent negative coverage and to find nothing there remotely connected to it.

→ **Remember that the Web is global in reach.** Spell out dates unambiguously. One European reporter in Jakob Nielsen's study dismissed a company's news as old because it was dated 10-3-2000, which to him meant March 10 rather than the intended October 3. Avoid country-specific acronyms and insert the kinds of background explanations that would be found in a quality news story.

PUBLICITY PHOTO TIPS

"You should build your publicity campaign around strong pictures," advises Joan Stewart, who spent more than 22 years working as a news reporter and editor before becoming a media relations consultant. "With pictures, your words become three-dimensional, and they leave a lasting impression." Great photos included in a media kit or online media room can persuade editors to cover events that they might otherwise skip over and can convey emotion that influences viewers to become customers. In fact, even if you're not ready to produce a full-fledged media kit, take the steps necessary to commission a professional portrait of yourself as soon as you put down this book. "Three out of four of the people I approach to publicize in my *Publicity Hound* newsletter have poor-quality photos or none at all," says Stewart. "Forget about snapshots that show you with friends or family. Editors won't bother to crop out babies, husbands, or friends. They just won't use your photo."

Your photo should fit the image you want to project without looking clichéd. According to Nat Starr of Troy, Michigan, who specializes in advertising for professional speakers, overdone poses include holding a trophy, posing on a platform with your mouth open as if you're talking, shaking hands with someone else, pretending to write or talk on the phone, and pointing at something, such as your product. To that list I would add, for highbrow types, the "Thinker" pose (chin resting on knuckles). Jeff Davidson, author of *Blow Your Own Horn* and 17 other books, updates his photos often and keeps different pictures on hand. "It's boring," he says, "to see the same picture of someone used over and over for years."

Here are some additional photo tips from Joan Stewart's excellent e-book, *How to Use Photos & Graphics in Your Publicity Campaign*, available from *www.PublicityHound.com*:

✦ Action photos help people identify with your company and feel as if they're part of the creation of your product—for example, when you show a photo of a site supervisor inspecting a house or a carpenter cutting a piece of wood. This convinces viewers that your company makes a difference in the way the products or services are delivered, Stewart says.

✦ Don't resize, crop, or touch up digital photos before giving them to media people. Leave such manipulation to their art departments—which are made up of pros.

✦ Photos can be sized down but not sized up. Magazines usually need 8×10-inch photos.

✦ Shoot products in both black-and-white and color. Yes, color shots can be transformed into black-and-white ones, but with a loss in sharpness.

✦ For trade magazine coverage, generic industry photos can win you brownie points with art directors. You'll earn photo credits and perhaps a chance for a starring role at the magazine.

✦ When photos feature people as primary subjects, obtain their signature on a model release to guard against legal claims later. (Google "sample model release" and you'll see how this works.)

✦ Provide a caption for each photo that identifies the people in it from left to right (with the correct spelling of everyone's names, of course), where the photo was taken, a brief description of the action and its result.

✦ Never ask for photos to be returned. It makes you look cheap, says Stewart.

Chapter 6

Letters That Pitch for You, Rattle the Public, or Roll Out Your Message

I f you're targeting just a few media outlets, should you still bother with the formality of a news release? Yes. It contains all the information they need in a format that enables them to appraise it quickly. But if you have some personal connection with a publication or radio/TV program, you may want to use a more personalized approach. Perhaps your college alumni notes inform you that a classmate hosts a talk show, your friend Franny's uncle lives next door to Rudy Reporter, or you once shook hands with the *Sentinel's* lifestyles editor after hearing her speak. Or perhaps you've read Carole Columnist for 10 years and feel as if you know her. In these kinds of cases, send a one-of-a-kind missive likely to be read with more attention: a pitch letter.

SAMPLE PITCH LETTER #1

Whatever the connection, lead off a customized pitch letter with a short statement of the link. Then concisely make your pitch, develop it, explain your qualifications on the topic of your pitch, and close the letter. Because you'll need more than a couple of paragraphs to fit all those ingredients, type the letter in standard business-letter format. Either use letterhead stationery or include your address and phone number at the outset. If you're sending the pitch by e-mail, include your contact information at the end. Here's a successful sample, sent by a friend some years back, slightly shortened and edited.

→→ ←←

Szifra Birke, M.S., C.A.D.A.C.
One Olde North Road, Suite 304
Chelmsford, MA 01824
(508) 250-1554

January 13, 1993

Paul Sullivan
WLLH Radio
44 Church St.
Lowell, MA 01853

Dear Paul,

By way of introduction, I'm Sally's daughter, from the noted Birke's Department Store, which after a mere 45 years in business now allows browsing! Your segments have brought my mother lots of attention. It's been fun to watch her reactions. Thanks.

I have a proposal for a show about Children of Alcoholism and Codependency to coincide with National Children of Alcoholics Week, Feb. 14-20, 1993. I hope you would be interested in doing an interview or somehow covering the issue. Besides the national scope, I've enclosed information about a Lowell-area poster contest and other local events scheduled for that week.

According to national estimates, 7 million children in the United States are living with at least one alcoholic parent, one of every eight school-aged children. Daily these youngsters face the fear, tension, and problems caused by parental drinking and codependency: They are children at risk. Possible angles:

○ Bill Clinton was raised in a home with alcoholism.

○ "Overage drinking" has as much impact on kids as teenaged drinking. The consistent focus has been adults advising kids, "Just say no." "Don't you ever do drugs." Kids need models, not critics.

○ Most resilient adults who grew up in alcoholic, troubled families can point to a person who believed in them—a grandparent, teacher, coach, clergy, Scout leader. A gift of attention or love from one of these adults to a child can change that child's future.

o   Many believe that children are fine once their parents are in recovery. But unless someone addresses their concern that the parents will start drinking or using again, the children's worry and hypervigilance will persist.

I have coauthored *Together We Heal: A Real-Life Portrait of Group Therapy for Adult Children* (Ballantine) and my articles on identifying and helping children of alcoholics will soon appear in the teaching magazines *Momentum* and *Teaching Today*. I am a mental health and alcohol counselor in private practice in Chelmsford, having begun my work with families of alcoholics in 1979.

Please let me know if this is a subject of interest to you; and if you can't use the ideas now, you might consider a story during Alcohol Awareness Month in April.

Thank you so much for your time.

Sincerely,

Szifra Birke, M.S., C.A.D.A.C.
(My name just looks difficult—it's pronounced "Shifra.")

→→ ←←

I don't recommend making up a connection where none exists—for instance by saying you read or listen to them regularly when you do not. Not only are the media's B.S. detectors the best in the world, but suppose your correspondent called you up and asked you something you could only answer from genuine familiarity with his or her work? Hence, even though your computer makes it easy for you to stick different editors' and producers' names and addresses into a standard letter, that doesn't count as meaningfully customizing it.

SAMPLE PITCH LETTER #2

Another publicity strategy involving a customized pitch letter is agreeing or disagreeing with a newspaper or magazine columnist. Here you latch onto a statement the columnist has already made and connect your expertise, experience, or convictions to an angle the columnist apparently hadn't considered. Your purpose is to provide corrective information or a challenging viewpoint that inspires or goads the columnist into mentioning you and your point in a future column. Whether you're writing to agree or disagree, maintain a respectful tone. Keep to one or two pages, enclosing supplementary materials you may have that back up your claims and introduce your work or organization more fully. The following is a sample letter I've been tempted to send.

❖❖ ❖❖

Marcia Yudkin, PhD
Creative Ways
P.O. Box 305
Goshen, MA 01032
(800) 333-8376
marcia@yudkin.com

Thomas Thompson, "Smarter & Smarter"
c/o *Big City Chronicle*
2578 Main St.
Big City, ST 55555

Dear Mr. Thompson:

I read your October 15 column with great interest. As a creativity consultant who teaches productive work habits, I have found that mindmapping is indeed a useful organizational or memory aid—for some people. Using bright-colored markers and a circular, web-like arrangement of ideas does reinforce ideas and make them more memorable for those who are visually oriented.

However, we're not all the same. People who are auditorily oriented may need to sort through and absorb material by talking it through with another person, whereas kinesthetically oriented people learn and remember best by using the material—putting it to work experientially.

I'd be glad to provide further information on creative styles, including additional experts in this area you could speak with, if you are interested. Enclosed are two columns I wrote on discovering one's idiosyncratic creative preferences for *New Writer's Magazine.*

Cordially,
Marcia Yudkin, PhD

→→ ←←

SAMPLE PITCH LETTER #3

In a third strategy involving customized pitch letters, you don't have to wait until a media outlet runs a story relevant to your purpose. You simply write to introduce yourself as a general source on a topic. Because this might not be acted upon right away, if possible, send a rotary file card indexed by your topic with your name, affiliation, and phone number along with your letter. Here's how this sort of introductory letter might run:

→→ ←←

[on organizational letterhead]

Willa Chu, Producer
WWWW-TV
45 Big Boulevard
Metropolis, ST 29999

Dear Ms. Chu:

If we can predict the future from the past, this summer the abortion controversy is bound to heat up again. Whether it's clinic blockades, demonstrations, abortion-related violence, or new court decisions, you'll probably be looking for a fresh point of view on this seemingly intractable issue.

Our group, Women for Dialogue, represents more than 700 women in the greater Metropolis area, both pro-choice and pro-life, who believe in mutual respect and civil debate on abortion.

I would be glad to appear on your show and discuss how productive dialogue on abortion is possible even when opponents are passionate about their positions. Or I could recommend two of our most articulate members, one on each side, to demonstrate this sort of discussion and interact with callers.

Please call me at (673) 555-1212 for more information or if you would like to arrange for us to appear on your show.

Sincerely,

Patricia James
President, Women for Dialogue

❖❖ ❖❖

Sample Pitch Letter #4

In Chapter 4, I mentioned the inadvisability of taking it upon yourself to subscribe media people to your e-mail newsletter. Instead, send a personal e-mail explaining how it would be to their benefit to subscribe, providing sign-up instructions and a link to a sample issue or your archives on the Web. Personalize it in some unmistakable way so that your e-mail doesn't come across as indiscriminate "spam." For instance, you could send an invitation such as this to a local newspaper editor or reporter:

❖❖ ❖❖

Subject: New "Living with Wildlife" Newsletter Keeps You in Touch With Community Concerns

To: Polly Person

From: Marty Mensch, "Living with Wildlife" Coordinating Editor

Dear Ms. Person,

If you'd like to easily keep your finger on the pulse of the more rural reaches of your readership, please sign up for our new weekly newsletter, "Living with Wildlife." Each week we report on what's happening in the hills with respect to environmental issues that often turn up in the headlines—conflicts with bears, beavers, hunters, birders who trespass without permission, new endangered species—as well as questions and discussion about animals and local wildlife sightings.

To subscribe, just go to *www.lwwhills.org*, insert your e-mail address into the box, and click "Send."

Thank you,

Marty Mensch

⇥⇥ ⇤⇤

PITCHING BLOGGERS

In June 2006, Jennifer Michelle of Fairfax, Vermont, was shocked while checking her Web statistics to see thousands more people visiting her lingerie Web store than usual. Investigating, she traced the surge in traffic to a post about her new "cell phone garter" product on the highly popular blog about gadgets, Gizmodo, which in turn seemed to have led to a mention by syndicated humorist Dave Barry. "Two years later, I'm still getting loads of visitors to my site and sales from those links," she told me. "I didn't know much about blogs then, but this taught me that they were valuable. I therefore began pitching blogs like KnickersBlog and The Lingerie Post, and they often printed my material."

Popular blogs not only have thousands or even tens of thousands of readers every day, but they also tend to have "must read" status with other journalists, other bloggers, and anyone else keeping a close eye on trends. In addition, links from blogs often get picked up by search engines quickly, sending more traffic your way when blogs are writing about you. But ask bloggers whether or not they enjoy having publicity seekers contact them and you're likely to get an earful.

"I receive around 25 pitches a day, and of those, about two per week are doing it right," says B.L. Ochman, an Internet marketing strategist for Fortune 500 companies who publishes the *What's Next Blog*. "The good pitches usually start with 'I saw you wrote about such-and-such last week, and I wondered if you would be interested in....'

Pitching a blogger is not that different from pitching anyone else: Know who you're talking to, what you're talking about; be succinct and don't send attachments. Don't send me a press release, just the 'who, what, when, where and why' in one paragraph."

To find influential bloggers in a certain niche, you can simply search for, let's say, "vegetarian blog" on Technorati (*www.technorati.com*) or Google Blogs (*www.google.com/blogsearch*). Or look at blog award Websites such as *www.bloggies.com* or *www.bloggerschoiceawards.com*. However, Brian Solis, author of *A Guide to Blogger Relations*, suggests that you may have more of an impact by seeking out not the bloggers who are most influential in their niche but those in the "Magic Middle," who have from 20 to 1,000 other people linking to them. "They help carry information and discussions among your customers directly in a true peer-to-peer approach. The true influencers are the peers of your customers."

Bloggers tend to favor products and ideas that will get their audience talking and creating links rather than straightforward news, so be sure you let any blogger you're pitching understand the significance of your story, not just the bare facts. Don't be pushy or overly familiar, and don't pretend you follow their blog if you actually do not. I often know instantly when someone falsely claims in an e-mail to be a regular reader of my stuff—something in the wording, or a wild mismatch with my ethics or preferences tips me off. If a blogger tells you your pitch doesn't fit what he's looking for, don't tell him he's wrong. "Unlike traditional journalists, who just ignore something that gets on their bad side, bloggers might print your e-mail and ridicule you," warns Ochman.

Often Overlooked: Letters to the Editor

Although pitch letters are not designed to be published, another species of letter is: the letter to the editor. Perhaps your junior high school civics teacher told you that the "Letters" column of your local newspaper represented democracy and freedom of the press in action. That's true, but she probably didn't tell you that the "Letters to the Editor" section of any magazine or newspaper also contains opportunities for free publicity for media-smart entrepreneurs and professionals.

And if you do have fervent views, or a cause to promote, why sound off only to the people you know when the media can carry your opinions to thousands or millions at once?

Newspapers, which run letters to the editor either right on their editorial page or very close by, usually offer readers a forum for topics of general concern as well as an opportunity to respond to articles they published. For example, if you're upset about the demonstrators who made you late for a job interview, a newspaper letters column might print your complaint even if the paper hadn't covered the demonstration. In contrast, most magazines run letters from readers in a special department up front, and stick to letters that respond to articles that appeared in recent issues. To contribute a letter to the editor at a magazine, then, you must read the magazine regularly and move quickly when you spot an opportunity.

Unlike call-in radio or TV shows, which ask you only for your first name and home town, both newspapers and magazines customarily publish at least the letter-writer's whole name and hometown, and often an organizational or business affiliation and title as well. And therein are chances to get your business message across to prime prospects at no cost to you.

Letters to the editor follow a simple format. Begin with "To the Editor:" even when you know the name of the editor. When responding to a published article, include the title and date of the article prompting your missive in the first sentence or two, in parentheses. Then agree, disagree, correct, comment, or amplify on the content of that article. When sounding off without specific provocation, include an indication of your topic's timeliness right up front before developing your idea. Here, for example, are some model openers:

- ✦ I couldn't agree more with Helen Jay's criticisms of the usual approaches to total quality management ("TQM: Harbinger or Hoax?," October)....

- ✦ Your article "Lawyers: Lowest of the Low to Some People" (March 28) did a real disservice to the 17.5 percent of attorneys in this county who provide at least some legal services without charge....

> ✦ As the summer fireworks season fast approaches, I'd like to share a story with adults and teenagers who think it's fun to defy the state ban on unlicensed fireworks displays. Five years ago my brother Bernie....

Below your signature, type your name, title (if any), affiliation (if any), and hometown, even if that information appears on your letterhead. Keep the letter to three paragraphs (up to 300 words) to maximize the odds that the publication will run it exactly as you wrote it. Make just one central point in the letter, back it up, and, if your purpose is professional visibility, emphasize your credentials within the body of the letter, not only at the end. For example:

> ✦ As inventor of a patented automatic umbrella drying device, I would like to defend umbrella owners....

> ✦ As someone who began working for animal rights in 1965, I have been gratified by the ever-increasing awareness of human abuses of animals....

> ✦ As a dermatologist who has treated hundreds of cases of severe acne, I disagree that parents should....

Stay on the lookout for these five kinds of opportunities to write publishable letters to the editor:

1. You agree with a writer. Don't simply express agreement. Add some information of value that shows off your services, products, programs, or general expertise.

2. You disagree. Even if you're ticked off, keep an even tone and explain why you think the writer was wrong. Insert some facts in your discussion that put your business or organization in a positive light for potential clients.

3. You're mentioned in an article and everything is accurate. Get double mileage from your good fortune by writing a letter of thanks for the mention and making a brief point that wasn't in the original article.

4. Something in an article requires correction. Because some readers who missed the article you're responding to will read your letter, never repeat the specifics of any damaging information or unfavorable claims, even to refute them.

Simply set the record straight, and reiterate the basic mission of your business or organization.

5.   An article overlooked you or your business. Instead of sulking when an article mentions competitors, horn in on their good luck. Use the fact that the publication covered your topic as an excuse to bring your existence to the attention of readers. If the article implied that your competitors had the field to themselves, gently protest. Otherwise just follow the previous guidelines in agreeing or disagreeing with an article.

If you happen to have extreme views on some topic unrelated to what you are attempting to publicize, I should warn you of a pitfall that didn't exist prior to the Internet and search engines. When print ruled supreme, you didn't have to worry that something you wrote for, let's say, *S&M'ers Unite!* would come to the attention of a mainstream journalist or a corporation thinking of hiring you as a consultant, or that a heated letter to the editor you wrote seven years ago on an obscure local controversy would be accessible now on the other side of the world. However, computer memories can be perfect, and very, very long online. You don't want something intemperate and potentially damaging in some people's eyes to pop up and put a dent in your reputation years later.

This scenario became real to me in 2002 when someone I had known on the online service CompuServe many years before contacted me out of the blue to say hello. He sent a series of several chatty e-mails, then revealed what must have been the real reason he looked me up. Back in 1995, I'd quoted him on a Website created by a then-colleague, and in the quote he'd disparaged America Online. Now his company was up for a major contract with AOL, and would I mind going back and erasing what he'd told me then? Sorry, I wrote back, but I don't have any control over that site. *Drat!* he replied. Don't let this happen to you—don't put your name to something you might not want to stand behind forever.

Fan Letters That Win You Traffic

Because of easy click-throughs possible on the Web, another kind of letter can pay off nicely now, although formerly it had little benefit for the writer. I'm referring to testimonial letters, which these days often get posted at the recipient's Website, complete with a link to you. When posted at a high-traffic site, or one whose readership perfectly matches your target market, that link can mean valuable traffic. The scales fell from my eyes on the value of doing this when I saw from my site's traffic logs how often someone searching for the name of a client of mine who had written me a testimonial arrived at my site, then read the testimonial and clicked through to the client's site. Presumably others reading the testimonials who didn't know my clients clicked through as well.

So each time you're happy with a service performed for you or a product you've purchased, instead of simply saying "Thank you" or keeping your contentment to yourself, consider writing a blurb expressing why you were satisfied, pleased, or ecstatic, and e-mailing it to the company responsible. End your message of praise with "And feel free to quote me on this," and very often the recipient will do just that. As with a letter to the editor, make sure that within the body of your praise, you mention what you do or what your company is up to. For example, "For anyone like us who helps recruit college presidents and other educational leaders, your service couldn't be more valuable." And add your site's URL when you sign off.

The same tips apply when you read a book you liked in your professional field of interest. Even if you bought it at a real-world bookstore, you can submit comments about the book at Amazon.com, Barnesandnoble.com, and elsewhere. In your review, find occasion to state how the book was valuable to you in your line of work. For example, "I read this book when our company, DocSafeT, was launching our portable document safes. It warned us away from so many pitfalls of new product introduction that the TravelSafe became an immediate success. Thank you!" So this doesn't sound like bald self-promotion, add a few more points that you appreciated in the book. After all, other Amazon customers can rate your comments, and you don't want to be tagged as unhelpful.

Chapter 7

Tip Sheets That Keep You in People's Minds, Files, and Favorites

Unlike some master networkers I know, I don't have much of a business card collection. To me they're usually utilitarian bearers of contact information without much other communicative value. Recently, however, I ran across a sheet of paper titled "How to Produce Photos With Impact" from Nat Starr Associates of Troy, Michigan, that I had picked up at a speakers' convention a decade ago. Because it was packed with useful tips, I saved it as I wouldn't have Starr's business card or brochure. You may not want to dispense with cards, but I hope you'll consider keeping tip sheets on hand as a basic publicity and marketing tool.

INTRODUCING THE TIP SHEET

A tip sheet is basically a list of, in most cases, six to 15 tips that show off your expertise and explain to the reader how to solve a personal or professional problem. The title should clearly indicate the content, and there should be an introduction of one to four paragraphs, followed by the numbered tips. Generally a tip sheet consists of only one page, written in a crisp, readable style. Later in this chapter, we'll consider its digital cousins, but for now we're discussing printed giveaways.

The title arouses interest among exactly the people you hope will become patrons of your business. Alliteration ("Five Factors"), surprise, and zippy numbers—7 and 12 have more snazz than 9 or 11—add appeal. These sample titles would work for tip sheets:

- → 12 Ways to Save on Property Taxes—Legally
- → How to Catch a Rich Husband in Less Than a Year
- → 5 Factors to Consider Before Choosing a Physician
- → What You Should Know About Stockbrokers and Why
- → Why Most Quality-Control Programs Don't Work
- → How to Check Out Your Dream House Before You Buy It
- → 7 Ways to Improve Your Golf Game—Off the Course

The following would not work for a tip sheet:

- → 17 Reasons Hanrahan, Hanrahan & O'Reilly Should Become Your Law Firm

Remember that a tip sheet is not blatant self-promotion. A good one promotes you in a subtle but compelling way because it offers information that only someone with genuine expertise could have delivered. It can contain examples, stories, or cases that embody what you've done for others, but these always remain subordinate to the tips. Use this question to distinguish an effective tip sheet from a marketing piece in the format of a tip sheet: Would this information be helpful to someone in my target market who couldn't care less about me and who might not ever buy my products or services? If the answer is yes, you're on the right track.

Because a tip sheet may have a long drawer life, it must be impeccably written. Polish it, edit it, and proofread it carefully. Unless you were an English major in college, find someone professional to go over it and make sure spelling, punctuation, and grammar are correct and consistent.

At a minimum, include your contact information prominently on the tip sheet. You can also soft-sell yourself on the tip sheet in a final paragraph that combines biographical information with what you offer clients and customers and how to get in touch with you.

It will look more official and impressive if you typeset your tip sheet in two or three columns. Most printing and quick-copy shops can do this for you for a reasonable fee. "Make it easy to read, so that you can take in what it is at a glance," says Barbara Winter of Las Vegas, who recommends tip sheets in the workshop she teaches around the country, "How to Establish Yourself as an Expert." "Don't worry about making it slick and glossy. I've seen excellent tip sheets printed on a letterhead," says Winter. I once ran across a tip sheet incorporated onto one side of a laminated bookmark, the other side promoting a new book. Brilliant—an attractive keepsake that simultaneously serves as promotional bait.

HOW TO USE TIP SHEETS

Let's count the ways tip sheets can earn you free publicity.

1. It's black-and-white proof of your expertise. Until you sit down to write your first tip sheet, you may not realize how much you know. "When you choose a small subject and decide to collect eight to 10 important points about it, that forces you to slow down and get organized. Then that builds your confidence," says Barbara Winter. It also builds up confidence among reporters and producers that you know your stuff. As a component of your media kit, a well-done tip sheet lends you at least as much added credibility as a photocopied clipping of an article by you in a non-prestigious publication.

2. You can use it as a handout at seminars or meetings. Unlike your talk, a tip sheet can be referred to again and again and passed on to others. The audience appreciates having the highlights of the presentation or additional pointers in a format that's much neater than their own notes. After the talk, the organization to which you spoke might reprint your tip sheet in its newsletter. Tip sheets come in especially handy on those occasions when you're speaking and the organization discourages you from selling products, giving your services a plug, or even passing out business cards. No one ever objects when you pass out beneficial information, and right there along the bottom is how to get in touch with you.

You can pass out tip sheets anywhere prospects have gathered, not only when you're up on the podium as the star. Enterprising folks have placed them on literature tables at conferences or handed them out personally at trade shows and exhibitions. Those who pick them up and keep them would not hang onto brochures or simple advertising flyers.

3. Material that you offer as a "freebie" can attract and identify potential customers. My most-used tip sheet originated in an article on getting published in big-circulation magazines. I wrote it for a writers' newsletter called *Minnesota Ink*, and it was later reprinted in the newsletter of the Boston local of the National Writers Union, to which I belonged. Shortly afterward, I transformed this article into a tip sheet and used it in a way that has worked for me many times since then. Having noticed that the Writers Digest Book Club bulletin included a column in which members asked other members for help or offered it, I wrote in announcing the availability of a free special report called "Breaking Into Major Magazines." To those who sent me their self-addressed stamped envelope, I sent my tip sheet along with a flyer for my *Freelance Writing* book and a promotional piece about my consulting services. One person from that promotion remained a valuable client for more than eight years after.

Many, many publications are delighted to run freebie notices at no cost to you. This is a tremendous deal, considering the credibility you receive because the offer isn't framed as an ad, and the fact that your fulfillment costs are minimal. Carefully select publications whose readers would benefit from your tips, and send them either a news release about the offer or a business letter, plus a sample of your item. To make it sound more valuable, consider pitching it as a "booklet," "tool," or "reminder card."

4. It's something you can send off to be published. Whenever you compile and print up a new tip sheet, let it do double duty by submitting its content to pertinent publications. Be sure you sell or give away only "one-time rights" rather than "all rights" so that you can continue to use your tip sheet in all the other ways on this list. Insist that the publication include your contact information at the end of the tips. If you offer the piece for free, it's hard for them to refuse.

5. It's appealing content for your Website. Naturally, post your tips on your Website. Steve Clark, a sales trainer in Gulf Breeze, Florida, used his tip sheet, "The 10 Most Common Sales Force Hiring Mistakes," as the centerpiece of a successful marketing campaign. He sent a series of three postcards to a list of business owners in his target market to entice them to find out more about his views on sales. One of the postcards read:

✦✦ ✦✦

Are you hiring salespeople who know how to sell?
That is Sales Force Hiring Mistake #3
Find out what's wrong with this and what to do instead in:
"The 10 Most Common Sales Force Hiring Mistakes"
Download it FREE at our Website: *www.saleswarrior.cc*

✦✦ ✦✦

For those who arrive at his site through some other means, the tip sheet serves as a free bonus for subscribing to his e-mail newsletter.

6. You can use a tip sheet as a panel of a brochure. Barbara Winter recalls a wedding consultant who took her advice and incorporated a list called "10 Ways to Have a Smoother Wedding" into her brochure. "People are more likely to hang onto your advertising piece when it includes valuable information that makes it more than advertising," she says. "I have a drawer loaded with little pamphlets on how to tie a scarf, take care of silk, decorate with baskets, and buy a new car."

BEYOND ONE-PAGERS

This chapter spent its first life as a tip sheet. At 853 words, it fit easily and nicely onto one page. If you could match that and develop 69 more tip sheets around the same size, voilà—you'd have a full-length book. Or just double the length and use larger type and you could have a four-page booklet. With at least four pages of tip-sheet-type information, you can even charge a dollar or two to defray your copying cost. New Jersey–based writer Robert Bly once charged as much as $7 for a booklet called "Recession-Proof Business Strategies: 14 Winning Methods to Sell Any Product or Service in a Down Economy," and sold more than 3,000 entirely through news releases to business magazines and newspapers. In case your math is rusty, that's a gross of $21,000. "The topic was timely," he explains in his book, *Targeted*

Public Relations. "The release was issued during the worst of the recession of the early 1990s."

The book you are reading now originated in a booklet. For a seminar I taught, I had created a four-page handout called "Six Steps to Free Publicity," and printed it up in an 11×17 folded format. Then I thought, *How can I use this to bring in additional business?* I offered it to the national newsletter *Bottom Line/Personal* for its "Freebies" column. At no cost to me, it ran six small lines describing the booklet and saying how to send for it. A staff person called me shortly before the notice ran to make sure I had 500 booklets on hand to satisfy anticipated demand.

That Number sounded like a lot to me, but I passed 500 five days after the first self-addressed stamped envelopes started to arrive. Then a blizzard shut down the post office, I had to go to New York for a day, and I returned to find 700 more requests waiting for me. And they kept on arriving. A postal clerk told me, as he fetched my daily bucket or two of envelopes, that I was receiving more volume than John Hancock and other mammoth companies that got their mail at that station. My husband set up an efficient system for the two of us to open the envelopes, type the names into the computer, fold the booklet together with my promotional offer, and stuff and send them all off within a few days of receipt. When three weeks had gone by, we had received 3,000 requests, and given my printer a Christmas bonus's worth of unanticipated business. And luckily, product orders and consulting jobs were bouncing back.

By the end of the second month, I had a good idea of who the 4,300 people were who'd written and why, and I wrote a book proposal. Without this bonanza, I'm sure I wouldn't have stopped to think whether I knew enough on the subject to write a good book. Nor would I have had quite enough credibility to make the case that I was someone who could get people to buy the book. But I explained to publishers that, because of the free publicity I'd received from *Bottom Line/Personal,* I now had a proven title and market intelligence on the kinds of people who were interested in free publicity. Of course, I had also amassed a list of prime customers for the book. When I began to negotiate a contract with Plume Books, I was still receiving an average of 20 requests a week. Even a full decade after the *Bottom Line/Personal* offer ran, I was still receiving about a dozen requests a month for the original booklet.

THE WHITE PAPER GAMBIT

If you serve business-to-business clients or sell complex, expensive business products, consider a sophisticated variant of a tip sheet that can help you spread the word about what you do to potential customers, both with and without the help of the media. A "white paper" is a nonselling piece, relatively objective in tone, that informs a certain audience about your area of expertise and subtly positions your organization as qualified to solve a problem for them. White papers often get passed around an organization that is actively considering major changes or investments in new technology. They usually run longer than tip sheets and either get posted on Websites for download in PDF format or are sent out upon request by phone, fax, or e-mail.

A successful white paper strategy begins with writing your document so that it reads well, uses a minimum of jargon, holds back on salesmanship, and truly educates the reader. Ideally, its title should mention both the problem it addresses and the solution. For instance: "Digital Printing Options for Companies Producing Annual Reports" or "Achieving Greater Participation of Underrepresented Minorities in Private Companies." On the last page of the white paper, following your educational presentation, include a profile of your organization and how you help clients solve problems, along with complete contact information. Format the white paper attractively, with lots of subheads to facilitate a quick read.

Once you've written and formatted it, send a news release modeled after Sample #3 in Chapter 4 to media in your industry. That is, don't merely announce that the white paper is available include meaty nuggets from it in the release. End by explaining how people can obtain a copy of the white paper. Also, create a bylined article related to the white paper, either by converting the news release into article format or by producing an edited excerpt from the longer white paper.

End the article with a biographical blurb that includes information on how to obtain the complete document.

To get the greatest mileage from the work you've done in creating the white paper, do three more things. First, send complete copies of it with a personal cover note ("Thought you'd appreciate having this") to current clients and hot prospects. Second, send tantalizing post-cards similar to Steve Clark's earlier in this chapter to companies and individuals in your target market. Third, look around on the Web for industry portals or noncommercial informational sites and topical link directories that might be willing to add a free link to your white paper. Consider also white paper repositories such as Bnet.com, which is free, and Bitpipe.com, which charges a fee for inclusion.

"A white paper is a wolf in sheep's clothing," says Andrea Conway, a Denver-based marketing communications specialist who has written more than 30 white papers for the computer industry. "You clothe the power and focus of your competitive message so that it looks and sounds like research. They're a terrific way to mar-ket to business-to-business customers who want to study a variety of approaches or learn more about a product without a direct sales encounter. When they request a white paper, they get to keep their distance and you get information about your product or service in front of a decision-maker."

ONLINE GIVEAWAY STRATEGIES

Because of the multimedia and interactive capabilities of the Internet, online giveaway strategies go far beyond what's possible with print. Besides offering bait pieces composed of written words, you can lure people with audio downloads, videos, and software tools as well as PDF files. With suitably appealing content, the dynamics of bookmarking and recommending items to a friend can quickly spread the popularity of your stuff to new audiences at little or no cost.

One popular strategy referred to as a "squeeze page" involves set-ting up a Web page that requires people to hand over their name and e-mail address before receiving your giveaway item, then automatically sending a series of follow-up e-mails until recipients either buy or take themselves off the list. Generally marketers send traffic to such a page via pay-per-click ads, postings on Web forums and discussion lists, and e-mails sent by affiliate partners. Be mindful that traditional media often refuses to help publicize a "squeeze page" giveaway because of the barrier before accessing the information. So I don't recommend issuing a news release for this.

Second, you can provide your freebie as a bonus that subscribers receive after signing up for your free e-mail newsletter. Here you post a tempting description of your bait piece on your home page and integrate the subscription signup form into a multi-page Website. You might be tempted to change your freebie offer frequently to see which giveaway item proves most appealing. That's fine—just realize that current subscribers may notice and email you for access to your lure, which they couldn't receive without unsubscribing and subscribing again.

Quite a different, very powerful way of giving away content online is dispensing with any requirement for the visitor to provide contact information by simply posting your tips, tools, or files for anyone to use or download. When the content has high value, this inspires bookmarks and links to your site, with individuals and media outlets recommending your page. As a result of such popularity, your site tends to rise higher and higher in search engine results, which in turn prompts even greater traffic from motivated searchers who might not otherwise know about you or your site.

For years, one information-rich page at my Website has received at least 400 visitors a day from search engines and from links at several business magazine Websites. I once challenged subscribers of my Marketing Minute newsletter to guess which page stood head and shoulders above all the other pages at my site in daily visits, and not one person guessed correctly! Learn how to monitor your Web traffic statistics, and you might notice such a gratifying, long-lasting appeal. Once you discover something like this, tamper with that page only at your peril.

Magnifying the effect of individuals marking Web pages as their favorites are social bookmarking Websites, such as Digg, Reddit, and

StumbleUpon, where people post links to cool items they've found. When that community votes en masse for a particular article, blog post, video or audio file, tens of thousands of others can stampede over to that link within hours. It costs nothing to submit your material to these sites and to encourage others to do so. According to Minnesota iconoclast Steve Olson, who writes a personal blog, what proves popular on one social bookmarking site may not appeal to members of another site. The Reddit audience, for instance, Olson found to be predominantly male, atheistic, leaning toward Libertarianism or Socialism in politics, and highly receptive to material on finances, psychology, science, and education, giving a poor reception to business advice, spirituality, and conservative points of view.

As broadband access has spread, more and more people and companies are using video in creative ways as their bait. YouTube, the third most visited site on the Web, and video-sharing sites it similar to, enable you to upload short videos for free that not only appear on YouTube, but also can appear on any other site that chooses to feature them. I got a taste of the so-called viral possibilities of video when I posted a video called The Internet Marketing Lifestyle on YouTube and invited people who knew me to go see it. (You can find it at *www.youtube.com/marciayudkin*.) Several people who knew me very slightly decided to embed my 2 1/2 minute movie on their sites, exposing me to totally new people, after which a perfect stranger did the same. Perry Lawrence posted it to his Video of the Week page at *AskMrVideo.com*, saying, "I love this because it shows another aspect of the IM [Internet marketing] lifestyle. I saw this and wanted to know more about Marcia and what she has to offer."

Harvard Medical School–affiliated therapist Jean Fain ventured into video at the urging of her husband, who works in high tech and told her that people don't read as much as they used to. For each of the four videos she created on the topic of mindful eating, she not only posted the video to YouTube, but also sent out a news release about it and contacted all the writers and editors she'd been in touch with throughout the years about her work. Results from the videos included "a larger audience, a bigger mailing list, way more Google listings, increased CD sales, and a client waiting list," she says—especially for the "Why a Twinkie?" video that was written up in the Boston *Globe*. Her local paper, the *Concord Journal*, published all the releases word for word, and "new clients mentioned reading the newspaper article, then looking at the video." Fain notes that unlike speaking engagements or even national radio/TV coverage, online videos can be easily watched again and again. Indeed, she designs her videos with that idea in mind and suggests visitors view them repeatedly.

Besides videos, miscellaneous Web tools called "widgets" are gaining popularity as a method of giving away something useful that prompts users to click to the site of the company that made the cool tool. For example, Babystrology.com enables expecting parents to post their Baby Countdown Pregnancy Ticker on their sites. Day by day, week by week, the widget baby grows and develops to match the real-life pregnancy. In the first five weeks, some 1,800 people added the 2 1/4×3 1/2-inch tool, which of course includes a link to *www.babystrology.com*, their site. Other widgets discovered in a random check of widget directories include a list of upcoming art show deadlines, a credit card payoff calculator, a yoga pose of the day, a healthy-living quote, and a map of which countries the hosting site's visitors come from. Combine creativity and usefulness in a quirky little widget, and you could have something people post and share that grows your traffic and reputation.

Chapter 8

Painlessly Publishing Articles Yourself

Publish? Me? I barely passed ninth-grade English!

Never mind. If you can create a list of useful tips, you can write a publishable magazine article. Getting published on your own is the fastest way to establish yourself as an expert, it helps you reach out to your target market, and it keeps on working for you forever when you include copies of your publications in your media kit or send them out to potential clients. In comparison with courting the media through news releases, you have more control of your message through article, writing. You also have the opportunity to develop your ideas in more depth.

Two major routes to publication exist: submitting a completed article and sending a query letter that proposes an article. It may surprise you to learn that the latter is the more common route to publication. But both strategies work, and I'll describe the steps involved in each.

GETTING FOCUSED

Both strategies begin with market research. Before you set pen to paper or fingers to keyboard, decide on your market, the group of people you'd like to reach. Here are some sample markets:

+ Women with enough wealth to afford diamonds.

+ Utility contractors who might need legal advice.

+ CEOs in the west.

✦ Travel agents who sell cruises.

✦ Training directors of companies with more than 500 employees.

At this stage, keep your publicity goal explicitly in mind. If you're writing articles to bring in new business, don't direct your writing toward your peers (other accountants, printers, restaurateurs), but rather toward your potential clients or customers. If you're hoping to get referrals from other physicians, roofers, or boat charterers who don't handle the specialized tasks you do, however, writing for your own professional or trade group makes good sense. With a goal of winning new converts to recycling, don't target a group that's probably already convinced. But with a goal of recruiting volunteers and donors for your nonprofit recycling initiative, by all means reach out to the converted.

After defining your market, think about and investigate which periodicals people in your target market read. The more specifically you've zeroed in on a target group, the more specialized the publications you approach should be. Then visit your public library, which contains numerous guides to publications of many types, or head out on your computer to the search engines. Think about these 11 categories of periodicals:

1. **Trade magazines.** Oriented toward practitioners of a narrowly defined business or profession, these magazines are rarely familiar to outsiders. But you'll find them listed in *Writer's Market*, the *Gale Directory of Publications and Broadcast Media*, and the *Standard Periodical Directory*. Two smallish online directories of trade magazines are Tradepub.com and tradewriter.freeservers.com.

2. **Regional business papers and magazines.** Examples: *San Diego Business Journal, Business Atlanta, New England Business*. These cover business and economic news in a defined geographic area. Be sure you have a local angle for this sort of periodical, and then check the listings in the *Gale Directory of Publications and Broadcast Media, Editor & Publisher International Directory, Bacon's Magazine Directory, Working Press of the Nation*, or the *Standard Rate and Data Service Business Publications*

Directory. Bizjournals.com provides an online gateway to more than 40 papers in this category owned by the same company.

3. **City newspapers.** Even the most casual visitor to your area soon learns the name of your city newspaper—the one sold in all the convenience stores and delivered to doorsteps. In addition, there are *USA Today* and *The Wall Street Journal*, two national newspapers. Larger papers have special sections for different topics, including food, entertainment, science, and education, and many accept contributions from people besides their salaried reporters. Look up newspapers outside your area in *Editor & Publisher International Yearbook* or *Bacon's Newspaper Directory*.

4. **Shoppers and community newspapers.** These tabloid-sized newspapers come free to your house or sit stacked ready for free pick-up at neighborhood supermarkets, libraries, and newsstands. Some include little but ads, whereas others contain local features and useful information for a broad base of local readers. They may be open to how-to articles on plumbing, real estate, cooking, or other subjects of general interest. Stick to those you can easily collect where you live and work.

5. **Alternative newspapers.** Some of these fall under the previous heading, because they're stacked around for free pick-up, but some cost from 50 cents to $1.50 at newsstands. Many include calendar listings. Boston has the *Boston Phoenix*, which covers politics, the arts, and lifestyles; *The Improper Bostonian*, an arts and entertainment biweekly for young professionals; *EarthStar*, a bimonthly guide for the spiritually minded distributed at New Age bookstores, health-food stores, and office buildings; and others. An excellent online directory of publications in this category appears at Altpress.org.

6. **Association magazines and newsletters.** Many trade, cultural, and activist organizations publish periodicals for their members. Look up any subject from abuse and neglect to

zeppelins in your library's copy of the *Encyclopedia of Associations* to locate prime candidates for your articles. I'm not sure why, but these publications often don't appear in any other directories.

7. **Subscription newsletters.** People buy subscriptions to these newsletters rather than receive them along with membership in an organization, and they're listed in the *Oxbridge Directory of Newsletters*, *Newsletters in Print*, and *Hudson's Newsletter Directory*. Often the publisher/editor writes the entire newsletter, but some subscription newsletters include material from outside contributors.

8. **Consumer magazines.** People buy consumer magazines for enjoyment and for information on hobbies, travel, people, and well-being. Readers usually comprise a distinct demographic subsection of the population, divided by ethnicity, sex, religion, age, region, or personal interests. The larger the circulation, the harder it will be for you to get articles published in these outlets; many deal primarily with professional writers. Look up this category in *Writer's Market* or the *Standard Periodical Directory*, and browse your local newsstands and bookstores for new broad-circulation and special-interest periodicals.

9. **Academic or scholarly journals.** If you possess proven expertise or academic credentials, try getting your work published in these volumes, which expect footnotes and other scholarly appurtenances. *Ulrich's International Periodical Directory* and the *Standard Periodical Directory* provide a guide for all subject areas.

10. **Websites.** Online publishing took a nosedive after the dotcom crash of early 2001, but a sizable number of Websites still welcome articles in their topical area. Hunt these down in a search engine using a search request such as this:

    "submit article" [keyword(s) for your topic]

    For instance:

    "submit article" wine

Using the keyword "wine" along with "submit article" turned up more than 300,000 sites to check out when I searched, and the phrase "pet care" along with "submit article" brought up more than 55,000.

11. **Company newsletters.** Publications in this category, published in print or via e-mail by privately owned companies large and small, are completely off the radar of the media directories, but they can provide a useful vehicle for reaching someone else's customers. Those charged with putting together and distributing these newsletters on a regular schedule are often desperate for prewritten, ready-to-go quality information relevant to their readers, and will often accept contributions from noncompeting colleagues, providing them with a brief credit line and contact information. You'll just need to be on the lookout for these opportunities when networking and in your mailbox.

For the examples I cited earlier, research would lead you to some of these periodicals:

→ Women with enough wealth to afford diamonds: *Vogue, Town and Country, Architectural Digest, The Robb Report.*

→ Utility contractors who might need legal advice: *National Utility Contractor, Underground Construction Magazine.*

→ CEOs in the west: *Boulder County Business Report, California Business Magazine, Oregon Business, San Francisco Business Times.*

→ Travel agents that sell cruises: *Star Service, Sailaway.*

→ Training directors of companies with more than 500 employees: *Human Resource Executive Magazine, Training.*

Another method of locating magazines that want to hear from you is to search for editorial calendars in a certain topic area. An editorial calendar is an issue-by-issue schedule of upcoming topics that editors use to commission articles, and that sales staff use to sell ads. Rather than let topics fall into place randomly, the editorial calendar provides for, let's say, cruises to be discussed in March, honeymoon trips in June, singles travel in September, and business trips in

November. By researching editors' plans, you can time queries and article submissions exactly right, and enjoy being featured in cover stories, special sections, and highly visible groups of articles.

Search engines can help you find editorial calendars on the Web. When I typed "editorial calendar pets 2008" in Google, for instance, writing opportunities at *Road & Travel*, *Whole Foods Magazine*, *Latitudes and Attitudes Magazine*, *Animal Wellness*, *Outdoor Woman* and many others came up. You can also hunt for editorial calendars at sites for particular publications. According to Meg Weaver, whose company Wooden Horse Publishing offers an online database of hundreds of editorial calendars, editorial calendars are often buried deep within a Website under a link called "Advertising Info" or "How to Advertise." Then look for "Media Kit," and, within that section, "Editorial Calendar." You may also obtain one by calling an advertising sales representative.

❖❖ ❖❖

After you've selected a target publication, decide what kind of article would be in line with your goal. Here are five kinds of articles that can serve as a vehicle for publicity:

1. **An opinion piece.** Journalists call these "op-ed" pieces because they often appear in newspapers *op*posite the *ed*itorial page. Magazines of all sorts run them, too. More carefully crafted than letters to the editor, these short pieces should be carefully reasoned and supported with persuasive evidence. Timeliness counts, and that includes tying your point of view in with general trends as well as with front-page news or holidays. Consultant Alan Weiss makes his submissions stand out by taking an opposite tack on hot topics. When the business world was excited about "quality," he wrote "The Myth of Quality Circles," and when "managing diversity" became a catchphrase, he succeeded with the theme, "Don't manage diversity, embrace it."

2. **A personal experience piece.** Writing about your feelings and experiences and observations may seem an odd route to publicity, but it pays off all the time for people seeking

publishers or literary agents. I see no reason why a personal essay couldn't lure customers and clients if placed in the right publication. Indeed, my first radio commentary had nothing to do with business, but it aired one weekday shortly before 8 a.m. on WBUR, Boston's public radio station, and at 9 a.m. sharp I received a call from someone who'd heard it who wanted to hire me to write a news release. She'd heard of me previously, and the radio piece prompted her to pick up the phone.

Examples of topics and publications would include a divorce attorney reflecting on the sadness and hope of his profession for a women's magazine or an ice cream store owner writing for a city parents' magazine, about the experience of serving kids in the town where she grew up. A memorable personal experience piece includes depth of feeling and dramatic detail.

3.   **A how-to or service piece.** See Chapter 7 to learn how to create a tip sheet that is also publishable as an article. Instead of six, eight, or 12 separate tips, you can also provide a series of steps that explain a process, or even just elaborate on one solution to a common problem. Whenever you tie your advice to pressing needs of a publication's readers, you'll meet with great demand. Include examples that show off your problem-solving prowess but avoid a self-promotional tone.

4.   **A round-up.** If you can't come up with enough stories and tips to fill an article, interview more seasoned experts and create a collage of their advice. The multiple voices cut down on the credibility and visibility you earn with this kind of article, but you still come off as well informed, and the piece offers a grand excuse for networking through phone interviews with the greats in your field.

5.   **A case study.** So long as your promotional purpose remains very, very muted, business magazines and Websites may be receptive to case studies in which you present a common challenge and provide the details of how an individual or

organization overcame it. If the case study focuses on your client, inject subtle reminders that the solution came about through your knowledgeable intervention.

✦✦ ✦✦

After deciding on a type of article, choose a subject. If you're just starting out, keep your focus practical and specific. Brainstorm what some of your major points about that subject might be. Then either organize those thoughts into an outline of the article or use them to write a query letter, following the instructions that follow.

IF YOU WRITE A COMPLETED ARTICLE

Polish and proofread your piece and make sure it's the right length for your target publication. Include a biographical sentence or two at the end of the manuscript with enough contact information that readers can easily find you. Although some determined readers will track you down without contact information accompanying the article, you'll get a greater response if the publication says where you live, or, even better, provides your phone number and e-mail address.

Send the article with a short cover letter offering "one-time rights" to the piece, along with a biographical paragraph explaining your credentials to write the piece. If sending by mail, enclose a self-addressed stamped envelope and wait a minimum of six weeks before following up with a polite inquiry if you haven't received a reply. Most editors will eventually answer you and send you a sample copy of the publication with your article if they do use it. If submitting by e-mail, remember that editors may not welcome attached files from someone they don't know, so cut and paste the article into an e-mail following a brief introduction along the lines of a cover letter. Wait a few weeks before following up.

Should you expect payment? I have mixed feelings on this issue. As someone who made a living from freelance writing for more than 20 years and who supports efforts to improve working conditions for writers, I believe that writing articles is work that deserves reasonable payment and respectful treatment. However, as someone advising you on how to get free publicity through writing, I have to tell you that some magazines and newspapers will find room for your work more readily if you accept the unpaid tradeoff of nothing but visibility in exchange for your article.

Indeed, I was once asked to serve as an expert witness in a case in which a business tabloid viewed publication in exchange for publicity as a fair quid pro quo. They even sent two editors to court for three whole days to wait for the case to come up. I attended the trial on the side of the freelancer, who won by showing the judge that the paper had told *Writer's Market* that it paid $150 to $225 for contributions. Yet to complicate the matter further, at the higher-quality, higher-budget publications, such as *Entrepeneur* or *The Wall Street Journal*, you would undercut your credibility by saying you were willing to forego payment. Perhaps the best policy would be to say in your cover letter that you're offering the article "on your usual terms," which leaves them the opening to tell you what their usual terms are.

Article fees, where they exist, vary widely. There are no standard rates. You may receive anything from an honorarium of $25 to $2,000 for a 1,000-word article (about four pages). After you receive sample copies, cut out your article, eliminating any advertisements that may share the pages, and paste it up nicely. You'll now have an impressive clip for your media kit. If the publication posts all its contents on its Website, you can link to your article as it was published there.

If You Send a Query

Most editors prefer queries because a short proposal allows them to provide you with input that ensures that your proposed piece comes to them with the length and the slant that they want. However, writing effective queries takes a little study and practice. Editors have three questions in mind when they read your query proposing to write a certain article for them:

- ⤙ What specifically is this person proposing to write?
- ⤙ Is this for us?
- ⤙ Can this person write?

Bolster your chances of receiving a go-ahead for the article by heeding these guidelines:

1. Make sure to address the query to a specific editor by name. Get the name from *Writer's Market*, or the other periodical directories listed earlier in this chapter, from the list inside the magazine, from the publication's Website or by calling the magazine.

2. Keep it to one page if possible—about 300 words.

3. Use a personal letterhead or include your address and phone at the top of the letter. If sending the query by e-mail, include your address, phone number, and e-mail address at the end.

4. The letter must showcase your writing ability, and evidence a mastery of spelling, punctuation, and grammar. The writing style must be compatible with that of the magazine you're querying.

5. One option: Write the first paragraph of the query letter as if it were the first paragraph of the article. Begin with an anecdote, startling statistic, interesting examples, or sparkling description.

6. Include the specific focus of the article and explain how you'll handle the topic. Naming one or two sources of information never hurts.

7. End with selected biographical information about yourself, including previous publications (if any), and any personal or professional facts that bolster your credibility to write on the topic.

8. Don't give everything away in the letter, but make it sound as if you already know a lot about your topic.

9. Enclose a self-addressed stamped envelope if using postal mail.

As with a completed article, wait at least a month before calling or writing to follow up.

SAMPLE ARTICLE QUERY

This was sent by e-mail to the editor handling the area of marketing after I caught the attention of *Business 2.0* editor in chief Jim Daly with a letter to the editor (see Chapter 13 for that story). Note how specific the proposal is. It won the assignment.

Dear Nancy Rutter:

UP AGAINST THE GIANTS

With long-established, famous dotcoms like garden.com failing, what hope is there for the "little guys" who have never attracted venture capital? Quite a lot of hope, in fact. Small businesses have these advantages and more vis-a-vis Internet Goliaths:

* Can more easily use a consistent personality to build a reputation.
* Can deliver true one-to-one customer service by e-mail and phone.
* With closer ties to clientele, can discern market trends without formal research.
* With no bureaucratic layers, can respond quickly to market needs and requests.
* By specializing, can build up deeper inventory for a small, profitable niche.
* Don't have to worry about investors suddenly getting cold feet.
* Can achieve actual profitability and an attractive return on investment.

I'll include quotes from and information about small online businesses that illustrate these points.

You can find seven articles on low-cost Internet marketing that I've done so far for ClickZ Today at *www.clickz.com/cgi-bin/gt/archives/author.html?author=184* as well as loads of articles on marketing in general at my Website, *www.yudkin.com*. My latest book is *INTERNET MARKETING FOR LESS THAN $500/YEAR*, published by Maximum Press.

I look forward to hearing from you about whether the above ideas hit the mark for *Business 2.0*.

Sincerely,

Marcia Yudkin
P.O. Box 305
Goshen MA 01032
Phone: 800-333-8376
E-mail: marcia@yudkin.com
Website: *www.yudkin.com*

THE "NICHE TO GET RICH" STRATEGY

Perhaps you service quite a varied clientele—everyone from attorneys to membership organizations to zoos. You'll feel tempted to write general articles and attempt to place them in magazines and at Websites. However, there is a much smarter way to accomplish your goal. Instead of writing in a generic way, which may prompt the response "Interesting but not targeted enough to us" from editors, choose three or four occupational or special-interest groups to target in a year, and customize a series of general articles for those niches.

Let's say, for example, that you're a physical therapist who has a strong emphasis on building habits that prevent injuries and chronic pain. From the long list of kinds of people who end up in your office and who could benefit from your advice, you choose three white-collar professions whose practitioners are often on their feet for long periods of time: trial lawyers, public speakers or trainers, and school-teachers. Each of these niches has publications and the ability to pay for the physical therapist's services, which would not be true of musical conductors (not enough of them to support magazines for the occupation), waiters and waitresses (who often don't get health benefits), and entertainers (ditto). You then develop several articles on aspects of being on your feet all day and sprinkle the proper terminology and relevant examples into customized versions for each niche. Choosing just a few niches at a time focuses your publishing efforts intelligently.

BEYOND ARTICLES

The ultimate publicity value from writing accompanies publishing a book. According to Larry Rochester, author of *Book Publicity for Authors and Publishers*, the greater media attention paid to authors than nonauthors has a logical explanation. Media people assume that anyone who has published a book has researched a subject thoroughly and thus can probably speak with authority and passion on his or her subject. Even when a topic isn't directly related to the book you've published, doors can open.

I experienced a strange confirmation of this principle after I wrote a pitch letter about my work on creativity to a business writer named Michael Pellecchia, whose column gets picked up by newspapers around the country after it appears in the *Fort Worth Star-Telegram*. After interviewing me by mail and phone, he told me that, because his column featured business books, he would mention the forthcoming paperback edition of *Smart Speaking* in the opening before turning to my ideas on creativity, which I was then currently researching and teaching about. In other words, the fact that I had published a book made me eligible for coverage on a completely different topic in his column.

Another publicity advantage of books over articles is that a book that lives on in libraries can keep your name before editors, producers, and the public forever. More than a decade after its publication, social worker Merle Bombardieri was still receiving calls from potential clients who had read her 1981 book, *The Baby Decision*, in their public library. She also received a call from Ande Zellman, editor of the *Boston Globe Magazine*, who asked how she could get a copy of *The Baby Decision*, which was out of print, for the *Globe Magazine* library. Bombardieri had been quoted a few times in that magazine, but she'd never written for it herself. Thinking quickly, she asked Zellman, "While I have you on the phone, are you the right person to send queries to?" Zellman replied, "Yes, but why don't you tell me what you had in mind to write?" Bombardieri made up an article idea that capitalized on the editor's interest in her book, and received a contract for her ad-libbed idea in the mail.

Finally, even in this electronic age, the depth of knowledge revealed in a book can make a direct, gratifying effect on readers. Tony Putman says that since publishing *Marketing Your Services*, he's received telephone calls and letters from every continent except Antarctica, representing hundreds of thousands of dollars in billings. The secret, he says, is writing something that makes a clear and distinctive point about the difference you can make with the problems readers have. "Write so that the reader will say, 'This is exactly what I've been looking for. I'll give this person a call'"—excellent advice to keep in mind for articles, too.

YOUR OWN E-ZINE OR BLOG

If you enjoy writing, you don't have to depend on the publishing industry to convey your latest chunk of thinking to your target market, of course. For minimal cost, you can attract subscribers and readers to your insights as published in your e-zine or blog. An e-zine, or e-mail newsletter, containing one or more articles, goes out on a regular schedule to people who have signed up to read it, whereas a blog features informal articles, tips, resources, rants, or anecdotes for readers on a specially formatted Web page with the latest entry first. Some people and organizations publish both an e-zine and a blog.

As a publicity vehicle, an e-zine helps a one-time encounter with you turn into longstanding familiarity and trust. The strength of a blog lies in conveying personality, enthusiasm, values, and perspective, as well as in attracting traffic to your Website from search engines. Either format can raise your public profile as long as you follow a few important guidelines.

> ✤ **Be consistent.** People don't respond only to the content of your e-zine or blog, but also develop a sense of whether or not you're disciplined and dependable. If you publish like clockwork, your audience believes you're the kind of person who delivers on promises. Letting months go by between newsletter issues or blog postings can give the impression that you're flighty and untrustworthy. From the point of view of a prospective client or a media person

looking around for sources, a visibly long interval between issues or postings triggers wondering about whether or not you're still in business.

→ **Be interesting.** Offer content that readers aren't getting elsewhere—original ideas or anecdotes, an entertaining spin on industry news, surprising case studies, or controversial advice. Keep a file of ideas, examples, and topics on which you can comment so you won't be facing a blank screen with a blank mind on publication day.

→ **Be professional.** Although it's fashionable for blogs to have a smart-alecky, looking-down-your-nose-at-others tone, this doesn't necessarily bode well toward readers thinking about hiring you or your organization. Likewise, confessing a run of bad financial luck, bragging about your kids or pets, ranting about politics, or sharing your religious commitments should have no place in your publications. Be provocative, yes, but never overly personal unless you're targeting only like-minded individuals or cultivating a beyond-the-pale image.

→ **Remember first-timers.** Ever visited a Website that impressed you enough to subscribe to its newsletter or read its blog only to feel like you've stepped into the middle of an ongoing conversation that means nothing to you? However long you've been at it, you'll always have people reading you for the first time. Avoid in-group references and unexplained abbreviations so that new readers feel included rather than like outsiders.

→ **Keep promotion proportional.** Subscribers and fans normally anticipate and pass along your stuff because of the content, not your promotions of products, services, and events. The latter can piggyback onto the content as long as it's decidedly secondary. My rule of thumb is no more than 20 percent promotional offers and at least 80 percent substance, to avoid turning away people who would otherwise remain within your sphere of influence.

→ **Be findable.** I'm not sure whether this is the fault of the most popular blog templates or people thinking it's cool to blog from the shadows, but many blogs I've visited make it difficult or impossible to identify and contact the author. That's foolish when you're blogging to increase your visibility. Likewise, make sure people who receive a forwarded copy of your e-mail newsletter can easily see who wrote it and how they can join the ranks of your devoted subscribers.

Chapter 9

Advertorials That Don't Cost You a Cent

From the time I can first remember reading the Sunday *New York Times*, I noticed copy by Albert Shanker, president of the American Federation of Teachers, in the upper-right-hand corner of an inside page of the "News of the Week in Review" section. The capitalized word *Advertisement* above the heading "Where We Stand" signaled that Shanker wasn't a *Times* editorial writer, but that the AFT paid to have his editorial appear in that space. Perhaps two decades ago, I began to notice pages-long article sections in magazines such as *The Atlantic Monthly* that were similarly labeled "Advertisement." Often they bore the sponsorship of the tourist boards of various countries, companies manufacturing beauty products, or special-interest groups. More recently still, I learned that a term had been coined for this sort of paid media feature: *advertorial.*

As you might guess from the word itself, an advertorial is a hybrid of an advertisement and editorial copy. Written by someone on the payroll not of the magazine but of the advertising company, a good advertorial looks like an article and reads like an article. So close are the verbal and visual resemblances, in fact, that most magazines insist on the word *Advertisement* in small print at the top of the advertorial so readers won't hold the magazine responsible for the content. Those that are well written and interesting lure readers who may not notice any difference with the publication's regular features, or who notice but may not care. Advertorials in this guise can cost more than 10 years of your advertising budget. But you can arrange the same kind of effect in all but the very most prestigious publications without paying a cent. Here's how.

An Advertorial by Another Name

Instead of calling it an "advertorial," you call it a "column"—or a "regular column." Choose a publication whose readers all constitute a target market, and define a subject area likely to interest that group of people. Low-priced publications such as newsletters and free alternative papers are especially likely to jump at a well-thought-out idea, but trade magazines that reach people in a particular business or profession (for example, *Concrete Dealers' News* or *Lawyers' Monthly*) can be receptive, too.

Linda Marks, a body-centered psychotherapist in Newton, Massachusetts, writes a regular column for *Spirit of Change,* a free quarterly on holistic healing and New Age ideas that is distributed in bookstores, libraries, and health food stores throughout much of New England. At the end of her column, which spans two pages, the paper lists her credentials, her special area of expertise, her book *Living With Vision,* and her phone number. Accompanying the second page of the article is a 5×5 advertisement for Marks's programs. Note that it would be prohibitively expensive for her to run a two-page ad, but, by combining an article on subjects of interest to her and readers with a traditional-looking ad, she gets great double exposure and much more credibility than if she only had an ad.

To maintain the trust of editors and readers, design your column so that it is truly informative rather than a disguised promotional piece. You need a relatively authoritative tone that showcases your expertise, not your opinions. Here are eight more angles:

- ✦ **For a restaurant:** A healthy-eating column in a local weekly paper or monthly magazine under the byline of the chef or owner (rather than a collection of recipes from the restaurant, so that the column comes across more as a public service).

- ✦ **For a hairdresser:** A column in a community paper on cures for common hair problems.

- ✦ **For a real-estate agent:** A column in the local newspaper or magazine for homeowners on ways to enhance and protect the value of their real estate.

⬦ **For a museum:** A column in a local paper of historical vignettes from at least 50 years back.

⬦ **For an adoption agency:** A column in a national parenting magazine on how to adopt.

⬦ **For a tax lawyer:** A monthly column in the regional business tabloid discussing developments in the tax laws affecting business.

⬦ **For an environmental group:** A nature-appreciation column highlighting local scenic sites, flora, and fauna for a community paper.

⬦ **For a mail-order office supplies company:** A column on running an efficient office for a trade magazine or newsletter read by secretaries and office managers.

An easy format to use consists of questions and answers. In the beginning, of course, you'll have to make up the questions as well as the answers, but the Q&A format invites more reader participation than the usual article style.

Jeffrey Lant constructed an information-selling empire whose foundation was a column he called "Sure-Fire Business Success." At one point it was reaching 1.5 million people per month through more than 200 different publications worldwide and some computer information services. He provided the copy for free in exchange for one hard-sell paragraph at the end of the article that promoted his books and consulting services.

Lant knew the column worked because orders constantly flowed in, and he received dozens of calls day and night from readers around the world, many of whom said they felt as though they knew him. His distinctive voice, that of a blustery, no-nonsense authority, certainly comes across in everything he writes. Although imbuing your column with personality helps get reader response, so does a steadfast focus on content that helps readers solve their problems. "If you're a plumber, think of yourself as a specialist with a technical body of expertise that people desperately need when they have a problem," Lant advises. In the days before e-mail became widespread, he would provide editors with 25 columns at a whack, on disk, for them to choose from, containing information that would be valid for the foreseeable future.

Jim Cooke, a Boston actor who executed a column on a much smaller scale, was also very satisfied with having done it. To promote his one-man show on Calvin Coolidge, he wrote 18 free monthly columns on Coolidge for the *Green Mountain Gazette* in Vermont, our 30th president's home state. Although he doesn't recall more than a few letters and inquiries about performances, "It helped me develop material," he says, "and I can still send out photocopies of the column. It's worthwhile because you never know where something is going to end up. Someone in a small town in Vermont who read the column sees my name later and says, 'Oh, that's the guy who wrote the column.' It's like a drop of water wearing away a rock. You don't know which drop of water will do it, but it happens."

For Linda Marks, the biggest motivator is the chance her column gives her to keep her hand in as a writer amidst a busy speaking, teaching, and counseling practice. Although she has received some 20 letters or phone calls from readers, that's just a warm, fuzzy bonus for her. Some of the feedback about her column is critical, especially when she writes about what she calls the "dark side" of human nature, and Marks feels fine about that, too. "To be a columnist, you need a point of view," she explains. "Not everyone will like it, but if it has enough substance that people can argue with it, then you have the chance to make a long-term impact. If all you get is positive feedback, you're probably not making a deep enough connection with the reader."

HOW TO DO IT

Before contacting an editor to propose a column, write at least one sample column. Send that together with a cover letter that explains the focus and title of your proposed column, the fact that you're offering to do it for free or in exchange for advertising space, and why you are the perfect person to write the column. If that editor doesn't show interest, try another. Remember that when your goal is reader response, the column works best for you if it includes explicit contact information at the end. If the publication's format allows, a photo of you topping the column each time can also promote reader involvement. When your goal is name recognition and reputation-building, give the column at least a year to produce an effect. The more you appear before your audience in your role of expert, the more your advertorial—whoops, column—promotes you.

Eventually, collecting your columns on a given topic gives you a book to sell. In fact, once you get your rhythm as a column writer, you might even create a book outline by listing and arranging the topics you've already done, filling in the conceptual blank spots, and then using the outline as a blueprint for future columns. Make sure that you don't sign a contract giving anyone all rights to your columns, because that gives them, rather than you, the right to create and profit from such a compilation. Surprisingly, people who like your column will often pay to own such a collection within book covers even if all of your columns are archived online. Paper still has its partisans!

To get your foot in the door at larger publications, propose a Web-only column, which would normally be under control of a special Web editor. Keep your eyes peeled for a page near the front of most print magazines, often just following the table of contents for that issue, and you'll see splashy copy and images spotlighting what readers can find on the Web. Magazines invest in Web-only features and columns to entice subscribers to visit their Website, not only to get exposed to more advertising, but also to participate more and become more loyal to the magazine's brand.

SYNDICATION SERVICES, ARTICLE BANKS, AND DO-IT-YOURSELF SYNDICATION

Before the crash of the dotcom boom in 2001, several companies were doing a thriving business in online syndication of articles, rather similar to what newspaper syndicates have specialized in for decades, but more democratically and inclusively. Newspaper syndicate services such as the Universal Press Syndicate, which handles "Dear Abby," take charge of distributing columns, comics, and other features to hundreds or thousands of newspapers, which each pay a monthly fee pegged to their circulation. The competition to get features into newspaper syndication is fierce and not for the flighty. Yet online syndicators such as iSyndicate.com and ScreamingMedia.com were distributing more and more specialized news and columns—including those by enterprising unknowns hoping to become the next Erma Bombeck or Tom Peters—to Websites. To the extent that these companies survived the Internet crash, they became considerably less friendly to fledgling content providers. When the economy recovers, look for a resurgence of online syndicating services.

Meanwhile, another option sprang up and remains active and open to do-it-yourselfers. So-called article banks or article directories serve as an online repository of articles that Websites, print publications, or e-mail newsletters may use without payment, so long as they also include the attribution and contact information provided with the articles. Some accept content on all topics; others specialize in articles on, say, Internet marketing, pets, or self-development. A variant of article banks, e-zine article distribution lists, enable you to send articles by e-mail to Webmasters and publishers who subscribe to their lists. Naturally, there's no guarantee that anyone will choose your material, but article banks and e-zine article distribution lists make it possible for you to offer samples of your column or one-of-a-kind articles to Webmasters and publishers you would not easily locate on your own.

Maria Marsala, a business coach in Poulsbo, Washington, credits her distribution of articles through article banks with coming up in the top 10 or 15 sites when someone uses a search engine to look for a "business coach." Each placement of an article online containing a link back to her site in the contact information increases her link popularity, an important factor in search engine rankings. Marsala believes that about one new coaching client a quarter has come to her from reading one or more of her articles. However, the effect may be much greater than that, because the wide distribution of her work makes her site more likely to come up when someone not looking at articles uses search engines to look for a coach.

"My articles have appeared in career magazines and newspapers as far away as the U.K. and I've appeared on cable TV and the radio because of them as well," says Marsala, who hires a proofreader to make her work comma-perfect before sending it out. Coming up with ideas is as easy as taking note of the questions her clients ask her or issues she is working on with her own coach. Based on responses to her submissions, Marsala creates her own list of publishers who seem receptive to her work. When she sends a new offering to that list on a regular schedule, in effect she is self-syndicating a column.

Houston-based information entrepreneur Marty Foley, who used a strategy similar to Marsala's to build his business prior to the rise of the Internet, says that e-mail has taken a lot of the tedious work and expense out of the article dissemination process. "In the early 1990s I would send out articles in printed form and in plain text on a floppy disk to print publishers, everything from those you might see on newsstands to obscure ones you've never heard of, published for just a handful of readers," he says. "In early 1996 I discovered that it was much easier to submit articles by e-mail rather than by the postal system. I now send each new article to 611 e-zine or Web publishers at one time." Foley estimates that at least several hundred online publishers—perhaps as many as a thousand—have used his work, along with several hundred print publishers. He sends articles as plain text within the body of the e-mail, not as an attached file.

An advantage of publication online versus appearing in print that Foley points out is that Websites often archive past articles indefinitely, whereas print or e-mail periodicals have a shorter life span. "This can snowball into more and more publicity, such as being published or interviewed in e-books and on the radio or being invited to speak at conferences and seminars," he says. To find appropriate candidates for your article distribution list, Foley recommends going to a good search engine such as Google and typing in "submit articles" along with another qualifying term that identifies your particular market (for example, wine, pets, computer security, or organizational development). "As you visit Websites or read e-mail or print publications, be on the lookout for places to submit your articles, and record this information in a file on your computer immediately—don't put it off. Make it a goal to send out each new article to more publishers than you did the last time. Results can occur as quickly as within a few days."

PART III

SPEAKING AND ACTING
FOR PUBLICITY

Chapter 10

Staging Magnet Events

January 19, 1989 was the 180th anniversary of the birth of Edgar Allan Poe, and Norman George, a Boston actor who portrays Poe in a show called "Poe Alone," was determined to make it a memorable occasion. Because Poe's birthplace, Boston, had treated the author shabbily during his lifetime, George decided that a good media hook would be "'The Raven' Comes Home to Roost," with Boston making amends to its famous son. George enlisted Poe scholars, aficionados, and prominent Boston businessmen into a Poe Memorial Committee charged with getting Carver Street, where Poe was born, renamed for Poe. The committee soon succeeded in securing a proclamation from Mayor Ray Flynn, a bronze memorial plaque, and a new street sign marking "Edgar Allan Poe Way." Meanwhile he planned a slide lecture and benefit performance of his show.

The October prior to the big anniversary, George mailed a first round of news releases about the celebration to monthly consumer magazines, airline magazines, *Amtrak Express*, detective and mystery magazines, newsletters, and literary journals. He also called or wrote producers and editors and contacted freelance writers he knew who had connections with *People* and *Yankee* magazines. In late December and early January, he sent releases and calendar listings to the Boston area dailies and weeklies, and TV and radio stations.

The national publicity blitz paid off. Because of pre-event coverage in *Yankee* and the *Boston Globe, Herald, Phoenix,* and *Tab,* among others, a standing-room-only audience of more than 600 people packed into the anniversary performance, and post-event coverage appeared in *People, The New York Times,* Associated Press newspapers, and elsewhere.

Because of the exposure, theater managers contacted George to book his show, documentary filmmakers and radio producers offered him related roles, and the state of Maryland, where Poe died, conferred honorary citizenship on George. In all, the media-savvy actor estimates that more than 10 million people read or heard about the story.

The Attraction of a Magnet Event

In Chapter 2, I suggested that a special event such as a lecture or free demonstration can add timeliness to an otherwise ongoing service or establishment. A magnet event includes some additional component that makes an event irresistible to the media. The extra ingredient might be one of the following:

1. **Celebrities/prominent people.** In Norman George's case, the featured celebrity was a dead one about whom most Americans had heard. Although Poe would not attend, George, his reincarnation, would give a speech and intone "The Raven" with the style, costume, and mannerisms for which Poe was known. The imprimatur of the mayor didn't hurt, either. Charity hosts and hostesses know well that the more glittery and well-known the people who attend their event, the more photos and column inches they're likely to get in the paper afterward.

2. **Curiosity/suspense.** In 1980, Bob Allen claimed that he could go to any city with $100 and in 72 hours would own several properties without using his own money. The *Los Angeles Times* took the bait and challenged him to do it. The free publicity Allen got when he delivered on his boast launched him as a phenomenon and kept his book *Nothing Down* on the best-seller lists long enough to become the biggest-selling real-estate book of all time. The curiosity/suspense factor came in when Allen predicted that he would do it, and the *Times* followed him to report on whether he could. As any street performer who announces, "And now I'm going to juggle five knives" knows, telling an audience what you're going to do is risky, no matter how many times

you've done it while practicing. Even Allen confesses that the days that earned him the headline, "Buying Home Without Cash: Boastful Investor Accepts Time Challenge—and Wins" were the most harrowing of his life.

3. **Colorfulness/humor.** Around the time of Bob Allen's exploit, I belonged to a group called Women for Survival that organized an annual Mother's Day march for peace through our town of Northampton, Massachusetts. By mentioning in our news release that the parade would include colorful banners and kids holding balloons, we easily enticed TV reporters and print photographers to show up at the march every year. Similarly, when TV reporters got wind of Ron Bianco running his singing dog Bilbo for president, they knew that the formal kickoff of his candidacy, which Bianco notified them would take place on the lawn of the Rhode Island State House, would be a howler for their viewers.

4. **Uniqueness.** Calculatedly, Jeffrey Lant stressed that no convention of consultants had ever taken place in Boston when he pitched the Boston Consulting Convention he and a colleague sponsored to the media in the 1980s. Even when it seems a stretch, creating an air of uniqueness can help, as when you're traveling to Chicago to give a speech and bill it as your "first and only Chicago appearance."

5. **Resonance.** According to Nell Merlino, creator and producer of Take Our Daughters to Work Day, some ideas turn into mega-events because they tap into what millions of people are thinking and feeling. "I don't think there's much of a difference between what the media is interested in and what the public is interested in," Merlino says. "Take Our Daughters to Work Day got so much coverage because people working at newspapers and radio stations heard about it and immediately wanted to bring their own daughters to work. Then it was natural for them to want to spread the word."

DANGER, DANGER

A magnet event involves much more than sending off a news release. "It takes money, time, creativity and nerve—all difficult," says Richard Falk, a New York City public relations consultant who holds the distinction of being the first inductee selected for the Press Agents Hall of Fame. Much can go wrong. Ron Bianco spent hundreds of dollars rallying supporters, printing T-shirts, and renting masks, banners, hats, and a police officer for the press conference to be held on the State House lawn in Providence. Then it rained and he had to reschedule.

For retailer Rick Segel, a great idea turned into a nightmare. He sponsored a contest for the best hairdresser in Medford, Massachusetts. The first year resulted in a photo of contestants wearing $20,000 worth of fur coats from his store winding up on the front page of the local paper. The second year he expanded the contest, renting a hall and selling 500 tickets. When one contestant complained that the fur coat bearing her contestant number didn't fit, coats and numbers were switched around, but without coordinating properly with the judges' lists. "As a result, some of the prizes were announced for the wrong people," Segel says. "Two of the judges walked out, and there were practically fistfights among the hairdressers."

When the gala event involves the Internet, technical glitches can disrupt its success or even turn it into a disaster. In February 1999, 1.5 million users attempted to log on to Victoria's Secret's heavily promoted online fashion show during a commercial break from the Superbowl. Most logged off in disgust rather than in admiration, because of a poor-quality video image or none at all. A client of mine who had a thriving market-research company ran her resources into the ground trying to get online focus groups, which appealed to many new clients, to run smoothly. Whether people from America Online who couldn't use the interface at her Website or corporate officers whose company's firewall blocked them from participating in sessions, the obstacles kept on coming and coming.

Sometimes the idea is so catchy and memorable that it gets separated from the sponsor who is supposed to benefit from the publicity.

On retainer for a refrigerator company, publicist Jim Moran proved wrong the saying that you can't sell an icebox to an Eskimo. For another client he investigated how long it took to find a needle in a haystack (82 hours). Other times, he led a bull into a china shop and hired actors to dress up as turnips and donate blood, verifying that you could indeed get blood from a turnip. Long after each hooha died down, people remembered the clever idea and Moran, not the sponsors.

The mischief inherent in stunts can also get out of hand. P.T. Barnum, the greatest showman who ever lived, created a magnet event when he hitched an elephant to a plow beside the train tracks to announce that his circus had come to town. This attracted both newsmen and the public, so much so that he composed a letter for those who wrote to him with questions about plowing with an elephant. Barnum explained: "In the first place, such an animal would cost from $3,000 to $10,000; in cold weather he could not work at all; in any weather he could not earn half his living; he would eat up the value of his own head, trunk and body every year; and I begged my correspondents not to do so foolish a thing as to undertake elephant farming."

In January 2007, blinking electronic devices planted in the Boston area as part of a guerrilla publicity campaign for the Cartoon Network triggered a full-fledged terror alert when law enforcement called in bomb squads and shut down the subway system and a major highway, causing commuter chaos. Far from laughing at the misconstrual, Mayor Menino was livid, attributing more than $500,000 in police costs to "corporate greed." Turner Broadcasting, owner of the Cartoon Network, and the New York City marketing firm they hired to place the devices, ultimately apologized and paid $2 million in restitution to local governments and law enforcement agencies.

Two generations ago, no Hollywood studio would release a movie without some wild, outrageous feat, and during the 1960s, simple political theater often lured the press, but the Boston debacle may have sealed the fate of humorously intended public events that are prone to misinterpretation. The phrase "publicity stunt" now carries a mainly negative connotation as an event with no apparent substance or value beyond attracting attention. Richard Falk, who sponsored

Publicity Stunt Day on April 1 for decades, died in 2008, and perhaps on that one day every year zany public exploits will continue to live on.

GUIDELINES FOR A SUCCESSFUL MAGNET EVENT

If you want to take on the challenge of a magnet event, keep these tips in mind.

1. **Be sure your concept is clear.** One of the reasons the Take Our Daughters to Work Day succeeded, says Nell Merlino, is that the title of the event named something simple that people could do to participate. If the success of your event depends on rallying participation, people must be able to "get it" from a headline, a calendar listing, or a snippet on the radio.

2. **Plan far enough in advance.** Timing is critical! Find out and meet the deadlines for key event listings, public-service announcements, and pre-event articles that will reach your target market.

3. **Consider enlisting the aid of cosponsors who can help spread the word.** Debbi Karpowicz proved a master at this for the swirl of events promoting her book, *I Love Men in Tasseled Loafers.* She arranged for book signings in Nordstrom's shoe department. She persuaded the Omni Hotel to host two book signing parties where they played foot-oriented songs and gave a prize (a shoe) for the best dancer. For free, the New England Bartenders School created a new drink, The Tasseled Loafer, to be served at the parties. She got loafer tassels and brand-name shoe boxes from the Allen-Edmonds company, and talked Pappagallo, a maker of women's shoes, into sending her a crate of women's shoes from which she could choose in dressing for her publicity events.

4. **Test, test, test your technology beforehand.** According to eTesting, a consulting firm in the United Kingdom, disasters such as the Victoria's Secret online fashion show and the June 2000 public crash of servers when the Cahoot online bank launched its operations could have been avoided by adequate testing. Besides the public humiliation

involved, such failures can cause big financial losses. You always need to be prepared in case publicity succeeds beyond your wildest dreams.

5. **Prepare contingency plans in case your event goes crazily or dangerously wrong.** During the Cartoon Network–caused terror alert in Boston, those responsible for planting the blinking devices waited way too long before revealing that the suspicious items were in fact harmless. Because of this, authorities will not take such behavior lightly in a future incident. Do everything you can ahead of time to head off problems and consider having an attorney on standby.

6. **Try for triple-barreled publicity—before, during, and after the event.** "Despite the best advance publicity in the world, some international leader could get assassinated and wipe everything else out of the news," says Nell Merlino. "You can't help it." Right, you wouldn't have gotten TV and newspaper coverage of the event itself, but if you had some pretext for post-event publicity—say, an award given out at the event— you might still get press after the fact, in addition to before. As the song says, two out of three ain't bad.

Chapter 11

Speaking, for Fee or Free

In survey after survey, public speaking turns up as the number-one fear of adults—more prevalent than fear of snakes, the tax authorities, or death. Even professional actors and accomplished orators confess to occasional attacks of the shakes before they step out on stage. For many people, performing before others represents the ultimate vulnerability. Suppose you forget what you wanted to say? Suppose people laugh when they're not supposed to, or fall asleep? Yet according to many who have mastered public speaking, acquiring comfort in front of an audience is worth the effort, because it represents the ultimate opportunity to win credibility and spread awareness of what you do.

"For selling books, speaking is much more effective than radio or TV," argues Jay Conrad Levinson, author of the "Guerrilla Marketing" series of books, and an active seminar leader since 1979. "Radio and TV segments are superficial—only seven minutes long or less. But if you speak for three hours, people learn and realize that there's even more to learn, so they buy books, and tell their friends. Company owners sit there and realize they need to buy a book for each of their marketing people. Had I not been out there speaking, I'm certain that my books would have ended up on the remainder tables long ago." Instead, Levinson's 1984 book, *Guerrilla Marketing*, has spawned more than two dozen sequels or spinoffs, a software program, a coach certification program, and a newsletter.

"Speaking is the least expensive way to promote your services," says Patricia Fripp, a former president of the National Speakers Association, whom *Meetings & Conventions* magazine called "one of the 10 most electrifying speakers in North America." She points out two multiplier effects that increase your impact beyond the number of people gathered in your audience. "If you speak to a group of 30, your signup statistics will be much better than if you talked to 30 people one-on-one. Regardless of how good you are at what you do, by virtue of being able to stand on your feet and give a speech, you're considered more of an expert than you probably even are. In addition, you can reach out beyond the 30 people by saying at the end of the talk, 'If any of you belong to any groups that might want a speaker on my subject, please give my card to your program planner.'"

When you link media publicity and public speaking, the multiplication of impact can become exponential. This includes classes, seminars, workshops, lectures, speeches, and panel discussions for either the general public or members of an organization. In at least nine different ways, even the humblest free speaking engagement sets up the possibility of or the pretext for media coverage.

HOW SPEAKING PRODUCES MEDIA PUBLICITY

1. **A printed catalog disseminates your name and qualifications.** Teaching adult education classes on freelance writing got me started, unintentionally, in consulting. A Harvard Business School professor whom I knew slightly called and said he'd seen the notice for my course but couldn't make the date, but would I be willing to come to his office and present the class to him privately? Sure! I plucked a per-hour figure out of the air and discussed writing with him for about seven sessions. After I received a second such request, from a stranger, I realized that I could call myself a writing consultant and develop that as a sideline to writing and speaking. Consulting now brings in 30 to 40 percent of my income. Others I know who teach in adult education programs say they regularly get consulting inquiries traceable to appearing in the catalog. In effect, any printed course catalog constitutes free publicity for your services as well as for your class.

2. **Journalists, invited or not, may attend your talk.** A freelance writer who attended Barbara Winter's "Making a Living Without a Job" workshop in Minneapolis published an article about it in *Minnesota Monthly*, the magazine of the area's public radio station. "The impact on my classes was extraordinary," she says. "At the next workshop after the article appeared, I had 80 registrants, more than a third of whom came as a direct result of the article. And there's been a residual effect. For the next five years, I consistently had 60 people per class, as compared with 45 before the article came out."

3. **Reporters or producers might call after spotting a notice about your talk.** My first appearance on a radio talk show came about because a producer saw my course listing in the catalog of the Learning Connection in Providence, Rhode Island. Similarly, I called to interview Laurie Schloff for an article in *New Woman* because of her course listing in the catalog of the Boston Center for Adult Education. After that interview, she asked if I'd be interesting in collaborating with her on a book, which we actually did twice. New York City therapist Linda Barbanel never leaves the publicity potential of speaking to chance. From the very first time she spoke on the psychology of money, at her temple, she would send an announcement of her lecture or workshop to the press. The first year she was quoted in *Money* and *Savvy*; the second year, in nine magazines. By continually building on her previous publicity, she now receives an average of three calls per week from reporters and producers.

4. **You can initiate pre-event publicity.** Jeanne Gavrin, a Weston, Massachusetts therapist and nurse who specializes in treating eating disorders, arranged to present a talk on how body image affects children at St. Anne's in the Field, a church in nearby Lincoln. She sent a news release to the local papers, and a staff writer from the *Lincoln Journal* came out and interviewed her. The resulting article and photo appeared before Gavrin's talk, and, she says, got concerned

parents to attend who otherwise wouldn't have come. Like-wise, whenever management consultant Alan Weiss has a speaking date in, say, Dayton, Ohio, he'll send a news re-lease to the Dayton newspaper. If it prints something, he clips it and adds it to his media kit. "When a client in Chicago sees that, they may pay more attention," he says. Don't forget to pursue free calendar listings, both online and in newspapers, which may reach as many people before your talk as a feature article.

5. **You can set in motion post-event publicity.** After your speaking engagement, send a notice or news release to your alumni magazine, your hometown newspaper, and the newsletters of local or national organizations to which you belong.

6. **The sponsor of your presentation can recommend you to the media or directly to clients.** Journalists and clients regard an organization that sponsors talks and seminars as a referral resource. Jay Conrad Levinson, who teaches through the University of California's community education system, says that when large organizations seek a presenter, they tend to contact universities first, rather than speaking agents, for recommendations. "A university has so much credibility, even though you don't need academic qualifications to teach in the extension program," Levinson says. By forming a relationship with such an educational organization, you have someone primed to pass the word about you at no cost to you.

7. **The sponsor of your presentation can publicize you in its own media.** Get copies of an organization's flyers or news releases announcing your talk and any pre-event and post-event publicity in its newsletter. When Alan Weiss presented a keynote speech to the Inland Press Association, the group produced an attractive 8 1/2 × 11 flyer with excerpts from Weiss's writings on the reverse. He secured permission to reprint it for his media kit. Because the flyer includes the organization's logo, it's more impressive than something Weiss could produce himself. Here, the coup to top all coups

is persuading a media entity to sponsor your seminar. Phillip Rierdan of Executive Briefing Sessions in Framingham, Massachusetts, had, as cosponsors of his seminar "How to Bring In New Business," WRKO (a talk radio station), and *Boston Business Journal*, both of which ran free advertisements for him to hundreds of thousands of listeners and readers.

8. **You never know who else might be in the audience.** I once gave a talk at a Borders bookstore in Framingham, Massachusetts, and happened to mention that someday I hoped to do commentaries on National Public Radio. After my talk, a bearded man introduced himself. "If you want to get on the radio, I can help. My name is Monty Haas." I recognized his name and his voice from news broadcasts on the local public radio station. True to his word, he referred me to his boss, who in turn referred me to the producer who handled commentaries on WBUR's morning show. Writing and recording eight commentaries for that producer remains, to this day, the most fun thing I've ever done in my career, and it raised my profile among well-educated professionals who were avid listeners of that station.

9. **You can painlessly produce a product whose launch gives you another excuse for publicity.** Large conferences commonly include the audiotaping of all sessions for the benefit of non-attendees and attendees who couldn't attend all sessions. Less commonly, some sessions are videotaped. They'll usually let you have or at least borrow the master tape for your session so that you can make copies to sell or use to prove your speaking prowess to other sponsoring groups. Although many organizations routinely slap their copyright on such tapes, insist on retaining copyright to your presentation so you have the way clear to sell the tape yourself. If your sponsor has no plans to record a session, you can also do so on your own dime, with the sponsor's permission. Usually you'll already be appropriately dressed, have a professional-looking setting in which you're performing, and

have an audience whose applause and questions can add to the perceived value of your tape.

Want to Speak? Let's Count The Ways

The terminology of speaking is somewhat fluid, with some people saying "workshop" for what other people call a "seminar," "presentation," or "class." Don't get hung up on what to call different kinds of speaking engagements. Instead, think strategically first about sponsorship:

✦ **Self-sponsored public seminars and talks.** If you have to hire a hotel meeting room and send out flyers to a mailing list, this option is risky. Regardless of what you may have heard about typical response rates, dramatic public seminar flops happen all the time. In 1982, Paul and Sarah Edwards launched a seminar on the topic that has since made them famous: how to start a home-based business. They rented hotel rooms and ran ads in major newspapers. In Sacramento, however, not one person enrolled, and in San Jose less than 10 people showed up. "We were ahead of the market, and we lost thousands of dollars—a lot of money for us at that time," Paul Edwards recalls. In connection with public seminars, send news releases to the media and invite reporters to attend as your guest.

✦ **Sponsored public presentations.** Sponsors range from adult education programs to nonprofit organizations, such as libraries, museums, churches, or interest groups such as the Historic Preservation Society or Pollution Control Advocates United. Professional or civic organizations that open their meetings to the public would fall under this category as well, as would for-profit businesses that sponsor lectures, such as bookstores. Usually the sponsoring organization takes care of publicity, but you should feel free to write your own lively news release or, for an out-of-the-ordinary talk, try phone pitches to key columnists and reporters.

If you have never taught in an adult education program, I urge you to consider it. Although high school and college/ university extension programs and independent adult education centers usually pay teachers just a small honorarium, their catalogs reach tens or hundreds of thousands of people. I know consultants and lawyers who normally charge $150 an hour or more who find the exposure valuable enough to continue to teach in these programs for one-fifth that amount.

Adult education also represents an opportunity to gain confidence in your expertise in an informal classroom setting before a small interested group. Programming personnel provide expert advice on your catalog copy, dates and times, and a free testing ground for new programs. On the other hand, because of a case in Florida in which both an unethical investment advisor and the institution that sponsored his class were sued, many adult education programs have strict guidelines controlling teachers' marketing, including distribution of business cards or brochures, at their classes.

To propose an adult education class, examine the program's current list of offerings and write a title and one-paragraph description that doesn't duplicate what they already have. Add a brief summary of your qualifications to teach the class and send it to the program director. To get maximum exposure with minimal time commitment, follow my policy of doing several one-shot programs at different locations, rather than four-to-10-week courses.

✦ **Sponsored organizational presentations.** These talks are publicized primarily to members of the sponsoring group, such as a chamber of commerce, Kiwanis Club, bar association, or state culinary arts society. Local lunch or dinner meetings on what is semi-affectionately dubbed the "Rubber Chicken Circuit" do not usually pay speakers, but many regional or national conferences do. Peruse the *Encyclopedia of Associations* (see Chapter 24) or the Yellow Pages under "Associations" to locate prospect groups, and contact the program chairperson, who will often be thrilled to hear from you. You can stretch the pre-event appeal and post-event impact of your talk to members not at your talk by contributing an article to the organization's newsletter.

❧ **In-house talks.** When a company engages your speaking services for its employees, you will almost always be paid, sometimes quite handsomely. Except for an endorsement or a notice in the company newsletter, however, these gigs have little publicity potential.

❧ **Teleseminars.** I hadn't heard of these when I wrote the first edition of this book, but I've appeared as a guest at others' teleseminars and run them on my own so many times that I now teach others to do so, also. A teleseminar (also called a teleclass) uses the telephone as the communication medium. At a certain hour, the seminar leader and participants call in to a special bridge line that accommodates multiple listeners. Via lecture and questions and answers from the assembled group, the leader makes an educational presentation. You can run these on a for-fee basis or free, to spread your influence. You can also arrange to record the telephone sessions for resale. If you venture into this arena (see the resources in Chapter 24 for some help), be sure you specify to potential participants that it involves nothing but a phone, because otherwise people will pepper you with questions about whether they have the right computer setup for access.

❧ **Webinars.** If you can iron out all the technical kinks, a Webinar enables people from all over the world to converge on a Website where a seminar takes place through video conferencing technology instead of or in addition to telephone call-ins. According to Steve O'Keefe, author of *Complete Guide to Internet Publicity*, "While the technology for hosting Web-based seminars has improved, live video and audio interfaces are still difficult to use and buggy. Just ask Oprah Winfrey. Her much-hyped Skype simulcast in 2008 went into digital meltdown when the software buckled under the traffic." Try canned video presentations, such as a video or audio podcast or slideshow instead, O'Keefe suggests. Even if the technology works perfectly, Webinars require three to five times as much preparation as a teleseminar, if my experience is a reliable guideline.

THE TALK ITSELF

Let's say you've volunteered to be the luncheon speaker at your chapter of the Lions Club, your first time speaking before a group since you blundered through an oral report in college. Patricia Fripp suggests keeping your presentation simple, calling upon skills you exercise all the time. "If you just stand up and say, 'The five questions I'm most frequently asked about [whatever you do] are...' and then answer those questions conversationally, that's a speech," Fripp says. "You've probably answered those questions dozens of times at cocktail parties, and the people you're speaking to are just like the people you meet at parties." As you gain experience and speak on more formal occasions, use these tips to keep audiences awake and involved.

1. **Plan your talk using a simple four-part formula.** You may have heard the advice, "Tell 'em what you're going to tell 'em, tell 'em, then tell 'em what you told 'em," but I think a slightly different schema works better. First, hook the audience's interest with a brief story, a set of questions that elicit a show of hands, or startling statistics. Then, state the focus of the talk and any background or practical details needed to orient the audience. Next, present your content. And finally, pull things together with a closing story, a restatement of your main theme, or an appeal to action.

2. **Customize your remarks for your audience.** No audience likes an "If this is Tuesday, are you the dentists?" attitude in a speaker. Listeners relax and like you more when you weave in words, examples, and names relevant to their industry, locality, and occupational concerns. But take special care with names and terms unfamiliar to you. I'll never forget the time a conference speaker offered praise of the organization's

president but pronounced his name wrong. You could almost hear a collective "ouch!" in the room.

As you speak in different places and for different groups, you'll notice that reactions to the same material may vary radically. I have a story about how I got started in writing that elicits out-loud laughs in Cambridge, just a few smiles across the river in Boston, and mostly blank looks elsewhere. I've also observed that, although working adults enjoy the real-world flavor of personal anecdotes, college students tend to find them egotistical and irrelevant.

3. **Include some form of audience participation when possible.** Studies show that when people participate in a presentation, the material becomes at least three times more memorable than if they merely listen to a lecture. With a small group, it's easier to encourage and manage comments and questions from the audience, but some forms of participation work even with a group in the hundreds. If your microphone arrangement allows, you can move off the podium and interact with individuals in the audience the way a TV talk-show host does.

    Fill-in-the-blank handouts, on which you provide the basic structure of your talk and numbered blanks for the key points, keep an audience involved throughout an information-rich speech. Even asking rhetorical questions (for example, can you remember what motivated *you* to go into accounting?) helps, as people answer in their own minds before you go on. In any group larger than 20 or 25, remember to repeat audience questions for the whole assemblage.

4. **Practice your talk out loud, either for a friend or in front of a mirror.** Just as familiarizing yourself with a musical score wouldn't necessarily get your fingers doing the right thing at the piano, having a great outline and good notes for a talk doesn't ensure a smooth performance. Actually saying the words in proper sequence helps immeasurably more.

5. **Don't get hung up on fancy visuals.** Although some circles expect slick slides, overheads, or other visual aids, use them only to clarify information that would otherwise be difficult to absorb. Jay Conrad Levinson confesses that he hired LucasFilms to make up slides for his seminars, but soon put those slides permanently away. "They were beautiful, but people were always so busy taking notes they didn't have a chance to look up," he explains. "Besides, I never say the same thing twice." If you're a spellbinding storyteller, would panic if a bulb burned out, or can never remember which button to press on the slide clicker, follow Levinson's lead and go solo up there.

6. **Know how to channel nervousness.** Expect some jitters and do your best anyway. In *Smart Speaking* (see Chapter 24), Laurie Schloff and I describe several easy ways to keep nervousness under control. With the "Pick-a-Tic" technique, for example, you choose how your body expresses the terror you feel. Out of the audience's line of sight, simply press your thumb and middle finger together for three seconds and slowly let go. Or interpret—"reframe," some psychologists call it—any physical symptoms in a positive, productive way: "I'm feeling excited because I'm eager to do a good job, and I will."

7. **Keep within your allotted time.** Run over, and you'll find word of mouth running heavily against you.

ADVANCED TACTICS TO ENSURE THAT SPEAKING PAYS OFF

→ **Write your own introduction.** Every experienced speaker has a story about the person delegated to introduce him or her to a group, who babbled irrelevantly, said something false, or even inflicted a mild insult. The solution: Type out exactly what you'd like the introducer to say and request that those few sentences be delivered word for word.

→ **Design your own evaluation forms.** Many organizations have either no evaluation forms or one that furnishes you with useless information. (See Chapter 19 for some questions that do better than others at eliciting usable blurbs.) If the organization distributes evaluation forms that include numerical scales, don't attach much importance to the fact that you achieved an average rating of only 3.9 out of 5 or an average of "very good" rather than "excellent." In my experience, such ratings are heavily influenced by the time of day, participants' expectations, and other factors beyond your control. The pattern of substantive comments tends to be much more revealing.

→ **Try to get a list of those present at your talks.** Do this even if you don't yet know what you would do with a mailing list. By the time you have a reason to recontact people who have heard you speak, you'll already be on your way to a substantial customer database. At a small to mid-sized class or workshop, send around a pad headed with "Name and Address if You'd Like to Be on Sara Speaker's Mailing List." For a sponsored talk, some organizations routinely present speakers with a participant list, although with other sponsors you need more creative tactics. Ask people to bring their business card to you or your product table after the talk, for instance, to be eligible for a raffled prize.

→ **Mention your services or special features of your business casually within your talk.** "No one really hears your bio when you're introduced," says Claudyne Wilder, who conducts presentation skills seminars that demonstrate Polaroid's LCD panel technology. "Allude to your expertise in the middle of your talk. They'll hear it more." To mention it naturally and without veering off into a sales pitch, simply work in occasional phrases such as, "As often happens when I help clients plan for their kids' college education..." or "Somebody who came to one of our Saturday morning computer workshops for kids said...." The more concrete, specific, and fleeting these references are, the better.

→ **Survey audiences.** If the setup permits, invite audience members to fill out a survey or questionnaire. From one large group or several smaller groups, you can collect newsworthy data that merits media publicity. (See Chapter 2.)

❖ **Cultivate your speaking skills** through private coaching, the National Speakers Association, or Toastmasters. (See Chapter 24 for contact information.) If you discover that you enjoy speaking, with professional feedback and exposure to master presenters, you'll learn how to deserve and command higher fees. Patricia Fripp started out as a hairdresser who addressed Rotary Clubs and other civic groups on motivational topics. At the suggestion of a friend, she attended a conference of the National Speakers Association, where she delivered 15 minutes of her motivational spiel and was "discovered" by an agent. "Wow," she said to herself as she soon faced an audience of 2,000 for the first time. "For this I could give up cutting hair." Through hard work and constant practice, she developed her skills to the point at which she could quit the hair salon and earn thousands of dollars per keynote speech.

❖ **Once you're successful, investigate speakers bureaus.** Similar to literary agents, speaking agents and bureaus become interested in representing you primarily once you're already consistently earning fees that would mean significant commissions for them. In fact, "representing you" is somewhat misleading, because their mission is to supply organizations with appropriate talent, not to market each and every speaker in their stable. Yet good bureaus and agents are extremely well networked with corporations and associations that regularly hire speakers, and can help you secure lucrative bookings. For partial listings of lecture bureaus and speaking agents, consult *Literary Market Place* or your favorite search engine.

Jay Conrad Levinson bypasses the bureaus with a speaking agent who acts more as a personal promoter, marketing Levinson's seminars aggressively and exclusively. "He's an angel from heaven," says Levinson of Bill Shear, who handles all the arrangements for Levinson's optimal quota of three appearances a month. So grateful is the "Guerrilla Marketing" guru for the carefree boost Shear's work has given his career that he not only pays Shear the standard commission for seminar bookings, but also, voluntarily, 10 percent of the royalties from all of his books.

Chapter 12

Hitting the Airwaves, on the Radio, TV, or the Web

Mention TV or radio in the context of publicity, and most people's minds lock on to being a guest on an interview show. But the airwaves hold a much wider band of opportunities for the publicity hound. Although being a guest of Regis Philbin or Tyra Banks may expose you to the broadest daytime national TV audience, some of the other options offer a more consistent, targeted impact, and more control.

In Macon, Georgia, for example, psychologist Amy Flowers had a regular 90-second spot called "Creative Coping" on radio station WPEZ for five years. Every Monday, Tuesday, and Wednesday, her voice came on the air just before noon and talked to listeners about common mental health problems such as handling stress or being more assertive. Starting with a teaser, such as, "Does your mother ever make you crazy?" she defined a problem, provided perspective on it, and supplied solutions, all in an optimistic, friendly, jargon-free tone. Flowers collected ideas from magazines, newspaper advice columns, and conversations in and out of her office.

Once, a woman driving through Macon heard the spot and called for an appointment even though she lived 45 miles away from the clinic where Flowers practiced. During the years "Creative Coping" was on the air, 75 people ordered free transcripts, yet Flowers was even more excited about another kind of response to her spot: "It gives me a chance to ethically educate people and to destigmatize therapy, so that people who need help aren't afraid to come in. If they hear me on the radio and that takes the fear out of counseling, then I've accomplished my purpose."

In 1999, changes in local media ownership led Flowers to move from radio to TV. Every Tuesday afternoon during the 5 p.m. newscast, she now has a two-minute mental health segment on WMAZ, the local CBS affiliate TV station, reaching an estimated 70,000 people. After her segment finishes, she goes into the station's back room and takes phone calls for about 15 minutes. People can and do call in for a handout on the topic of the day.

Amy Flowers's "Creative Coping" format can work for almost any expert, whether your field is cars, country living, or creativity. And additional options for exposure on the air abound, some of which are almost as accessible as an old-fashioned soapbox.

The Most Accessible TV Opportunity of All

Some media critics like to say that freedom of the press belongs to those who own the presses, but in the case of public-access cable TV, you as Joe or Jane Public, in effect, own the medium. To receive a license that gives them a monopoly to provide cable service for a certain locality, cable companies must provide a channel open to any qualified person or group in that locality that wishes to air a program. Here "qualified" means "technically qualified," and cable companies must also provide training so that those who wish to can learn to produce their own programs.

According to Geri Michael Hackel, who produces a news show for the Boston public-access station, the free training, which at her station takes 10 to 12 weeks, can be worth thousands of dollars. Beyond requiring that you have technical competence and that you live in or have a business in the subscription area of the station, these stations are not allowed to impose any other qualifications. Whether you want to sermonize about the right of companies to pollute the environment, present your off-color comedy act, or interview all your law partners about their areas of expertise, the station must allow you on the air when your turn comes up.

Unlike with broadcast TV or radio, your potential viewing audience is limited to cable subscribers in a strictly delimited area, usually your town or city. In a metropolis the size of Boston, that adds up to a significant opportunity, especially if you will be offering something likely to build a regular audience or catch the attention of channel cruisers. In a smaller area, a public-access cable show gives you excellent exposure if your primary target market is local. If you'd like to reach a regional or national audience, this medium still might be worthwhile: You'll get precious practice, and can try to interest other areas in using tapes of your show.

As Valla Dana Fotiades discovered in the first year and a half that she produced her interview show, *Valla &...*, in Worcester, Massachusetts, other benefits can trickle in from a regular cable program: "I'm just launching my speaking career, and having my own show gives me an opportunity to make easy cold calls, inviting people on my program. I help them, and it has come back in speaking business for me. Also, two consultants I had on the show asked for a copy of the tape, which they are sending to their clients and prospects around the world."

On the other hand, stations don't furnish a crew to shoot your show. Although they may give you a list of volunteers, it's up to you to spark enthusiasm, commitment, and quality in at least three and preferably five or more technically qualified people each time you shoot a show. Some of the skills needed, such as with graphics, is simple enough that Fotiades has been able to use her 13-year-old son and her director's 11-year-old daughter as part of the crew.

Bill Costley, who lives in the 6,000-subscriber town of Wellesley, Massachusetts, streamlined his crew for *Author!*, a 12-part interview series on writers with Wellesley connections. He got by with a crew of three: the interviewer (and co-producer), the studio manager (and director), and himself on two cameras (one stationary), as floor manager and coproducer. Shoots never had to be cancelled for lack of volunteers. A local author himself, Costley deliberately remained off camera in the series. "If you try to glorify yourself, crews and audiences gradually drift away," he says. "Those who crave stardom should seek it somewhere else." Costley's nonstarring participation in community-access TV, dating back to 1986, had previously led to a front-page feature story in the *Wellesley Townsman*.

Because Costley's *Author!* series had archival value for his town and wider appeal, he donated a videocassette of the programs to the Wellesley library's audio-visual department, which circulates it among a network of 22 public and two academic libraries along Route 128, west and north of Boston. "Despite budgetary problems, public libraries are busily expanding their video holdings," he says. Valla Dana Fotiades adds that tapes from Worcester sometimes "bicycle" around to stations in four smaller Massachusetts towns before returning to Worcester. Create connections with big city stations, she suggests, and you could exchange your way to a major effect on cable.

If public-access programming seems to you like a good launch pad for publicity, just call the station that serves your locality and find out when the next training course begins.

Being an Interview Guest

Participating in someone else's interview show takes much less work than producing your own show. When the show has a large audience, the payoff can be huge. Publishing analyst John Kremer says that one appearance on *Oprah*, when the reigning queen of the talk show world expresses enthusiasm for a guest's book, could sell 50,000 copies. "If you're up there with nine other people, though, it may not do much," he says. Yet, everyone with whom I've spoken who's appeared on one of the major interview shows reports that their prestige skyrocketed. For this reason, Jeff Slutsky, who calls his experience with *The Sally Jesse Raphael Show* "horrendous," nevertheless says he'd do it again in a minute. "When people look at my bio, they don't know it was a lousy show," he says. The cumulative effect of many smaller shows can be significant as well.

Within the category of interview shows, formats differ. Sometimes, for TV, you'll sit with the host in a fake living room and trade pleasant, mildly informative banter. Other times a studio audience participates in the show with questions and comments. You may be on alone or with a long lineup of guests. Both radio and TV shows may include anonymous callers who sound off, ask for information, or try to put you on the spot. For radio, you may either do the show in the station's studio or by telephone from your home or office. Any show can be either live or taped.

Think about which kind of show seems best for you and which medium (radio or TV) you prefer. Therapist Szifra Birke worries much more in connection with TV. "I get caught up with what image I want to put across—casual Cambridge, sporty sophisticate, or power broker," she says. Social worker Merle Bombardieri finds call-in shows fun because she gets a sense of the audience, but risky because callers can get the show off-track. "On TV people get to meet me, not just my voice," adds Bombardieri. "I like that." Therapist Linda Barbanel likes *Good Day New York* best because it positions her as a featured expert who explains the taped man-in-the-street comments on the issue of the day. Many other shows put more emphasis on the testimony and emotions of the guests.

As I discussed in Chapter 4, your library probably carries some of the media directories that contain contact names, addresses, and phone numbers of radio and TV shows across the United States. You can also find excellent talk show directories on the Web at Radio-directory.com and TVtalkshows.com. For any shows you especially hope to get on, it's prudent to call and confirm the name and spelling of the person who should receive your information.

Once you've selected a show or shows to target and learned the name of the producer, try one of three approaches to becoming an interview subject: Make a phone pitch, being especially conscious that you may be interrupting someone working on deadline (see Chapter 16); write a pitch letter, explaining what you'd be able to discuss and how it would benefit listeners or viewers (see Chapter 6); or send a news release, either alone or accompanied by your media kit (see Chapter 5).

According to broadcast media maven Larry Rochester, many talk-show producers look down their noses at potential guests calling on their own behalf. So, for this purpose alone you may want to enlist a friend, relative, or employee to call on your behalf. Whoever calls must be enthusiastic, clear, concise, and prepared to elicit and keep track of many nitty-gritty details about the show in case the pitch wins a yes. After your first yes, read Chapter 15 especially carefully so that you make the most of being a guest on the airwaves.

APPEARING ON THE NEWS

Although much of radio and TV news focuses on governmental and political developments, it includes coverage of business, scientific, and entertainment innovations; profiles of community problem-solvers; and stories about special events—indeed, most of the topics you'd find in the newspaper. You'll do best on radio and TV news with either a happening-right-here-this-very-week hook or what media people call an "evergreen" topic, such that there's no more reason to run it this week, last week, last month, or even last year. Timeless topics such as what to do about varicose veins come in handy when a station has several gaping minutes to fill on a slow news days.

I remember a piece at the very end of the evening news on one of the networks about a professor who runs a grammar hotline, where he gives authoritative answers to callers asking, say, about "like" versus "as" or whether "impact" should be used as a verb. By cutting back and forth from the reporter's statements, filled with typical mistakes, to the professor's good-humored, pedantic corrections, the reporter made an undramatic topic thoroughly charming—to a writer, at least. I don't remember, however, the professor's name or at what college he taught, much less his hotline number, which embodies the weakness of broadcast news as compared with print. From a newspaper, I'd have that information in black and white.

Although some organizations plant themselves on TV by spending tens of thousands of dollars on video news releases—prepackaged features that include a very subtle sell—you can match their success with nothing more than shrewd thinking and good communication skills. Either through a pitch letter, a news release, or a phone call, stress the timeliness, the visual (for TV) or auditory (for radio) drama of your hook, and the importance for listeners or viewers. Lila Ivey, former producer of the 5 p.m. news on WLNE in Providence, Rhode Island, recalls a pitch that won her over because it met all three of those tests: "A publicist from the University of Rhode Island told me how colorful their jellyfish tanks were, that July was Jellyfish Month and that it was important to tell beachgoers which jellyfish to watch out for, which ones sting."

Bill Costley, who serves as publicist for the Wellesley Symphony Orchestra in Massachusetts, says that he usually beats out other organizations competing for air time to tell listeners on WBZ Radio about upcoming events by sending stories with more depth and timeliness than the average event announcement. For a concert featuring the composers Dvorak and Tchaikovsky, for instance, he tied the program to political turmoil going on in 20th-century Czechoslovakia and Russia.

If a radio or TV station does send a crew to you to prepare a news story, some guidelines apply in addition to those discussed in Chapters 14 and 15. "Never call and cancel," advises Lila Ivey. "If you do, you've burned your bridges for a long, long time. If an emergency comes up, get someone to fill in. Have a backup plan." Provide clear, accurate directions for the crew to find you, and when they arrive have two people, not one or five, available for interviews. Feel free to make suggestions, "but don't tell me how to do my job," warns Ivey. "We're not MGM Studios. I know what we can do and still get on the air at 5 p.m." The worst and most common blunder, she says, is grabbing the microphone. Assume that the technicians know more about what they're doing than you do. Finally, if a crew arrives and then rushes off because a big fire breaks out, "Don't whine. They'll try to get back to you."

To get on to news programs in a more consistent and controlled fashion, consider proposing a regular spot, such as Amy Flowers's "Creative Coping." Lila Ivey's former station, Channel 6 in Providence, has local movie reviewers, a nutritionist, a chef, and a master gardener who appear weekly at a regular time for two minutes. Ivey says that credentials count most in a potential regular, then whether they can write their own material and have a personality that can come across well on TV. If this option grabs you, research which station in your area might be receptive to your idea, call the receptionist to find out to whom to send your proposal, and write a captivating query letter, similar to the sample in Chapter 8, detailing your concept and your qualifications. Just as with a newspaper column (see Chapter 9), you have a good chance of a station running your segment for free if you design it to be informational and entertaining, and meet viewer or listener needs.

Other Publicity Opportunities on Radio or TV

1. **Public service announcements (PSAs).** Most radio stations and many TV stations air announcements of events of interest to their audience that are sponsored by nonprofit organizations. Follow the format of the sample that follows, which Bob Piankian of Boston wrote and sent to the local classical music stations. Use all capital letters, with reading time indicated. For TV, it's worthwhile to send along a prop, such as a customized mug or T-shirt, that the station can hold up while making the announcement.

Sample Public Service Announcement

Press contact: Bob Piankian
(617) 254-3088

FOR IMMEDIATE RELEASE
MAY 16, 1993
KILL DATE: JUNE 5, 1993

METROPOLITAN WIND SYMPHONY HOSTS 5TH ANNUAL BOSTON FESTIVAL OF BANDS

PUBLIC SERVICE ANNOUNCEMENT/COMMUNITY CALENDAR

15 SECOND: THE METROPOLITAN WIND SYMPHONY HOSTS THE FIFTH ANNUAL BOSTON FESTIVAL OF BANDS ON SATURDAY JUNE 5 FROM 10 AM TO 6 PM AT FANEUIL HALL, ADJACENT TO QUINCY MARKETPLACE IN BOSTON.

EIGHT BANDS WILL PLAY A WIDE VARIETY OF MUSIC. ADMISSION IS FREE. FOR INFORMATION CALL (617) 522-2849.

20 SECOND: THE METROPOLITAN WIND SYMPHONY HOSTS THE FIFTH ANNUAL BOSTON FESTIVAL OF BANDS ON SATURDAY JUNE 5 FROM 10 AM TO 6 PM AT FANEUIL HALL, ADJACENT TO QUINCY MARKETPLACE IN BOSTON. OTHER BANDS PERFORMING INCLUDE THE AIR FORCE BAND OF LIBERTY, THE AMERICAN BAND, AND THE CONCORD BAND. THE BANDS WILL PLAY SELECTIONS RANGING FROM BROADWAY SHOW MUSIC TO SOUSA MARCHES TO CLASSICAL MUSIC. ADMISSION IS FREE. FOR MORE INFORMATION CALL (617) 522-2849.

45 SECOND: THE METROPOLITAN WIND SYMPHONY HOSTS THE FIFTH ANNUAL BOSTON FESTIVAL OF BANDS ON SATURDAY JUNE 5 FROM 10 AM TO 6 PM AT FANEUIL HALL, ADJACENT TO QUINCY MARKETPLACE IN BOSTON. OTHER BANDS PERFORMING INCLUDE THE AIR FORCE BAND OF LIBERTY, THE AMERICAN BAND, THE METROWEST BAND, THE STRAFFORD COUNTY WIND SYMPHONY, THE NEW ENGLAND BRASS BAND, THE CASCO BAY CONCERT BAND, AND THE CONCORD BAND. MUSIC DIRECTOR DAVID MARTINS OF THE UNIVERSITY OF LOWELL DIRECTS THE MWS. THE BANDS WILL PLAY SELECTIONS RANGING FROM BROADWAY SHOW MUSIC TO SOUSA MARCHES TO CLASSICAL MUSIC. RADIO STATION WCRB IS COSPONSORING THE EVENT AND PETER ROSS OF WCRB WILL AN NOUNCE IT. ADMISSION IS FREE.

THE CONCERT IS WHEELCHAIR ACCESSIBLE. TO GET MORE INFORMATION CALL THE MWS CONCERT LINE AT (617) 522-2849. A PART OF BOSTON'S MUSICAL COMMUNITY SINCE 1971, THE MWS IS A NONPROFIT SEMI-PROFESSIONAL ENSEMBLE COMPOSED OF APPROXIMATELY 70 TALENTED MUSICIANS FROM THE GREATER BOSTON METROPOLITAN AREA.

❖❖ ❖❖

2.   **Editorial replies.** Another opportunity especially open to nonprofit groups is free air time to respond to a station-sponsored editorial that presented only one side of an issue. The federal Fairness Doctrine mandates that stations provide balanced coverage, so that, if the station does not respond reasonably to your request, you may appeal to the Federal Communications Commission (FCC). If you can make a case that a feature show, documentary, or news item constituted unbalanced coverage, you may have the same right of reply. Call the offending station and find out to whom you should send your letter requesting reply time. In your letter, be as specific as possible about what was unfair and why and how you propose to remedy the lack of balance.

3.   **Bulletin boards.** Some commercial and noncommercial TV stations that do not broadcast 24 hours a day may fill their screen with rotating community announcements during off-hours. Again, contact the station to find out its guidelines.

4.   **College radio and TV stations.** Some college stations open the airwaves to local people unaffiliated with the college. On Wellesley College's WZLY-FM, students get first choice of time slots, Wellesley residents next, and finally others living in the 10-mile listening radius. From 1983 to 1988 Bill Costley did arts interviews live on the station in a slot no one else wanted: Sunday mornings following the broadcast of a local church service for shut-ins. "Since the service

ended anywhere from 11 to 11:45 a.m. and the next program started at noon, I had to be adaptable," he remembers. "But church listeners stayed tuned, and I developed a regular audience who recognized my voice years after the program went off the air."

5.   **Public radio commentaries.** "All Things Considered," the evening news show on National Public Radio, regularly airs recorded essay segments that offer personal and observational commentary from people who are not public figures and may live anywhere in the United States. Call the station, based in Washington, D.C., to find out who considers commentary submissions, then send both a transcript and a recording running less than three minutes. Because the purpose of the sample is to hear how you sound, don't worry about its technical quality. If the producers like your piece, they'll arrange for you to re-record it professionally at one of their stations. Local NPR affiliates may also have slots for commentaries. I did one for the national business show "Marketplace," as well as eight for WBUR, the Boston public radio station.

6.   **Game shows and reality TV.** Many game-show hosts introduce contestants to viewers by their whole name, occupation, and hometown. On shows such as *Jeopardy* or *Who Wants to Be a Millionaire?* the host often gets contestants talking a bit about their work or hobbies. Don't pursue this avenue, though, unless you believe a particular show is consistent with your image. Reality TV shows are far dicier because of their relish for sleaze and predictable unscriptedness. During the finale of the Survivor China show, contestant Denise Martin claimed she was being demoted from lunch lady to janitor back home at Douglas Intermediate Elementary School in Massachusetts. Not true, retorted school officials, who were deluged with angry e-mails from as far away as South Korea. Martin's local reputation plummeted.

7. **Exposé shows.** *60 Minutes,* one of the longest-running shows on television, has spawned numerous imitators, such that a reporter and camera crew pursue allegations about individuals, businesses, or organizations. It's hard to come off well if they choose you as a subject. Unless you enjoy swimming in piranha tanks, keep your distance from shows of this sort.

8. **Your own show.** Who says you can't create your own show for commercial radio or TV? It's a traditional ploy for office-less politicians who hope to remain visible to the public between elections. The guidelines earlier in this chapter on getting a regular spot on the news apply, but, because you'd be on the air for 30 minutes at a time or more, you need a good deal of performance polish, and, usually, broadcast experience to pull this off.

9. **Web and satellite radio.** If you peruse the directory of radio stations at Radio-directory.com, you'll notice a category called "Internet only." These are radio stations that don't broadcast over the bandwidths picked up by the radio in your car or kitchen, but can be heard exclusively over the Web. Similar to other radio stations, these break down into various formats, such as Alternative Rock, Adult Contemporary, and Classical. You're looking for Internet stations in the category "News-Talk." Sirius satellite radio also has several talk channels. Then there are free-standing podcasts, which may or may not ever go on the air at a certain time but get distributed through online syndication sites and often make an archive of past programs available on demand.

10. **A segment within a feature show.** In 1998, Jeannine Graf, who had hosted a radio show on which I had twice appeared, launched a Saturday morning TV program to air around New England, *The Job Show,* and invited me to do a weekly one-minute segment. I called it "The Marketing Minute," and, except for one week when I went to the TV studio and appeared on camera, I would deliver my one-minute, prewritten, pre-polished tip by telephone while viewers saw

different parts of the show's Website. It was terrifically impressive to be able to say I was on regional TV every week, and as part of the deal I got unlimited space at the show's Website to do whatever kind of promotion I wanted. That spelled the start of my weekly newsletter, "The Marketing Minute," one of my most productive publicity tools, still going strong although the TV show that spawned it no longer airs.

PODCASTING AND ONLINE VIDEO

If you think of podcasting and online video as homegrown, open-to-anyone versions of traditional radio and TV, you'll have a handle on much of the potential of these fast-moving publicity tools. Both add another dimension to what words and still images can communicate. Donna Maria Coles Johnson, CEO of Indie Business Media in Charlotte, North Carolina, considers video unparalleled in its impact, citing a client who'd done business with her for nearly seven years. "When I started adding video, she called me crying, telling me that she was so moved by my passion and sincerity that she felt like I was speaking directly to her. Then she gave me her credit card number to purchase more services," says Johnson.

Likewise, Susan Daffron, founder of the National Association of Pet Rescue Professionals, says her weekly audio podcast showcasing animals that need adoption, "Take Me Home," has an emotional impact that's not possible in any other medium. "Every rescue organization has an animal who's been with them for too long," she says, "and every animal has a story. When they tell that story on my podcast, you can hear the love in their voices, which doesn't come through on a Website." Daffron celebrates the fact that the first dog featured on the show was adopted, and also notes that her program has attracted members to her association, as well as subscribers to the association newsletter who might, through time, become members.

Even for a non-emotional topic such as auto equipment, video packs an extra dose of persuasive power. Veteran videographer Bill Myers was once trying to sell a diesel tuning module through an eBay auction. "There were 12 watchers for the auction, but nobody bid," he recalls. "So I took my camera out to my workshop, set it up on a tripod, and shot and uploaded a short video of me installing the diesel tuning module. I then re-listed the item. Same price, same description—the only difference was a link to the video. Within an hour, a buyer paid my full asking price. Potential bidders could see that the item was real, and they could see how easy it was to install."

Do online video and audio require a lot of specialized equipment? Not necessarily. Daffron's half-hour weekly podcast takes little preparation beyond lining up the guest to interview, and no investment in technology other than a new $45 headset. Christopher Penn spent a mere $70 for a microphone that, in conjunction with his laptop, lets him podcast to a regular Monday-through-Friday audience of more than 1,200 students, parents, and financial professionals about college loan and scholarship opportunities. For each 10-minute episode, his Financial Aid Podcast takes Penn 30 minutes of research, 10 minutes of recording, and then 10 minutes to upload the podcast recording to the Web.

Although Penn started the podcast as a hobby in April 2005, it soon developed into a core publicity vehicle for his company, generating approximately $25 million in requested loans for his firm, The Student Loan Network, in 2007 alone, not to mention sparking media coverage in CNN, the *Wall Street Journal*, the *New York Times*, *BusinessWeek*, and more. "Our little company could never in a million years have afforded the exposure we've gotten through podcasting," he says, adding that opportunities still exist in most industries to launch a similar success without much competition.

Whereas most podcasts model themselves on talk radio shows, online videos use several different formats, and rarely imitate TV shows or Hollywood films. Hypnotherapist Jean Fain created her first mindful eating video as a slide show, combining stock photos from Microsoft Office with an audio narration, assembling the components via Microsoft Movie Maker, a program built into Windows. "It was free and easy to do this," she notes. Many information marketers use a program call Camtasia Studio to create so-called screencasts—videos that capture and enhance what appears on a computer screen, accompanied by explanatory audio narration. Technically, these are a bit more complicated than a slide show, but they offer broad potential for explaining how to do something on a computer.

"Creating a screencast can be surprisingly easy if you start with the right tools," says Bill Myers, who produces a one-minute how-to screencast in 15 minutes using only Camtasia Studio, a Plantronics USB Headset Microphone and his computer. He simply captures the computer screen activity and his voice describing the steps involved while performing a specific task on his computer, then edits the screen capture movie. Then he converts the completed movie into Flash format, which can be published on the Web for anyone to view or loaded onto a CD that will play in either Mac computers or PCs.

Once you've acquired those tools and learned how to use them, you can produce and upload screencasts to video sharing sites such as YouTube, where strangers can discover them, as well as to your own site, where such videos, in Myers's words, "serve as the ultimate 'learn by seeing it done' information delivery system."

Other video techniques include animated shorts, which provide ample scope for creativity and humor, and talking heads, in which someone speaks to the camera for several minutes. Nancy Marmolejo, who has posted her own instructional videos on YouTube, says she's tired of looking at people's cluttered bookcases and stacks of papers in the background of talking-head videos. "Have a nice backdrop and use a real camera on a tripod instead of a Webcam," she advises. "Bring energy into the shoot by holding up a prop or by moving in and out of the frame." Finally there's the documentary style of video, consisting of action scenes accompanied by on-screen dialogue or voice-over narration—the approach I used for my YouTube video, showing me sweeping snow off our Internet satellite dish, conducting a teleseminar in my home office, hiking, and more, while I made the case for wealth as freedom rather than as showy luxuries.

Whichever kind of video you create, Bill Myers offers these tips for maximizing its publicity reach and impact:

> → **Include a title screen and closing screen.** Start and end each video with a graphic featuring the name of the video, your name, and the URL of your Website. Myers also ends every video by saying, "To find more videos like these, visit

www.bmyers.com." This gives viewers an impetus to go to his site, without any heavy-handed promotion that discourages others from embedding the video in their site or recommending it.

❖ **Allow embedding.** While uploading videos to YouTube or another video sharing site, select the option, "Yes, allow external sites to embed this video." This enables anyone who loves the video to share it on another Website, while keeping the video exactly as you made it.

❖ **Require approval for comments.** "I once forgot to set this option correctly, and within minutes of my video going live on YouTube, spammers and flamers started loading up the comments section with obscenities, racial slurs, and political rants, none related to the video. Because these comments would be objectionable to most sane people, I quickly removed them and reset the sharing options to prevent this," Myers says. "Almost every video I post generates legitimate new messages to me each day. I try to reply because I have found that many of the people asking questions end up joining my member Website or purchasing my videos."

❖ **Pay careful attention to keywords.** YouTube and similar video sharing sites ask for a video title, description, and keywords so that they can properly index your creation. Include the words and phrases someone would most likely use to find your content in each of these fields, Myers recommends. Google picks these up and rewards you with top search engine listings for those phrases, often in two hours or less. "As video becomes the preferred content on the Internet, more and more Google searchers use Google's video search to narrow the results to videos that include the keywords being searched for," he says. "Rarely does a day go by that I am not contacted by someone wanting to pay me in some way as a result of viewing my videos on YouTube, including product manufacturers, TV producers (who paid me $300 for a one-minute clip), publishers, and DVD distributors. Learn the tools of video communication and you have the advantage—now and in the future."

Chapter 13

Schmoozing That Puts You in the Public Eye

A nne Boe of Encinitas, California, took the idea of being her own best press agent farther than most. Everywhere she went—meetings, airports, parties—she introduced herself to strangers and invited them to do the same. As a way to create unpredictable opportunities, it worked. During a speaking engagement once in Washington, D.C., she left the banquet to get something from her room upstairs and found herself in an elevator with a man she'd never met. "I wasn't going to waste 10 floors," she remembered, "so very quickly I said my usual, 'Hi, I'm Anne Boe. I do career management and networking. What do you do?' The man saw my speaker badge and said, 'I'm not a speaker. I write about speakers.' He worked for the magazine of Meeting Planners International and invited me to send my press kit and demo video, which I did. Six months later, I spoke to his group in Phoenix, and a year later was asked to keynote their conference, a real plum for speakers."

The man in the elevator wasn't wearing a name tag and could have been a tourist from Walla Walla, but Boe wouldn't have been discouraged if he was. "Everything in life is an opportunity, yet I don't see many other people reaching out the way I do." In her book, *Is Your "Net" Working?* Boe discussed the art of making and keeping connections with people. Because for many people the word *networking* has taken on a shallow, opportunistic connotation, I'll talk instead about "schmoozing"—ways of cozying up with people that can pay off in publicity, even if the idea of starting a conversation in an elevator feels to you like an ordeal.

STRATEGIC SELF-INTRODUCTIONS

Speaking with strangers does sometimes lead to spectacular results. John Kremer tells a story about one author traveling by plane who talked to her seatmate about the guidebook she'd written for handicapped travelers. The seatmate was none other than Abigail Van Buren, and after "Dear Abby" mentioned the guidebook in her syndicated column, more than two mail sacks full of orders for the guidebook materialized. I'm sure the author was glad she hadn't spent the flight with her nose buried in a novel.

But whether or not you make the first move, it's essential to have handy a quick, comprehensive, and comprehensible way of introducing yourself. How can people help spread the word about you if you say just your name or the fact that you live in Kalamazoo or work in computers? Steve Schiffman does it this way: "I'm president of DEI Management, a sales training firm in New York City. We do a lot of business with companies like IBM and Pitney Bowes." Schiffman says he uses this self-introduction everywhere. "It can be as obnoxious as hell," he admits, "but the reality is that everyone knows someone, and it cascades."

Some schmoozing specialists take the art of strategic self-introductions one step further by recommending that, instead of using an occupational title, you use your six seconds to present the benefits you or your organization produce for people. For instance, instead of saying that you're a CPA, you can say, "I specialize in helping people dramatically reduce their tax bill." Instead of saying, "I'm vice president of the Earthwise Foundation," you might say, "I work for an organization that helps local communities throughout the country carry out curbside recycling programs." Doesn't that grab you more? The real test, Jeff Slutsky explains in his book, *How to Get Clients*, is to rattle off your carefully honed self-introduction at a cocktail party. If you've done it right, people will lean forward and ask, "No kidding! How do you do that?"—inviting you to say more.

San Franciscan Patricia Fripp says it's a great conversation starter when she's asked what she does and replies, "I make meetings and conventions more exciting." Usually that provokes another question, to which she replies, "You know how meetings are supposed to be dynamic and exciting and they're usually dull and boring? I have some practical ideas I present in an entertaining way, with the results that people stay awake, have a good time, and get the company's message. I'm a professional speaker." Fripp says this approach works especially well by making what she does for a living meaningful even to the eight out of 10 people who have no idea professional speakers exist. It works just as well, she says, if you do something more familiar, such as sell real estate, because it implants the idea that you can solve problems more creatively than competitors who merely say, "I'm a realtor."

Those who are on the shy side can cut down on fear flutters by circulating at parties or business gatherings with a friend. Patricia Fripp often attends meetings with Susan RoAne, author of *How to Work a Room* and *The Secrets of Savvy Networking*. "When we meet someone, Susan will say, 'This is Patricia Fripp. She truly is one of the best speakers in the country,' and I will say, 'What Susan is too modest to tell you is that she's a best-selling author.' We act like each other's press agents." Not only is it easier to tout a friend than yourself, consider how much better an impression each of the duo makes than if Fripp said, "I'm one of the best speakers in the country" and RoAne said, "I'm a best-selling author."

Gerontologist Ruth Jacobs of Wellesley, Massachusetts, has found a way to introduce herself and invite curious questions before she even opens her mouth. She often wears customized T-shirts that bear the legend "R.A.S.P.: Remarkable Aging Smart Person" or "Outrageous Older Woman." Both relate to her book, *Be An Outrageous Older Woman,* and the purple version of the "Outrageous Older Woman" shirt especially attracts a lot of attention. "People come up to me and want to know where I got the T-shirt. I hand them a flyer for the book, and when they call the 800-number of my publisher they usually order the T-shirt *and* the book." She also has buttons with both slogans and wears those when she's going around town on errands. "Sometimes in the supermarket someone will come up to me and get so excited about the button that I have to give it away on the spot," Jacobs says. When she speaks at conferences, a display of the buttons often draws to the book table people who end up buying the book.

BEING MEMORABLE

Besides meeting people and talking with them, artful schmoozing involves making yourself more memorable than happens in the average encounter. A catchy business name helps accomplish this. Professional organizer Cheryl Norris of Washington, D.C., calls her business name, Order Out of Chaos, "a tremendous asset." If you counted yourself among the desperately disorganized, just hearing that business name would make you prick up your ears and remember what you heard. Similarly, "Nancy Friedman, The Telephone Doctor," is more likely to stick in your mind than "Nancy Friedman, consultant on telephone skills." Another telephone skills trainer, Stan Billue, goes by the nickname "Mr. Fantastic" because of his standing offer that if you ask him how he is and he doesn't say, "I'm fantastic," he will give you a 100-dollar bill. (In the 16 years that he's told this to hundreds of thousands of people, he's had to pay up exactly four times.) Entertainer Ron Bianco feels strongly that the name he gave his singing dog makes a difference in the response to his act. "Bilbo" has a ring to it that, for example, "Rover" does not, he says.

You might think that your personal name is not within your control the way your business name and the name of your pet are, but some disagree. Don't you find "Kirk Douglas" easier to remember (and spell) than "Issur Danielovitch," the name the actor was born with? Likewise, the public-radio star and best-selling author of *Lake Wobegon Days* who goes by Garrison Keillor was born with the less distinctive first name of Gary.

Those loath to tamper with the name your parents gave you still have choices. If your passport reads "Margaret Fox Viglioni," are you going to go by all three names, by "Margaret Viglioni," "Margaret F. Viglioni," "Meg Viglioni," "M. Fox Viglioni," or "M.F. Viglioni"? I believe that if you want people to remember your name and cite it accurately, a middle initial is an encumbrance rather than an asset. Most ordinary people and many reporters will drop it out, and you'll have an inconsistency in your press clips. If you've already become well-known by a certain name, however, whatever its flaws, stick with it.

Your appearance might form a part of your strategy of becoming unforgettable. Patricia Fripp nearly always wears a hat when she attends business meetings. "I have about 70 hats and let's just say they're very memorable," she says. "People race over to me when they see my hat and say, 'Hi, Patricia, I knew it had to be you.'" Although Fripp argues that women have an advantage in being able to dress with pizzazz, a man can stand out by always wearing a bowtie, elegant suits, or, in some careers, an unusual hairstyle. If you met boxing promoter Don King, with his electric, stand-up-by-itself hairdo, wouldn't you remember him?

Or what makes you stand out in people's memories might be your opinions. Rick Segel, owner of Ruth's, a dress shop in Medford, Massachusetts, appeared on the Sally Jesse Raphael show because of a referral from someone he hadn't spoken with in three years. The show concerned people who wore clothing and then tried to return it to the store from which they bought it, and the person who referred him remembered that he took a much harder line on the practice than the majority of retailers. Similarly, what got Anne Boe on Phil Donahue's show was an oft-repeated wish. For eight years, she got laughs by telling audiences that she wanted to be on the Phil Donahue show. Then she had a good laugh herself when she received a call from Donahue's producer and found out that one of her clients had sent him her video.

SCHMOOZING WITH THE MEDIA

Although the first two steps (meeting people and being memorable) can land you eventually in the path of the media, you can sashay there directly by visiting their watering holes. Larger cities have press clubs that may have events open to the public. In the summertime, writers' conferences abound, and either there or at some other program of a writers' organization you can stay alert for on-the-move freelancers who might view you as their ticket to *American Health, Inc.*, or *Parade* magazine.

Parties help, too. In the early 1980s, I had the opportunity to write a cover story for *Psychology Today* after a friend and I crashed the housewarming party of one of its at-large editors. Peter Desmond, a writer in Cambridge, Massachusetts, who also works as a tax preparer, says he was quoted in the *Boston Globe* because he met a freelance writer at a party who remembered him when she was writing about the changed home-office deduction rules for the *Globe's* real estate section.

Try the time-honored friend-of-a-friend approach if there is a specific writer, host, or magazine you want to approach. A generation before networking came into vogue, social psychologist Stanley Milgram established that you have a 50-50 chance of being able to construct a chain of acquaintanceship from yourself to any randomly chosen person in the United States with only two intermediaries. That is, if you're dying to do lunch with NBC anchor Tom Brokaw, syndicated columnist Ellen Goodman, or former talk-show host Rosie O'Donnell, the odds are one in two that you know someone who knows someone who personally knows him or her. If you find those odds promising, start schmoozing away.

I can't even count the number of times I've interviewed acquaintances, or met people by interviewing them, became friends, and then interviewed them more. In one case, I began doing some editing work for a consultant who decided she wanted more visibility. She asked me if I knew any freelancers who might want to write about her. I gave her the names of three writers who wrote a lot on business topics, and she contacted them, but nothing developed. Because I had the chance to learn about her work, however, *I* ended up quoting her in three articles for national magazines. The lesson for her, I suppose, is that familiarity breeds citations.

You can also get on board with the media by taking advantage of free listings of all sorts. For special events, investigate calendar listings in all the papers serving your area, taking note especially of submission deadlines and whether photos are accepted. Send your vital information off for mention in your alumni magazine or organizational, club, or church newsletter. Some trade magazines and others for the general public include resource lists, such as of vocational training programs, computer suppliers, or vacation spas. If you spot such a list that omitted you, contact the magazine and ask if it's a repeated feature and how to submit information for inclusion next time.

If you belong to a national or regional professional organization, find out if it maintains a resource database for the media. To locate people to quote for magazine articles, I regularly used the services of the media relations department of the American Psychological Association in Washington, D.C. I would call and describe the topic I was working on, and receive four to six names and phone numbers of association members with expertise in that area who had volunteered to speak to the media. Less than 2 percent of APA members make themselves available for publicity in this way, however, even though it costs them nothing. If your professional organization does not have such a service, suggest it as a great way to spread awareness of what members do.

You can get a direct line on media people's current needs by subscribing to a leads service, such as Profnet if you are a company, educational institution, or nonprofit organization, or PRLeads if you would be promoting yourself. (See Chapter 24 for contact information.) For an annual fee, a leads service sends you brief notices of sources and stories for which reporters and producers are currently looking, along with the deadline. It's then up to you to follow up appropriately. Help a Reporter works much the same way, except that it's free.

If you're more of a joiner, volunteer to be press liaison for any organization to which you belong. By becoming a spokesperson or just doing the legwork for a group, you get to practice your publicity skills, experience how the media operates, and make contacts of which you can later take advantage. With that idea in mind, communication consultant Claire McCarthy served as the public relations chair for the Greater Lawrence, Massachusetts Rotary Club. "That meant that any time there was an event, I was publicly thanked and acknowledged in the newspaper. It elevated my whole credibility in the community," McCarthy says.

Getting to know the leaders of organizations can pay off in publicity, too. For young chocolate-maker Kim Merritt, a great organizational go-between with the media came to her unbidden. Someone in the Association of Collegiate Entrepreneurs read about her and contacted her. "Because I was female and one of the youngest entrepreneurs they knew of, whenever ACE sent out press releases, I was one of the people listed," Merritt recalls. A similar connection with someone in the leadership of the National Federation of Independent Businesses led to Merritt being featured in *Money* magazine.

Whenever you do schmooze your way to a good media connection, seize the day. Ruth Jacobs remembers the day an Associated Press reporter showed up at the Wellesley College Center for Research on Women, where Jacobs worked, looking for stories about women. "Luckily, I had the presence of mind to give her a copy of my book," Jacobs says. Not only did the reporter gratefully read it, but her story also went out on the AP newswire and appeared all over the country, with a photo. Likewise, at a meeting of the New York chapter of the National Association of Professional Organizers, Ilise Benun schmoozed with a writer who was working on a piece for *New York Magazine*. Benun sent her information about what she did and ended up mentioned in print as someone who helped people promote themselves. "Five years later, I was still getting calls from that article," she says. "It was the type of thing people clipped and saved."

SCHMOOZING ONLINE

If the prospect of getting dressed up to work a room strikes dread into you, never fear. Technology now gives you the option of schmoozing with the media while shuffling around at home in your bathrobe. Numerous writers and producers locate sources by posting notices in online forums or e-mail discussion lists devoted to specialized topics. Paul Edwards estimates that he found 20 percent of the guests for the "Home Office" show that he and his wife Sarah presented on the Business Radio Network through online forums. "We also refer people we've met there to reporters who call us," says Edwards. "People have wound up on the covers of national magazines because of contact with us online. Yet when writers leave messages on forums, the rate of response is nowhere near what it could be. As a general rule, people are missing the boat on opportunities to get media exposure."

When responding to a reporter or producer's online plea for sources, be quick, because they are almost always working against a deadline. Be forthcoming. Instead of simply noting that you fit their stated criteria, explain how, and provide some details as well as your contact information. And be relevant. My fellow writers complain bitterly about people who e-mail them with stories that have only a far-fetched or no connection to their request.

You can also often initiate contact with a writer, columnist, or producer more easily and more informally online than by phone, fax, or mail by sending them a comment, anecdote, or brag about yourself that you believe will pique his or her interest. Sometimes reporters' e-mail addresses are published at the end of their articles. More often, you find these e-mail addresses not in the print version of a publication but accompanying the article on the publication's Website. Of the four times I have been featured in the Sunday *Boston Globe*, the easiest appearance came about simply by e-mailing someone who wrote a column on what Bostonians were up to on the Web. I told him about my e-mail newsletter. He recommended it in his column a few weeks later, and, among the dozens of new subscribers that brought me, was the marketing manager of a local bank, who a year or two later hired me to present a seminar.

Indeed, sometimes even routine e-mail correspondence with the media gets to the top because it can be forwarded with just a click. In September 2000, as moderator for the ClickZ Forum, a discussion list on Internet marketing, I wrote a message to subscribers about an article in an issue of *Business 2.0* that had arrived the previous day in my mailbox. I wanted to include a link to the article on the *Business 2.0* Website, and I went there only to find the previous month's issue touted as the current issue. Annoyed, I dashed off an e-mail complaining about the problem and sent it to the "letters to the editor" e-mail address for the magazine. Two hours later, I was astounded to receive a reply from the editor in chief, Jim Daly, explaining why the new issue wasn't yet up at the Website. Of course, I recovered quickly and sent back an e-mail along the lines of, "Now that I have your ear, let me introduce myself properly and offer to write something for you." Within two weeks I had my first writing assignment for this prestigious business magazine.

Besides schmoozing online with media people, you can expand your reputation by getting to know what the communications consulting firm Burson-Marsteller has dubbed "e-fluentials"—an 8-percent segment of Internet users who tell an average of eight others when they get excited about a product or service. When they spread the word to other e-fluentials, this quickly produces an avalanche of interest through an exponential multiplier effect. Although they may not have any formal title or official role anywhere, they post heavily to online discussion groups, obviously enjoy spreading their discoveries, and make speeches, write letters to the editor, and serve on association committees much more often than the average person. Often their opinions are highly respected by online communities because people know they have no vested motive in their recommendations other than sheer enthusiasm.

To get an idea of the self-selected character of many e-fluentials, browse the reader reviews at Amazon.com. Occasionally you'll encounter reader comments submitted by someone labeled a "top reviewer." In contrast to formally appointed book critics in the newspaper or on radio, this is someone who provides well-informed, in-depth reviews of books just because he or she likes to do so, and whose reviews are highly rated by Amazon.com shoppers. If you were publishing a book, it might be worth your time to figure out which top reviewers gravitated to your topic, and to make sure they knew of the existence of your book.

Similarly, in your niche, a top e-fluential might not be a popular keynote speaker, CEO, or trade association official, but someone who simply knows everyone else who's active online in that niche and communicates like crazy with them. Almost always you'll find e-fluentials responsive to e-mail contacts, so long as you approach them personally in a spirit of colleagueship. Agree or disagree with something they said. Flatter them mildly and sincerely. Ask questions about what they do. In short, schmooze them up the way you might at a networking event. After expressing interest in them, you'll often find them receptive to what you do.

Schmoozing Through Social Media

If you're under the age of 35, you don't need me to tell you about the widespread use of social media sites such as Facebook, MySpace, and Friendster, where anyone can create a free multimedia profile and collect and create links to other people's profiles. A 2008 study by Rapleaf showed that 87 to 90 percent of users of those three sites were 35 years old or younger. Among the most popular social media sites, LinkedIn had the highest proportion of older users, with 24 percent of its population age 36 to 45 and 16 percent age 46 or older. If you have left age 35 behind, you may wonder if becoming active on such networks is worthwhile.

"For me, as an author, I want to be communicating with the next generation, and that's where they are," says Susan RoAne, author of *Face to Face: How to Reclaim the Personal Touch in a Digital World.* "Besides, many of my business colleagues and clients are going on Facebook, and it's convenient to reconnect with them that way." Accordingly, RoAne created profiles on Facebook and MySpace and tries to keep them updated.

Because the unique appeal of social media sites is the interpersonal connections they facilitate, you need to consider how best to issue and respond to invitations to set up a connection. "Write your invitation so it's the one you would send, not the one provided by the site," advises RoAne—an important point because upwards of 95 percent of all the invitations I've received to link up on the networking site LinkedIn used the same boilerplate wording. That's off-putting, like getting a robotic phone call. "Make it sound like you, so that you showcase your authenticity," RoAne says.

When she receives a social media message from someone wanting to become a contact whose name she doesn't recognize, RoAne writes back, "Please forgive me, I can't seem to place where we met, can you please remind me?" If the person replies, "I read your book and I like it," then RoAne knows that's a fan and accepts them. "If there's a request from someone where you can't find a link, don't accept that invitation," she says. "You don't want someone using your name to get access to someone else and then find out there's some kind of screw-up."

Anaheim, California–based PR strategist Nancy Marmolejo, who works with women entrepreneurs, agrees that it's essential to personalize social media introductions. "Otherwise it's like someone shoving a business card in your face and saying, 'Here, be my friend.' I like to break the ice by posting a comment on someone's video, picture, or profile, which starts a conversation. Then after a few exchanges, we're ready to do business. There's also an eavesdropping effect because these exchanges can be read by others. Focus on relationship building first, then let business flow from that." More than half of Marmolejo's income comes from clients she met or befriended on social media sites.

Fern Reiss, author of the "Publishing Game" series of books, went one step deeper in social networking when she started a "Writing and Publishing" group on Facebook, which accumulated more than 1,000 members in the first six weeks. "It took me about five minutes to set up and takes perhaps another hour a week to moderate. It gives me another 'pulpit' from which to share my wares. Unlike industry discussion lists, which can be tricky to post in, with a Facebook group, you control it." Reiss attributed a surge of requests for consultations to her initial Facebook activities and expected that to keep growing with time.

As with all the new and old publicity media discussed in this book, be mindful of your business image when sharing photos, contacts, stories, and videos on social media networks. A 2006 University of Dayton study found that, nationally, 40 percent of employers consider Facebook profiles relevant to hiring decisions, even though 42 percent of students considered that a violation of their privacy. For entrepreneurs, the same dynamics undoubtedly occur when committees are seeking keynote speakers or deciding which professional firm with which to sign a contract.

"I once looked up the profile of someone who has a good name in Internet marketing, and his top 'friends' all looked like strippers," says Nancy Marmolejo. "Now every time I run across his name I think, 'You certainly have a double life.'"

A final pitfall to avoid in turning social media to your advantage is spending too much time on it. "You can easily spend all day doing online networking, if you don't set limits," notes Biana Babinsky, a Chicago-area consultant. "You need time to work on other aspects of your business."

PART IV

POLISHING YOUR PUBLICITY SKILLS

Chapter 14

Cooperating With Reporters

Interview shows such as *60 Minutes* and *20/20* that seem to show reporters at work actually present a very misleading picture of the job of the journalist. Unless you're a celebrity, public official, corporate spokesperson, or criminal, the reporter will not usually function as your adversary, trying to coax or trick you to reveal information you'd be better off concealing. Instead, the reporter ordinarily tries to get out of you the story or expertise that is yours to share, in a form that makes sense to the audience.

Other erroneous expectations may come from horror stories you've heard from others who claim to have been grievously misquoted. But rather than approaching the prospect of being interviewed with paranoid apprehension, you can take steps to improve the odds of being accurately quoted. Also, even indisputable misquotations are not always the disaster you might assume they'd be. Years ago, a consultant I know was the subject of a long, front-page feature story in *The Wall Street Journal*. Disgusted at the snide tone and inaccuracies in the story, she showed me a copy of the story with more than a dozen factual errors circled. Yet she also revealed that, years later, she was still receiving calls from potential clients and press inquiries traceable back to that story from as far away as Tokyo.

Similarly, book publishers have long claimed that any review, even a blisteringly negative one, works better than silence—because it gets the word out. Readers are quite capable of disregarding the writer's attitude and making up their own minds.

As someone who has sat on both sides of the interview encounter, I can clue you in on the agenda, methods, and constraints of reporters, as well as preventive measures you can take as an interviewee to ensure that the story ends up serving you. I'll be focusing here on print interviews; Chapter 15 presents additional tips for TV and radio interviews.

Do's and Don'ts for Print Interviews

Call the reporter back as soon as possible. Even more fundamentally, call him or her back, period. For the first edition of this book, I wrote to 12 individuals who had listings in *Chase's Calendar of Events*, and of the 12, only four got back in touch with me. Because I explained there could be more free publicity in store for these people who had already gone out of their way to get some, I was shocked at the low rate of cooperation. Other journalists confirm this measly rate of response. When Gordon West, a contributing editor for *Boating Industry* magazine, was updating a marine electronics buyer's guide, he contacted 84 companies, of which only 20 responded. The other 64 missed out on an opportunity for an accurate listing and free editorial space. Putting a journalist first on your list of call-backs or write-backs isn't merely polite. Because every one of them has a deadline to meet, it's essential.

Discuss a mutually agreeable time and place for the interview. When you receive a call from a reporter, don't assume that you have to begin the interview on the spot. Scheduling the interview at a time convenient for you puts you more in control of the situation. Even if the reporter says he or she is up against a tight deadline, ask if you can call back in 10 minutes. That gives you the chance to become mentally and practically prepared.

Although many good interviews take place on the phone, some types of articles and some reporting styles require an in-person meeting. The setting sometimes ends up in the story, so if your office or home won't corroborate the image you hope to project, arrange to meet in a hotel or restaurant instead. If you do suggest meeting over lunch, coffee, or a drink, reach for the check. It sends the message that you understand who's doing whom a favor and that you know reporters don't make princely salaries. The reporter might have to refuse your offer to pay because of the employer's gift policy, but your message gets across nevertheless.

Feel free to set time limits in advance. If your time is scarce, tell the reporter during the initial call how much you can spare. A half hour should be plenty for a phone interview, an hour sufficient when you meet in person. During the set-aside time, don't take calls, check your e-mail, or allow other interruptions. Be understanding, though, about the time a photographer needs for a shot worthy of a national magazine. Kim Merritt says that the four or five times magazines such as *Money* or *People* have featured her, their photographers spent nearly the whole day at her chocolate factory. "Some people find that bothersome, but I know it helps a lot to have my picture attached to the story. It's making me money as much as if I spent that time with customers," Merritt says.

Ask the reporter's agenda. Before hanging up from the initial phone conversation, ask something along the lines of, "Would you mind telling me the scope and focus of the article you have in mind?" Sometimes in following up on a news release you've sent, the reporter plans a feature article that spotlights what you wrote about in the release. Other times the reporter merely needs a few additional facts to run a small informative notice. Still other times a topical piece that quotes many people, including you, is in the works. If a journalist has called you on his or her own initiative, it's fair to inquire about the audience, emphasis, and circulation of any publication with which you're not familiar, as well as whether he or she is on staff or a freelancer. Freelance writers have a greater chance of their stories being rejected, but I still recommend cooperation if you can find the time.

Sometimes the reporter's reply reveals a slant that may not be favorable to your business or point of view. If, for example, your release concerned the opening of a new paper mill and the reporter says the article is about the environmental effects of paper mills, warning lights should go off in your brain. Ask more questions, and follow your instincts! You do not have to cooperate with any journalist working on a story bound to portray you in a negative light.

Know your own agenda, and prepare. Before you speak at length with a reporter, be clear on the essential points you want to get across in the interview. Write down these points and have them with you during the interview. A few times, people I've interviewed have even handed me their typed list of important points, which I found helpful.

Otherwise just resolve to steer the conversation toward your agenda, gently, if you have to. Study how politicians do this in debates and press conferences. Henry Kissinger once opened a press conference by asking, "Does any reporter have any questions for my answers?"

Preparing at least one example or story for each of your major points beats having to tell the reporter, "Well, let me see...um...gee... gosh...." To get ready for her first major interview, *Lions Don't Need to Roar* author Debra Benton thought up as many questions as she could that her interviewer might ask, and an effective answer for each, and she spread them all out on her desk in anticipation of his call. "I was swimming a lot in those days," she says. "I would swim for an hour and rehearse questions and answers while I was going back and forth in the pool."

Be cooperative during the interview and grateful afterward. A writer told me about a man who'd suggested she write a story about him, and then sat there like a lunk during the interview, offering little more than monosyllables. I've never encountered that, but I do recall one interviewee who told me how to do my job, and several who complained that I quoted them too briefly. They thereby eliminated themselves from the list of people I would ever contact again. You can stay in your media contacts' good graces by understanding the constraints under which they work.

When a reporter interviews for an article, he or she rarely knows exactly how the article will be structured or what the major points and examples will be. That depends on what interviewees say. After gathering information, the writer figures out how to weave it all together in a way that fits the publication's format, focus, and length. Great quotes from nice people sometimes do not make it into the article, and, after the writer finishes with the piece, editors can compel other cuts and changes. Instead of reproaching the reporter because an hour-long chat yielded three printed sentences, thank him or her and express your willingness to be helpful again.

Be specific and colorful during the interview. General statements, lofty observations, and clichés are useless to a journalist. Speak naturally, but improve your quotability with these media-pleasers:

➔ *Precise statistics, dates, figures, events, and names.*

> INSTEAD OF: "Most older men worry about losing their hair."
>
> SAY: "According to the National Council on Balding, one out of every two men older than age 40 has experienced significant hair loss."
>
> INSTEAD OF: "Pretty soon I was doing all right."
>
> SAY: "In just half a year, I went from ending up in the red every month to making $5,000 over expenses every month."
>
> INSTEAD OF: "I used to be in the hair business."
>
> SAY: "From 1972 to 1976, I owned the priciest women's beauty salon in North Umberland, called Pinkie's."

➔ *Fresh ways to say ordinary ideas.*

> INSTEAD OF: "Well, you know, when the going gets tough, the tough get going."
>
> SAY: "When I eat my 2,000th peanut butter sandwich of the month is when I always get my best ideas."
>
> INSTEAD OF: "Everyone needs to look their best at a job interview."
>
> SAY: "You should dress for a job interview as carefully as you would—no, even more carefully than you would—for your wedding."

➔ *Interesting examples or stories to illustrate general points. For example:*

"One of my teachers said I'd either end up on Easy Street or in jail."

"My at-home wardrobe in those days was mostly the quality-control rejects, regardless of what size they were."

"When I was 7 years old my next-door neighbor, Flossie, was saved from death by emergency surgery. The day she came home from the hospital was the day I decided to be a doctor."

Spell out and/or explain any unusual terms or names you bring up during the interview. If your vice president of human resources is named Sam Smyth—with a "y"—tell the reporter. Monitor yourself for any jargon (words used only by insiders to your field or institution), and explain the meaning of any technical terms that are unavoidable. One artist I know who had created an extraordinary flower garden referred to a man who worked in the garden as her "partner." She was upset when the published article upgraded the man's status to "co-owner," when in fact she paid him to work in her garden and she was the sole owner. She called him her partner because they often worked alongside each other pulling up weeds and transplanting bulbs. The reporter probably should have realized it was a leap from partner to co-owner and checked that with her, but the artist should also have realized she might easily have been misunderstood and have explained what she meant by "partner." Reporters can't be mind-readers!

Don't let anything out of your mouth that you wouldn't want to appear in print. Some people get so caught up in establishing rapport with me that they say things during an interview such as, "Just between you and me—I wouldn't want to see this published...." I'm not the kind of person who gets a kick out of turning on the spotlight when someone's pants are down, but how could they know that? Besides, I might stick the taboo information into the article by mistake. A reporter is someone doing a job, not your chum.

Repeat your main points. "Reporters don't listen very well sometimes," says Alan Weiss. "You can compensate for that by saying the same thing nine different ways." An especially good time to recapitulate key points would be at the end of the interview. Lay out the overall context for your comments as well for the reporter, either at the beginning or the end of the interview. Jeff Slutsky learned this lesson the painful way. In one of his earliest interviews, he told his favorite funny stories to a cub reporter in Cincinnati who took them in a way he didn't intend. "She slammed me, and I have a lot of relatives in Cincinnati who read the article and thought I was some kind of shyster. Luckily, within a year, *Inc.* magazine wrote about me and used the very same stories in the right context. I became careful to tell reporters how I use a story, and this works. In the 12 years since then, this didn't happen again."

Don't ask to approve the story before it's published. Only a very foolish or inexperienced journalist grants you the right to review the entire article before it's submitted. Because you do have a legitimate concern about accuracy, ask instead that the reporter check back quotes with you. Newspaper reporters, though, may not have enough leeway before deadline to do this. If you have some special concerns that the reporter ought to know about, mention them. For example, a psychologist I interviewed reminded me several times during one interview that he can lose his license if he appears to have diagnosed someone he has not seen as a patient. Therefore it was important that his comments about possible psychological dynamics in the lives of certain public figures be worded in the way he suggested. Not only was I receptive to the reminders, but I also passed them on to the fact-checking department of the magazine for which I wrote the article, alerting them to the importance of not changing certain quotes without checking with the psychologist again.

To help ensure accuracy, I tell reporters at the end of every interview, "If you're not sure about something, please call me back and I'd be glad to clarify it for you." One young reporter was very intimidated interviewing and writing about me, because I'd written a book on writing. She did call me back three times for clarifications, which I pleasantly provided. If I hadn't invited her to call me back, or if I'd been impatient at her first call, the article wouldn't have been as good and as useful to me as it was. I also sent her a note afterwards thanking her for having done a great job—a gesture that can never hurt even with veteran writers.

Ask to be identified in a way that allows readers to find you. Don't assume that the reporter will include any of the details you were so careful to enumerate in the news release: your company name, your address, your phone number, your URL, or the precise neighborhood in which you're located. If you have a phone number listed under your name or your business's name, the minimum would be your name and the city, unless you're "J. Williamson" and the city directory contains five. Sure, someone who wants to find you can call all five, but how many would bother? Think this through beforehand, and ask the reporter to include the appropriate identifying information, if possible.

According to Joel Goodman, executive director of The Humor Project, when the media makes it easier for readers to find you, it's "a win-win-win situation—great for you, helpful for the readers and a relief for the magazine or newspaper because they don't have to use their staff time responding to inquiries from readers." For instance, when a 1989 *Better Homes and Gardens* article mentioned that readers could receive a free information packet about the positive power of humor in exchange for a self-addressed stamped envelope sent to The Humor Project at 110 Spring Street, Saratoga Springs, NY 12866, 25,000 requests poured in almost immediately (and continued to arrive at the rate of 25 a week many years later). Imagine how long it would take for the magazine to respond to even one-tenth that level of interest!

Don't ask for payment, and don't offer gifts. Although I've never been asked for money from an interviewee, other writers have been. That's probably the quickest way to get a reporter to hang up on you. Unless you have witnessed a political leader in adultery with a minor of the same sex and the reporter is from a sleazy tabloid, it wouldn't be done. And it's gauche to ask. Most publications have strict policies preventing employees from accepting gifts or money from sources or anyone they might ever write about. So don't create a predicament for anyone in the media by offering or sending a gift with any value more than $10 to $25.

Fax, e-mail, or send collateral information. A final way you can increase the chances of in-depth, accurate reporting is to fax or send items such as your business bio, articles you've published, tip sheets, and other written materials you have on hand. The reporter might use additional examples, stories, and facts from what you send, and refer to them as a check while writing the article. The extra material also makes it more likely that something you didn't mention to the reporter will stick in his or her mind and prompt another call for a related story. Marketing experts say it's easier to keep an old customer than to make a new one; the same goes for your media contacts. Be courteous, cooperative, and interesting, and you'll find yourself quoted more and more.

Journalists' Horror Stories

When I asked writer colleagues for their peeves about PR people and publicity-seekers, I received a flood of stories. Every one of the misbehaviors that follows, described in the journalist's own words, actually occurred and deeply annoyed the media person involved. Laugh if you like, but please don't make these blunders.

- ❖ "This morning I got a call from a PR person saying, 'Did you read the e-mail I sent you Friday?' (He was calling from San Francisco, where it was barely 6 a.m.) Because I had 120 messages in my inbox, I asked him to call back next week. He called again at 3 p.m. This guy goes in my 'clueless' file."

- ❖ "Once I put out a request for sources for a specific story. A PR person was very aggressive, saying her client was the absolute expert in a specific topic. I didn't think so from the bio she sent, but I gave her specific questions, which she assured me he could answer at length. So, we set up the interview, and when I was introduced to her client, he said: 'I don't know why I'm on this call. I don't know anything about this.' You can bet I automatically delete any messages I see from that PR person."

- ❖ "Don't try to go over the reporter's head. I'm a freelance writer and don't work in the office of the publication for which I'm writing. I've had PR people call and leave messages for me at the publication. This annoys the editor; it's a waste of their time to take messages for someone who's not on staff. I don't need a PR person jeopardizing my relationship with the publication. Only use the contact numbers and addresses I provide."

- ❖ "A PR agency recently called me to be sure I received their release (sent by e-mail) about a new management position filled in a dotcom company (their client). Have they ever bothered to check out my publication and see the things I cover? I don't give a rat's tail about a new post (unless it's really, really important) in some company. Some media have sections about new posts and so on, but my publication does not. Because of their follow-up phone call, I went to their client's Website and tried out the service. Guess what... the first link I tried was empty! I stopped right there."

➔   "Don't offer to help me find another story if I'll only drop the story I'm working on or leave out some information because it's damaging to people you represent. Don't call to say you've bought a long-term advertising contract, expect a story to be done on your firm and that the managing partner won't understand my attitude if I refuse to do the story. Don't ask me to report to you on how some of the other PR people in your company conduct themselves with me. I've experienced all those things and more."

➔   "I hate it when PR people offer me a source, expert—whomever— I research it, decide it is worth the time, come up with questions, maybe even tell an editor about a potential source, and *then* they tell me their client isn't doing interviews. This I just don't get. Why not find out before you pitch me?"

➔   "I've had a couple of PR people tell me that the publication for which I was writing wasn't important enough for them to waste their time and effort on. Saying something like that might give them a nice thrill, but as a freelancer, I work for a lot of different publications. And I'll remember these people and their comments when I work on publications they might consider important."

➔   "A company that shall remain nameless invited the media to an 8 a.m. news conference and the sponsors ran out of food and coffee before 75 percent of the media showed up. We were not happy. Plan ahead!"

➔   "At around 10 a.m. on September 12, 2001, I got two press releases from a PR person representing a 'scenic trails' highway program. This was when there was still hope that people remained alive in the rubble at the World Trade Center and the Pentagon. I e-mailed the person and asked if she was really as callous as her e-mail indicated. She e-mailed back that she hadn't meant to offend anyone, but thought we could put this information in our 'As things get back to normal' file. I have never opened another e-mail from her or her agency."

❖ "A guy who'd just launched a high-tech company wanted to dictate a lengthy release over the phone. I didn't find this appealing. The following conversation ensued:

Me: Can you fax it?
Caller: I don't have a fax machine.
Me: Well, can you e-mail it?
Caller: I'm not on the Internet yet.
Me: Well, can you FedEx it?
Caller: I don't have a FedEx account, either.
Me: So just mail it then!
Caller: It's really important. There isn't time."

IF YOU FACE HOSTILE PRINT REPORTERS

Janet Jordan, president of Keynote Communications in Cambridge, Massachusetts, says that people can usually get the hang of dealing effectively with hostile reporters in a daylong workshop or just a few coaching sessions. Much of her work consists of preparing executives for situations in which the company's credibility might be at stake, such as when activists have chained themselves to the company gate or a fire has broken out at the plant. "The more you know what to expect from reporters, the more confident you'll feel and the more you'll be able to move from a defensive stance to an offensive one," she says. "Remember that whatever the reporter is doing, it's part of his or her job. Your job is to come across as authoritative and credible, and that's a learned skill." Roleplay with a friend who pretends to be Mike Wallace, and practice staying alert for these classic reportorial tactics:

❖ Goading you to comment on something you really shouldn't discuss. Never use the phrase *no comment*, which has unsavory connotations left over from the days of Watergate, Jordan says. "People will assume you're hiding something. Instead say, 'I'm not in a position to talk about that,' or explain why you can't talk about it."

❖ Trying to put words in your mouth. Listen carefully when a reporter says something along the lines of, "So what you're saying, in essence, is...." If that's not something you'd feel comfortable reading in the paper attached to your name, don't agree. Say No, then restate the idea in words that do represent your view well.

✦ Asking unfair questions, comparable to "When did you stop beating your wife?" If you don't agree with the assumptions or information built into a question, say so. Don't get trapped into admitting something you shouldn't, or that isn't true.

✦ Asking the same question again and again. If a reporter persists with the same question, worded a little differently perhaps, you're just as entitled to give the same answer. Don't get annoyed at being poked in the same place from different angles; stay composed and polite. At one point during the Clinton years, *60 Minutes* presented unedited footage from their pre-election interview with Hillary and Bill Clinton that revealed that Hillary had made her infamous and controversial comment about not wanting to stay home and bake cookies only after she'd been asked the same question several times. Simply repeat your answer as many times as you're asked the same question.

✦ The silent treatment. Most people feel uncomfortable with silence. A reporter may pause and look at you expectantly in an attempt to get you blabbing. During a hostile or high-stakes interview, don't fall for it. Just look expectantly back.

✦ Having a friendly chat after the tape recorder or notebook is put away. As I explained earlier, assume that everything is on the record—including anything you say after you think the interview is over. According to Janet Jordan, after interviewing Marlon Brando, Truman Capote told Brando some tales about his sexual escapades while they were walking to the elevator. Brando reciprocated with some stories of his own, and then was furious—at himself, it should have been—when that material ended up in Capote's article.

Keep all these warnings in perspective, though. If you're a small-time operator making an inoffensive, honest living, the reporter's goal is probably in tune with yours: informing, inspiring, or just interesting the public.

Chapter 15

Performing on Radio and TV Like a Pro

I made my television debut at the age of 7. The station in New Haven, Connecticut, had a show on which a man named Admiral Jack joked around with an audience of kids sitting on bleachers, and then showed "Popeye" cartoons. Occasionally, a featured boy or girl would demonstrate a talent by singing or doing magic tricks. One afternoon, I stood at the microphone in front of the cameras and read poems I had written.

I recall being intimidated by the waiting room at the station, but not any attack of nerves when I took the spotlight. I must have done fine because no one in my family remembers it otherwise. Because I was young and so was the medium of TV, expectations were low. By the 2000s, however, the typical American adult has logged tens of thousands of hours watching smooth, professional performers on the small screen. In any TV appearance you or I make now, we have a lot to measure up to. But there is a simple trick to success on the airwaves, and it begins with a "p."

PREPARE, PREPARE, PREPARE

Find out the format of any show for which you're scheduled, and watch or listen to it, if possible, to get a sense of the atmosphere. Is it live or taped? Will you be on alone or part of a panel of guests, and if so, who will the others be? Is it a call-in show, or is there interaction with a studio audience? Is the host cozy or confrontational, liberal or conservative? Negotiate ahead of time whether they will announce your telephone number, mention a freebie offer, or flash a close-up of your book cover. Ask what you need to do to obtain a tape of the show, and, if they say you should bring your own blank tape, find out what kind. Taping is essential to improving your performance. I was astounded to learn from the tape of one of my speeches that a clip-on microphone picked up and amplified the sound of my lips coming apart each time I began a thought.

Confirm all the arrangements, date, time, directions, transportation, and parking in writing, by e-mail, or by fax. Someone I know was told by her publicist that a show would be taped at 8 o'clock. When she arrived at 8 a.m. on the appointed day, however, the studio was all locked up. Puzzled, she went home and learned later that day that the taping would be at 8 *p.m.* Fortunately, she had the evening free. Bring the confirmation sheet with you when you go to the station. I've heard of guests showing up in an office lobby and not having the faintest idea who should be buzzed about their arrival.

You probably already know that white shirts and plaids or other busy patterns won't show up well on TV. Do plan what you'll wear ahead of time and make sure your outfit is clean, pressed, comfortable, flattering, and consistent with the image you want to convey. Men, wear over-the-calf socks that stay up, and women, choose either pants or a skirt that's long enough that you won't have to worry about the cameras embarrassing you. For radio, leave any noisy jewelry at home.

At least as important as planning what you'll wear is practicing what you'll say. Don't wing it! Decide on the points you want to get across and roleplay with a friend who takes the part of the interviewer. Ask the friend to toss you some pre-scripted questions and some out of left field, so you can try seguing from an unexpected probe to one of your three main points. Merle Bombardieri says that before beginning her first publicity tour, she rehearsed fitting in the phrases, "In my book, *The Baby Decision*...," and "When I work with clients, I...," so that they felt comfortable and sounded natural. If you have to practice without a friend's help, talk to the mirror or play both roles yourself.

I can't emphasize enough the difference between actual practice and just thinking about what you're supposed to do. Greg Godek remembers that when he worked in PR, he would tell corporate clients to make only two or three points and keep hammering them home—"but that's easier said than done. When you're actually interviewed, time goes by so fast. It's easy to get carried away with a story, and then the whole thing is over." The more you practice, however, the more likely the rehearsed behavior is to kick in automatically on cue.

For TV, rehearsal should include practicing what you need to do to look good on the video screen. Put a camcorder in the hands of a friend who films you while you speak. Note anything you do that's distracting, which might not be as noticeable in real life. "Hand gestures can look wild on TV," says Laurie Schloff, of The Speech Improvement Company in Brookline, Massachusetts. "Your movements should be smooth and controlled. Remember that people will be seeing you large and up close."

As if you were an athlete in training, take special precautions the day of a broadcast appearance. Get enough sleep the night before, and the day of your appearance don't rev yourself up with too much coffee, try to brace yourself with alcohol or tranquilizers, or consume dairy products, which can make your voice unpleasant, according to Schloff. Eat just enough so that your stomach won't be rumbling and you won't feel sluggish. If you'll be taking part in a taped show, bring along some fruit and a book or crossword puzzle to keep you occupied in case you're kept waiting for hours in the so-called green room offstage. This happens sometimes when the station records more than one show in a session.

WHEN YOU ARRIVE AT THE STATION

Assuming you've arrived on time, duck into the restroom to repair your windblown hair and make sure you don't have a piece of lunch stuck between your front teeth. Larger TV stations provide guests with a complimentary makeup session. *They* don't look good if your nose is shiny or the pouches under your eyes would make you look raccoon-like on screen. On both TV and radio, many producers or hosts sit you down for a "pre-interview," in which they go over a few areas they want to ask you about on the air, explain any technical things you need to know, and generally attempt to make you feel comfortable about the interview. Now is the time to hand over your list of sample questions or to ask about anything that concerns you, from "How will I know we're on the air?" to "Who's going on just before me?" They may explain who all the people are who may be scurrying around, or, on radio, tell you about the "cough button," which shuts off your microphone if you're desperate to make throat noise. In any case, from the moment you walk into the station, don't touch any piece of technical equipment unless invited to do so.

While you're waiting to go on, the most important thing you can do is to center yourself so that you feel calm (though energized) and ready to be 100-percent present in that studio. "Daydreaming is not conducive to good interviews," says Larry Rochester in his *Book Publicity for Authors and Publishers*. "When in front of a microphone or camera, the guest must mentally be there and nowhere else at that time." Rochester's book describes an extended but simple-to-execute process that enables you to feel and project confidence and well-being, and says that it helps him ignore the multitude of just-off-camera distractions at a TV studio. My own centering technique is to place my hand on my lower abdomen, which helps me be composed and steady. While you're waiting is also the ideal time to practice the relaxed, pleasant facial expression you want to be wearing during your first seconds on the air.

DO'S AND DON'TS ON THE AIR

Once on the air, assume you're always on camera, and that your microphone is always on. Without a doubt, you will get an urge to scratch a most inconvenient itch; even if someone else is speaking or you think you're still in the middle of a commercial break, restrain yourself. During one of the 1992 presidential debates, some viewers got a bad impression of George Bush Senior when the camera caught him looking at his watch while one of his opponents was speaking. He's the same man who somehow avoided a public relations disaster when he threw up in the lap of the Japanese prime minister, but don't count on being so lucky yourself! Lesser folks have had to scale down their ambitions because of offensive jokes told when assured that the microphone was off.

Sit carefully and strategically. Lillian Brown, a TV producer and makeup artist who wrote *Your Public Best*, says that, although the ideal chair for a talk-show guest would be hard and straight-backed, you usually encounter "upholstered armchairs, which you can easily cope with by sitting slightly forward on the front edge. Then there is the soft, fat, over-padded sofa, which can be a hazard in that it tends to swallow you up and overpower you. If you sit back in it and cross your legs, you will completely lose control of your breathing and speaking apparatus. You can overcome all that by perching as best you can on the front edge, ignoring the armrests and finding some way to anchor your body." Whether on radio or TV, avoid any position that might put any part of your body to sleep. It's difficult to be charming and articulate when numbness is spreading along your limbs.

For TV, be conscious of your body language and facial expressions. Some people frown when they listen or concentrate, and if you don't want to convey disagreement, strive for a neutrally attentive expression instead. Contrarily, a good many people nod their heads when they listen even though they disagree, and this is very confusing on television. Save nods for situations in which you agree with what's being said.

Understand the rhythm of the medium. According to Al Parinello, co-host of the nationally syndicated radio show, "Your Own Success," the vast majority of guests he's seen can do a *good* interview but not an *effective* one, because they fail to take into consideration how and why people tune in to radio and TV. To truly exploit your radio or TV appearance, Parinello says, remember first that the audience will change while you speak. On radio, the audience changes from minute to minute and you must repeat yourself rather than assume listeners stay with you. On TV, the audience changes significantly if your appearance crosses the half-hour mark, and you must repeat yourself after the commercial break. Second, you can't simply lift your performance from another medium. "That's the biggest mistake of speakers and seminar leaders— they start to spin a story and then just before they get to the climax, it's time for a commercial break," says Parinello. "Afterward, the momentum is lost." Third, you need to earn the interest of the audience before you give out your address or phone number or the title of your book. "Not until the audience is saying to themselves, 'This guy is interesting' should you tell them how to get in touch with you," he says.

Try to match the energy level of your host. "If the host is talking a mile a minute and you answer in a normal speaking voice, you'll sound dopey," says Greg Godek. On the other hand, if the host is a dud, you can pick things up if you put out just a bit more energy, adds Larry Rochester: "Enthusiasm is contagious."

Give substantive answers, but stay alert to signals from your host that you're talking too long. Szifra Birke calls this her biggest challenge during broadcast interviews. "Some hosts don't want you to say more than two sentences at a time. It's hard for me to be short and compressed, because I like to go on and on. If I'm succinct, I can't be engaging, but I'm working on it. You don't look good when the host has to shut you up," she says.

Remember that you have two audiences: the host with whom you are conversing, and, more importantly, those viewing or listening to the show. Don't get so bent on building rapport with the host that you forget to hook the interest of those tuning in. According to Jeffrey Lant, electronic media offer the opportunity of a uniquely contemporary kind of intimacy of which he takes advantage by addressing his prospects directly when he's on the air, as in, "Now listen up, all you home-based entrepreneurs and people who are thinking of starting a business...." Lant explains, "The host is just a prism. You need to talk *through* him or her to the audience. To get a response, talk to the audience about themselves, not about you."

Use your normal conversational volume. The technicians running the show know how to adjust their controls if necessary.

Be yourself at your most scintillating. Unless you're a proficient actor, don't try to come across as someone you're not. Audiences don't respond well to phoniness.

Difficult Moments, Special Situations

An Incompetent or Uncongenial Interviewer

Sometimes you find yourself paired with a host or reporter who asks bumbling questions or acts as if he or she woke up on the wrong side of the world. If you want to come off well, you'll have to compensate for his or her shortcomings without seeming to take over. Laurie Schloff remembers one interviewer who was very cold. She maintained eye contact, a smile, and a warm tone of voice anyway, telling herself, "This person is not going to help me out. I still want to come across well."

REMOTE RADIO BROADCASTS

Many radio shows include the participation of guests by telephone from their own home or office rather than from the studio. Whenever you have this kind of publicity opportunity, make the most of it by isolating yourself from interruptions. Put a do-not-disturb sign on your door, keep dogs who might bark or babies who might cry in another room, and, most importantly, temporarily disable call-waiting if you have it. (Ask your phone company for instructions.) Paul Edwards, co-host of "Home Office" on the Business Radio Network, says that once when he was interviewing a guest by phone, the call-waiting signal came on the line. "Maybe I'd better get that," said the guest. "Please don't," retorted Edwards. "You're live on national radio." Greg Godek installed an extra-long cord on his telephone that enables him to stand, walk around, and gesture animatedly whenever he does radio interviews from home. "That really helps me come across," he says.

Win brownie points with producers and listeners by calling in with good-quality equipment on a land line—not your cell phone, not a cordless phone, not an Internet phone, and not a speaker phone. A couple of times, I've had teleseminar guests whose voices sounded tinny and thin because of a bargain-basement phone or headset. Don't let that be you!

CALL-IN SHOWS

The unpredictability of a media interview multiplies when a show includes people who call in and can make brilliant, stupid, relevant, or wildly off-the-point comments. Be as courteous to anonymous callers as you would be to your host. You won't have to worry about responding on the air to any really offensive calls, however. Live call-in shows are set up with a seven-second delay that enables the host to cut off anyone making obscene or threatening comments.

A Panel of Guests

Getting at least your fair share of airtime can become the challenge when you fill just one of several guest slots for the same segment. Knowing the atmosphere of the show beforehand helps you plan appropriate tactics. If the show tends toward brawling free-for-alls, in which everyone speaks loudly at the same time and the camera eventually zooms in on the one who is the loudest, politely waiting for your turn won't get you airtime. You have to interrupt noisily just as everyone else does. On a one-person-at-a-time show, in which the host orchestrates contributions, you can graciously cadge extra time by speaking up the instant another panelist has finished, with "May I add something to what Dr. Brothers said?" or "If I can add something quickly...." On a radio panel, you can help listeners keep the voices straight if you identify yourself when you break in uninvited. When Laurie Schloff was promoting our book *Smart Speaking* on a half-hour TV panel segment, I noticed that twice she got extra attention by saying something especially tantalizing just before a commercial break. Both times the host couldn't help saying, "When we come back, Laurie will tell us...." Although she says she didn't do it purposely, *you* could.

A Camera Crew at Your Special Event

In Chapter 12, I recommend that if a news crew comes to you, you should put yourself 100-percent at their disposal. But if a TV crew wants to shoot your special event, you may have to execute a delicate balancing act. Joel Goodman, executive director of The Humor Project, has had video crews from PBS and Turner Broadcasting filming his conferences on humor and creativity, and says unequivocally that conference participants come first. "I try to head off problems by making sure I talk to the person who would be in charge of shooting on site and going over my concerns. First, I don't want them shining bright lights in the faces of participants. Second, I don't want any camera person standing in the way of a seated participant. I also try to get a sense of their goals. The PBS producer was already familiar with my work, and I felt that we were sympatico."

The PBS crew produced a stand-alone five-minute spot that was disseminated nationally to PBS stations, many of which aired it. As worked out in advance, the Turner Broadcasting crew got more "up close and personal," Goodman says, sometimes filming what felt like four inches from his face. Because they came to a workshop limited to 50 participants, Goodman notified attendees ahead of time. "I thought some people might have concerns, but I told them about my excitement and they were excited, too."

EDITED SEGMENTS

When a reporter for an investigative, news, or magazine-type show comes out with a microphone or camera crew to interview you, he or she will intersperse snippets of what you said with quotes from others. Although you have absolutely no control over how much and which parts of your conversation will appear in the report, a simple defensive maneuver reduces the possibility that you'll be quoted with a clip that leaves out your side of the story. Radio and TV editors hate to cut someone off in the middle of a sentence. Thus, couch anything negative you might have to say in a sentence that includes the spin you want listeners or viewers to hear.

For example, suppose a confrontational reporter challenges you with, "People who didn't get what they ordered told us that you're a classic rip-off artist." If you protest, "That's not true! We were overwhelmed with demand and everyone eventually got their merchandise," the editor could cut you off after "not true" and before your explanation. If you say instead, "Although it did take some extra time to catch up with orders, we eventually filled them all," the whole sentence will probably make it on the air. Whether or not you're on the hot seat, the more you can deliver concise, colorful "sound bites," the more you'll find snippets of you on the air.

Chapter 16

Pitching Over the Phone

In the early 1980s, Colorado consultant Debra Benton decided she was ready for serious media coverage and kicked off her campaign with a call to a Chicago-based columnist whose style she admired. "Mr. X, this is Debra Benton of Benton Management Resources in Fort Benton, Colorado," she said. "I know you must get 100 calls a day from people who say they have a story for you, but I think you really would be interested in what I do." Then she shut up.

"What is it that you do?" the columnist asked.

"People describe me as teaching executives how to have charisma," Benton replied.

The columnist took her number and called her back a week later. They spoke for an hour, and 10 days after that she knew his article had appeared because she received a call from a brewery in the Chicago area. The same day she also received calls from both *Time*, which eventually ran its own story, and *Newsweek*, which didn't. Someone else called and hired her sight unseen "for something I would normally have had to work very hard to get," Benton says. Of the dozen and a half calls she received that first day, 80 percent turned into business.

As a direct result of the story about her in *Time*, a printing company brought her to New York City to give a speech. "The company had a very good PR department and sent out releases inviting the media to attend my talk," Benton recalls. Reporters from *The New York Times*, *Barron's*, and *Financial Weekly* attended and wrote her up in their papers. That led to six minutes on *CBS This Morning* and a segment on *Good Morning America*. In addition, both the *Time* and the *New*

York Times pieces were syndicated internationally, and Benton got calls from South Africa, Germany, and France.

This may sound like a positive version of the nursery rhyme that traces the loss of the war to the want of a nail, but I've given you only a snippet of the results Debra Benton can trace back to getting up the nerve for a 30-second phone call. If just this much inspires you to want to try your own phone pitch, read on.

REACHING OUT TO CALL THE MEDIA

An effective phone pitch to the media starts with the recognition that, whenever you call someone associated with radio, TV, newspapers, or magazines, you are interrupting them. Sometimes they're not just busy, they're hell-bent on a deadline that waits for no one. If you have enough slack to plan the time of your phone call, do it. Call the station or publication to learn its deadline, and call either way before or just after it. For a monthly, one week a month will probably be most frantic; for a weekly, one day a week will be frenzied; and at a daily show or paper, the pace quickens from crazy to berserk during certain hours.

In preparing to call, make sure you know who to call as well as when. Usually if you call the main number and ask, "Who should I call about a [blank] story?" (fill in the blank with a category of story, such as business, travel, health, or human interest), they'll give you a name or title and an extension number or direct number. You can also find the names of section editors and producers in many of the directories listed in Chapter 24. Remember that, for radio and TV, you call a show's producer, not the host.

Plan a spiel that dispenses with small talk, quickly introduces you, and states what the story is that you think will appeal to them. Practice your pitch until you can say it clearly, enthusiastically, and comfortably. "You need to sound better than, more exciting than, 95 percent of the people who call them," says Stan Billue, a telephone sales trainer in DeBary, Florida. "You'll be more memorable if you rhyme or compare your name, such as 'Evan Gold, like the metal.' People often remember that even years later. Then when you state the purpose of your call, try to provide a benefit for that person's readers or listeners, such as, 'I can share six techniques with your audience that will immediately increase their self-esteem.'"

Go beyond rehearsing your initial pitch by trying also to anticipate objections or uninterested responses. Prepare comebacks that make a second appeal to their interests. According to Steve Schiffman, author of *Cold Calling Techniques That Really Work*, cold calls break down most after the callee responds, because the caller doesn't know how to turn around a response in a positive way. "Odds are that the person you're calling won't be interested," Schiffman says. "So if they say, 'Sorry, we're not interested,' ask, 'What kind of stories *are* you interested in?' Then see if you can fit yourself into what they say. Even if only one out of 10 people you call respond positively to that, you're still better off than simply hanging up when they say they're not interested."

Stan Billue used exactly that strategy once when he moved to a small town in Florida. He called the nearest paper and said he had an Arabian horse farm and did professional speaking. "Within an hour a photographer showed up at my place," Billue recalls. The paper ran a half-page article with a color photo, and Billue took that to the Orlando *Sentinel*, the major paper for that part of the state. "They said, in effect, that I wasn't important enough for them to do a feature on. So I offered to give them the names of other speakers in the area, and sent a list of all the professional speakers in and around Orlando. Two weeks later they had an article about us in the business section, and almost half of it was about me."

If you take a bit of extra trouble to set up a cold call, you may find that it goes more smoothly. TV producer Lila Ivey says that when she receives a letter or a news release that includes the line, "I'll be calling you next week," she puts that correspondence in a separate pile to read more carefully. "I want to be prepared when they call, to have an answer ready." When the promised call comes in, she responds with more attention than when an unknown person calls to make contact for the first time.

Nancy Michaels warns not to take it personally if media people seem rude or abrupt; they're just reacting to occupational pressures for efficiency. And don't be discouraged if your first all-out effort goes nowhere. There are tens of thousands of other media people who might respond just as you'd dreamed.

CHECKLIST FOR ACHIEVING PHONE FINESSE

Tape-record a practice session and your first few cold calls to the media. If your phone setup doesn't include a record-while-talking feature, you can buy an inexpensive device called a "telephone recording control" at Radio Shack or elsewhere that easily attaches your phone line to any ordinary voice recorder. Then rate yourself according to the following criteria.

1. **Articulation.** Do your words come across clearly? Because your phone call will be coming out of the blue, you may have to pronounce words more precisely than usual. One person I called while researching this book asked for clarification of the title and told me he thought I'd said "Six Debts," not "Six Steps."

2. **Tone.** Do you sound friendly and natural? Avoid a monotone or sounding cold or computerlike. It may help to imagine the person listening on the other end of the line.

3. **Pace.** You should start right in without fumbling, then keep up an even, brisk pace. Speak a bit faster than you usually do, but don't race.

4. **Relevance.** Do you provide an obvious answer to that all-important question: Why would our readers/listeners be interested in you now?

5. **Length.** If your opener goes on for longer than 20 seconds, that may be too much. Say just enough to whet the media person's curiosity—and not a syllable more.

6. **Volume.** Can you be heard without strain or recoil? A former colleague of mine used to start her sentences with such a sharp burst of sound that it hurt my ears. If you're too soft, try standing up, which gives you access to more air and breath support.

7. **Intonation.** Do you sound confident? A rising intonation, as in, "My name is Marcia Yudkin?" makes you seem tentative and timid.

8. **Poise.** In an actual call, did you have a smooth rejoinder ready when your callee responded?

Chapter 17

10 Pitfalls in Publicity Writing— and How to Avoid Them

Crafting material that impresses the media takes work. Plan to write a news release in two stages: first, a rough draft that captures and develops your idea, and second, a final draft that you've ruthlessly and rigorously polished. Once you're satisfied with content and organization, test your text against this checklist, which also helps you fine-tune any marketing copy, including ads, brochures, flyers, bios, and sales letters. Remember to write news releases and bios in third-person, objective style, in contrast to the "you" that belongs in materials directed to clients and customers. Whatever the occasion, you'll make the most of a reader's limited attention span if you root out the following 10 flaws from your promotional materials.

10 Pitfalls in Publicity Writing—and How to Avoid Them

1. Vague Phrases

Every word and sentence you use should plant a specific meaning in the mind of the reader. Consider these common kinds of statements:

→   Hillside Inn is a wonderful place to spend a winter weekend. *(Why is it wonderful? Is it cute and cozy or huge and luxurious? Is it wonderful because it's cheap, or remote, or exotic, or full of media stars on vacation?)*

→   Dr. Henry Kissinger has consulted with a variety of individuals and organizations facing unique challenges in many parts of the world. *(If Kissinger put out a news release, do you think these generalities would do him justice?)*

→ Addicts, Anonymous provides help to people who struggle with their need for various substances. *(Really? If I need enough money to pay next month's rent, or a swatch of fabric to match my grandmother's torn antique shawl, is Addicts, Anonymous equipped to help?)*

Compare the following more specific versions of those weak sentences:

→ Hillside Inn offers a quiet, affordable refuge from city pressures. *(No product or service can be all things to all people. By being more specific, you increase your attractiveness to customers who will be happy with what you have to offer.)*

→ Since leaving the office of U.S. Secretary of State, Dr. Henry Kissinger has advised numerous leaders of foreign governments and multinational corporations on how to adapt to a world rife with terrorism, revolution, and protest. *(Because of the confidentiality of his services, Kissinger might not be able to be more specific than this. But it's an improvement!)*

→ Addicts, Anonymous provides help to people trying to eliminate their dependence on alcohol, cocaine, marijuana, heroin, amphetamines, tranquilizers, and other harmful or illegal substances. *(That eliminates people needing money or fabric swatches, doesn't it?)*

2. Negative Language

Notice the difference between these negative assertions and the positive versions that follow each:

Negative: Don't imagine that smart businesspeople shouldn't be aggressive.

Positive: Smart businesspeople must be aggressive.

Negative: Whether or not dieters have already failed with other weight-loss programs, Diet-Eze makes sure that they are not disappointed.

Positive: Diet-Eze guarantees satisfaction with its weight-loss program.

Negative: Hillside Inn makes it hard for urban dwellers to resist the chance to inexpensively escape the pressures of the city.

Positive: Hillside Inn offers a quiet, affordable refuge from city pressures.

Any use of a negative word, including *not*, words starting with un-, dis-, or mis-; *failed, resist, escape, avoid,* and so on, forces the reader to perform a mental somersault to arrive at your meaning. As more negatives pile up in a sentence, the more likely the reader is to become dizzy. Be nice to your reader! You'll communicate more clearly by being direct and positive.

3. PASSIVE VERBS

As you may recall from high school English class, "Jim hit Bob" uses an active verb, whereas "Bob was hit" or "Bob was hit by Jim" employs a passive verb. Instead of saying directly who is doing what to whom, passive constructions start off with the whom that is being whatted and often leave out altogether the who that's doing it. For example:

> ❖ Before formulation of a training plan, interviews are generally conducted with problem employees. *(A weak, indirect statement, this doesn't say who conducts the interviews.)*

> ❖ Pasta lovers are satisfied by P.L.aghetti's fresh, authentic taste. *(Again, weak and wimpy.)*

> ❖ Merchandise can be special-ordered by Boombox City's knowledgeable, helpful clerks. *(This is not only indirect but also unclear. Are the clerks doing the ordering or are they the ones entitled to special orders? Surely you don't want customers confused about that!)*

When you substitute active verbs for passive ones, you get more lively writing. Here are punchier, clearer versions of the same sample sentences:

> ❖ Before formulating a training plan, Teletrain's experts interview problem employees and determine specific needs.

> ✦ Pasta lovers rave about P.L.aghetti's fresh, authentic taste.
>
> ✦ Boombox City's knowledgeable clerks help customers place special orders for hard-to-find merchandise.

4. Meaningless Superlatives

Are you fond of words such as *best, newest,* and *freshest*? They actually don't carry much credibility unless you explain how your goods or services are the best, newest, or freshest. Consider these sentences:

> ✦ Tri-Tech is world-famous for the newest ideas in high technology. (*Anyone can claim that, can't they? Says who?*)
>
> ✦ Ideal Game Corporation has been one of the major forces in the game world for more than a generation. (*This sounds grand, but how has it been a major force? By suing all of its competitors?*)
>
> ✦ Winsome Widgets, Inc. solves all those quality-control problems perfectly. (*All of them? Even the boss's grandson Benny, who is prone to fall asleep on the job?*)

The following restatements carry more weight with readers:

> ✦ Since 1959, Tri-Tech has received at least 17 new patents for technological innovations, and cumulatively more than three times as many as any competitor.
>
> ✦ For more than a generation, Ideal Game Corporation has sent competitors scrambling with games including XXXX, YYYY, and ZZZZ, named "Best Game of the Year" in 1975, 1986, and 1999 by the World Toymakers Association.
>
> ✦ With Winsome Widgets, Inc., manufacturers and consumers never need to worry about poor quality nuts and bolts again.

5. Jargon

At a seminar for would-be consultants, I listened carefully as participants introduced themselves and the focus of their consulting. Despite my education and worldliness, I could not understand the self-descriptions given by more than 90 percent of them. They relied on gobbledygook, insider buzzwords, and jargon instead of clear, comprehensible language. Sure, you can use technical terms you're certain that everyone in your target market knows, but "in" language used merely out of habit or to sound superior and "with it" leaves many readers out. These sentences use jargon and need rewording:

➢ QCA Videos Teach QC Excellence. *(A cute headline, but it's more considerate of readers to spell out "QC" as "quality control.")*

➢ With strict third-tier sales quotas, TTT's telemarketers get results. *(Maybe people inside your company know what "third-tier sales quotas" are, but the rest of the world doesn't.)*

➢ BestPost offers best-of-breed, robust solutions for mission-critical delivery in the e-mail technology space. *(Be more direct about what the company does—that is, makes sure your e-mail gets delivered.)*

Although some business and high-tech journalists use jargon in their publications, a good number of others scorn made-up buzz words so much that every chance they get, they lampoon companies guilty of sabotaging human communication in this fashion. You can get a taste of the ferocity of this contempt from the journalists who created the site *www.buzzkiller.net.*

Along with mealy-mouthed, pretentious jargon, stay away from culturally insular metaphors for materials to be posted on the Web. Americans tend to understand "end run" and "extra innings" when used outside of sports reporting, for example, but the rest of the world isn't familiar with football and baseball terminology.

6. INCONSISTENCIES IN TENSE, PERSON, OR VOICE

Through carelessness or ignorance, you may be guilty of distracting grammatical inconsistencies. Can you diagnose the problems in the following sentences?

➢ Their special training and experience is geared toward the needs of the customer. *(The phrase "special training and experience" consists of two things and should be followed by "are," not " is.")*

❖ You need not climb Mount Everest in order for one to deserve a pat on the back. (*You shouldn't mix "one" and "you" in the same sentence, or even the same passage. Choose and be consistent.*)

❖ Dr. Kate Hollins-Rollins's odyssey begins in 1952, when she is born to a husband and wife team of pediatricians in a suburb of Chicago. In 1980 she received her own medical license. (*Don't mix present tense [is born to] with past tense [received] in the same passage. Use one or the other consistently.*)

If you couldn't pinpoint and correct those mistakes, I recommend you hire a professional wordsmith to proofread and edit your copy. *Literary Market Place* (see Chapter 24), most writers' organizations, and many university English departments, can help you locate editorial assistance.

7. WORDINESS

Always assume that you've used a lot of extra words in whatever you've written, and didn't find them. Search for and destroy all verbal clutter.

Wordy: From 23 years of past experience, Martin Goode derived a system of formulating future plans. (*Wouldn't the experience referred to here have to be in the past, and the plans in the future?*)

Better: From 23 years of experience, Martin Goode derived a system of formulating plans.

Wordy: Needless to say, various different employees follow up on each and every complaint. (*If it's needless to say, don't say it! If it needs saying, say it just once.*)

Better: Several employees follow up on every complaint.

Wordy: Personal coaching is designed to provide individuals with professional encouragement at convenient times. (*Can you find three unnecessary words that weaken and lengthen this thought?*)

Better: Personal coaching provides individuals with professional encouragement at convenient times.

8. Mistakes in Emphasis

Suppose someone told you, "It'll be easy to identify the important people at the party. They'll be wearing red ties," and at the party *every* man was wearing a *red tie?* You foist a *similar* kind of frustration on your reader when you emphasize *too many words.* Go *lightly* on underlining, italics, extended capitalization, and bold face, and the *rare* word or phrase that *must* stand out *will.* (The reader would understand my meaning perfectly with no italics at all in this paragraph.)

The opposite problem occurs when you bury your most important information in the middle of a paragraph. To make sure your strongest points get the attention they deserve, either lead with them or save them for the end of the paragraph.

Weak: Michael Gepdale, Wysdec's top troubleshooter, brings unique qualifications to his work. He won the decathlon in Olympic competition in 1984 and 1988. Now he puts his energy and persistence at your service.

Stronger: Two-time Olympic decathlon champion Michael Gepdale now puts his energy and persistence to work for you.

9. Clunky, Awkward Rhythm

Although people usually look at your promotional copy rather than read it out loud, prose that would trip up an announcer or sound terrible aloud frequently needs improvement. As a last test of whether you've polished your paragraphs enough, read the whole text out loud. If you have trouble reading any sentence in one breath, it's probably too long. If you hear a series of short, choppy sentences, as you would with the "weak" version in #8, you probably need to combine sentences and vary your sentence patterns. Wherever you trip up while reading out loud, you're likely to have identified a sentence that needs smoothing out. Endings should sound conclusive; if yours don't, tinker with the order of various clauses.

For example, to my ear the preceding paragraph would sound much better if it ended this way: Endings should sound conclusive; tinker with the order of clauses if yours don't.

10. ABSENCE OF CREDIBILITY-BOOSTING INFORMATION

I once received an invitation to a free evening seminar with a trainer who promised participants measurable improvements in their presentation style. It sounded good, but my question was, *Who is this guy?* Although he referred to himself as a "renowned international communication and public speaking coach" and he included some testimonials from well-known people, nowhere in his six-page bulletin of seminars or his one-page sales letter did he mention any education, training, or awards in speaking or communication skills. When you leave out credentials, as this man did, readers rightly become suspicious that you haven't any. As you review your publicity materials, look for and remedy omissions that put claims about your qualifications or your products into question.

→→ ←←

Did you notice that this whole chapter violates one of the foregoing 10 rules? Look at the box that follows for a rewrite that takes account of guideline #2.

---

10 KEYS TO PUNCHY, PERSUASIVE PUBLICITY COPY

1. Specific language.
2. A positive approach.
3. Active verbs.
4. Meaningful boasts.
5. Phrases understandable by all.
6. Consistent grammar.
7. Crisp, concise prose.
8. Subtle, effective emphasis.
9. A lively, forceful rhythm.
10. The inclusion of credibility-boosting information.

Chapter 18

77 Ways to Get Unstuck When Trying to Write

Writer's block is not terminal—unless you allow yourself to use it as an excuse. Whether you're biting your pen because of an article, a news release, or a brilliant opening line for a pitch letter that eludes you, try one of the following block-breaking strategies instead of simply giving up.

77 WAYS FOR WRITERS TO GET UNSTUCK

1.   Warm up for writing by putting your pen to paper without stopping for at least five minutes. Then throw away what you've written.

2.   Write a letter to someone about what you would say if you could only get started.

3.   Meditate.

4.   Stretch and relax.

5.   Imagine writing as an obstacle course, then draw it, labeling each obstacle.

6.   Interview your obstacle(s), on paper or in your imagination.

7.   If you've been concentrating hard, drop the problem; take a walk, do the dishes, go running or swimming, read the newspaper.

8.   On paper or in your imagination, interview your future self looking back at how you solved the problem.

9. Notice any particular feelings in your body while you're stuck. Describe them precisely and free-associate about them.

10. Remember times that you succeeded in doing difficult things and give yourself a pep talk: "You can do it. Just try!"

11. Look at the actual results of your past successes; this may in itself pep you up.

12. Concentrate on an ordinary object for five minutes, giving it all your attention; then write about how something you noticed about the object is similar to your problem with writing.

13. Ask yourself, *What am I afraid of?* and write down everything that comes up, no matter how silly or far-fetched.

14. Ask yourself what's wrong and write out the explanation with your "other" hand.

15. Complete this sentence: "I should be able to..." and then ask, "Why?"

16. Try writing in a different, unexpected place: the laundromat, the kids' room of the library, the train station, the top row of empty bleachers.

17. List all the wrong ways to write your piece, and if you get inspired to start one of the "wrong" ways, go for it.

18. Doodle randomly with colors and see if you can see something in your picture.

19. Find a "writing buddy" and give each other deadlines.

20. Think of someone you admire and ask yourself, *What would that person do now?*

21. Read some great piece of writing, put it down, and imitate it on your topic.

22. Decide on a reward to give yourself if you write a page (or even half a page); then get started and really give yourself the reward if you earn it.

23. Sing! (It may wake up a part of your brain you need to use.)

24. Wake up your senses by smelling flowers, looking at art, or listening to favorite music.

25. Make a list: What would you need to know or learn in order to quickly solve this problem?

26. Ask yourself, *Is there any payoff for me in getting stuck right now?*

27. Visualize the problem being gone. How do you feel then?

28. If you had 500 pages in which to tell your story, how would you start? If you had to fit it all on one page, what would your first sentence be?

29. Open your dictionary randomly, and, without looking, point to a word, and use that word in your first sentence to get started, even if it's silly.

30. Talk your piece into a tape recorder.

31. Write a book review, or blurbs, for your book, by real or imaginary people.

32. In your imagination, line up your critics, then put a wall between them and you so you can write without them seeing or hearing you.

33. When you can't think of the right words, make gestures that express what you're feeling, then try to translate those into words.

34. Take a walk and imagine being able to see from the back of your head.

35. Imagine writing or speaking your story to someone who doesn't speak English, or communicate it in gibberish.

36. Ask yourself what color you feel within yourself. If this color were to speak, what would it say?

37. Write sideways or in a circle or some other pattern.

38. Imagine being the topic or problem. How would you prefer to be written about?

39. Don't sit still to write; pace.

40. List all the solutions to writer's block you've tried in the past; if any ever worked for you, try them again; think also, though, about whether any of these solutions might be part of the problem.

41. Begin in the middle or the end if the beginning is too difficult.

42. Wear a patch over one eye; wear earplugs or sound-blocking headphones; block up your nose; wear scratchy or sexy clothes; do a headstand.

43. Breathe alternately through one nostril at a time, a yoga technique that may help you balance both sides of the brain.

44. Take a break and slow down all of your activities during the break (washing dishes, reading the newspaper) to half speed.

45. Try writing the opposite of what you really want to say.

46. Think of something else besides writing that you are just as stuck on, and attack that problem, then see if writing becomes easier.

47. Set a specific time (at least a few days) during which you are not allowed to write the troublesome piece, no matter what (reverse psychology).

48. Turn your difficulty with writing into an elaborate and truly funny sit-com, then think about the truths revealed in the funny parts.

49. When you sit down to write, pretend you are someone else, complete with name, costume, mannerisms, motivation, and so forth.

50. Use an inappropriate form to record your ideas: a menu, shopping list, computer instructions, legal indictment, dictionary definitions, publicity flyer, personal ad, dialogue.

51. Tell your troubles to a shoe, a pen, or a flower, then sit down to write.

52. When you're procrastinating, make a list: What Am I Waiting For? Then find one item on the list that you can accomplish right away, to break the block.

53. Write it very badly, then see what's salvageable from this attempt.

54. Brag about what a great writer you are, on paper or out loud, then notice any objections, images, or feelings that come up.

55. Ask yourself, *If I did know how to get started, how would I do it?*

56. Write about your attempt to write in the form of a fairy tale.

57. Invent the rhythm for what you want to say, then fill in the words.

58. Find a noun or adjective to describe who, what, or how you are when you can't write. Is that an identity you are trying to hold on to?

59. Consider how much energy you've been expending in not writing.

60. Try writing with colored markers on huge poster paper.

61. With a tape recorder going, have someone interview you about what you'd like to say, then transcribe the tape and use that as a rough draft.

62. People from Planet X understand only pictures and symbols; write something for them.

63. Visit a toy store or a playground, knowing you'll find something there that will help you write.

64. Do something that makes you bored for twice as long as you think you can stand it, then go to write.

65. Think of the writer you could be but are not: What would that writer do? Then do that.

66. Write a letter to The Muse pleading for help.

67. Indulge yourself with your favorite forbidden pleasure, then sit down to write when you're feeling happier.

68. Imagine your writing problem as an opportunity in disguise. If you unmask it, what do you see?

69. Think of the most unreasonable way of writing you can imagine, then modify that in a workable way.

70. Make a "pep tape" of others talking about your real strengths, talents, and triumphs, and play it before you sit down to write.

71. Build a model in aluminum foil, clay, or office supplies of what you're trying to say, then describe in writing what you've built.

72. Find another area of your life where you get things done easily, naturally, and well, and transfer strategies you use there to writing.

73. Imagine that you're writing for a reader who can only pick up your meaning and can't notice errors in spelling, punctuation, grammar, or word choice.

74. If you're immobilized by having to correct everything as you go, get two hats: one labeled "writer" and the other labeled "editor"; tell yourself you can't edit when wearing the "writer" hat and vice versa, and switch at increasingly longer intervals.

75. Allow yourself to feel a strong emotion—for instance, anger, grief, love—then immediately begin to write.

76. Examine your stuckness again and again, until, TV's Lt. Columbo, you see something in it.

77. Invent your own way to get unstuck and write me about it.

Chapter 19

Getting Sizzling, Forceful Testimonials

One Thursday evening, while I was setting up for a one-session workshop at the Boston Center for Adult Education, a woman who had been in one of my other classes burst in the door and exclaimed, "Boy, am I glad to be here!"

I looked at her, surprised.

"I went to the doctor on Tuesday, and he wanted to schedule me for surgery today, but I told him, oh no, it will have to be Friday. I couldn't possibly miss Marcia Yudkin's workshop. I've taken a lot of writing workshops, and you're absolutely the best. You give 110 percent. You don't hold anything back."

Heat spread across my face, and my ears began to buzz. If I heard the rest of her accolades, they slipped right on through without sticking in my memory. The idea that someone would postpone surgery on account of my teaching seemed almost beyond belief, and I wasn't sure how to extend sympathy while she was showering me with praise. Other participants began to arrive, and I recovered enough to murmur concern for her health and add in a whisper, "Would you write that down for me—everything you just said?"

She took that right in stride. "You mean as in a recommendation? Sure thing." At the end of the workshop, she handed me a folded piece of paper, and I wished her well.

Had I overstepped some boundary of appropriateness? My nagging worry shifted when I unfolded the paper and read what she had written. Instead of the pointed praise that had made me flush, she had offered three paragraphs of vague raves about my generosity and helpfulness. I smiled and tucked the whole incident away for later reflection.

In retrospect, this episode crystallizes for me some of the challenges standing in the way of testimonials that convey a powerful wallop in your publicity. Even when compelling praise spontaneously comes your way, you have to capture it, and occasionally the process produces embarrassing moments. More often, you have to go out of your way to solicit, collect, save, and purify nuggets of acclaim. But whether you own a car dealership, sell scholarship information, or produce children's parties, whatever trouble you have to go through is usually worth it. Dynamic blurbs inject strength into any media kit, news release, or brochure.

WHAT MAKES A BLURB COMPELLING?

In an effective third-party endorsement, someone offers independent testimony about you, your product, or your service. This testimony persuades insofar as it is attributed, enthusiastic, pithy, and specific. Let's look at each of those four requirements in turn.

ATTRIBUTED

Floating quotes, attributed to no one, or those credited merely to initials, a title, a company, or a place don't carry much oomph. How can people know that you didn't make them up? At a minimum, testimonials should be accompanied by the person's full name and an identifier, such as a city or organization. The person's occupation or title provides added credibility, and helps whoever is reading the blurb decide on the relevance of the praise to his or her own purposes. For many purposes, blurbs from unknown people and organizations work fine, but your reputation rockets ahead when Dr. Ruth Westheimer endorses your couples counseling program, or the president of the American Truckers Association plugs your anti-dozing device.

ENTHUSIASTIC

The tone of the comments can range anywhere from mildly congratulatory to zealously fervent. Make sure that each word in the testimonial actually carries the weight that the person who praised you intended. For example, the training director who wrote, "We got nothing but good reports about your presentation" undoubtedly meant that as a forceful tribute, but someone reading that might wonder about the weakness of the adjective "good": *only* good, not "excellent"? When Laurie Schloff and I were collecting blurbs for our book *Smart Speaking,* one of her corporate clients wrote, "It can help you get through the day." Perhaps he meant that the book was so useful you'd want to refer to it for all kinds of different daily situations, but I thought it sounded as if the book was for someone who was depressed and dragging through the day. We asked if he would feel comfortable changing that to "it can aid anyone in getting ahead"; he agreed.

PITHY

For publicity purposes, each testimonial should be three sentences or less. But those few sentences need to be as tightly packed as the doll in a jack-in-the-box. The first time I tried to get blurbs, I sent a copy of my *Freelance Writing* manuscript to Michael Curtis, an editor at the *Atlantic Monthly,* with a cover letter reminding him of the time we had met. He left a message on my machine saying that he'd written "a couple of sentences" that he hoped would be useful to me. Because I was brand new to the business, I thought, *just* a couple of sentences? But this was what he had written: "Anyone who buys Ms. Yudkin's book can count on a huge return on his or her investment. I don't think I've ever read a dissection of my profession that was as thorough, as fair-minded and as full of genuinely helpful information." In just two sentences Curtis motivated the reader to buy the book with a distillation of its merits. Not only did those two little sentences land on the top of the back cover, but they also appeared in a box on the publicity flyer, and were picked up as the complete description for the book in a catalogue for writers, as well as quoted on Amazon.com.

SPECIFIC

Here is where most of the well-intended commendations you receive fall down. Consider these blurbs, taken from printed materials about various seminars. I've followed each with a question that shows how it could become more powerful.

"The power of this is truly amazing." *(What did the power consist of?)*

"I am proud to say that this seminar has made a real difference." *(In what?)*

"There wasn't a session that I didn't take away something." *(For example?)*

"Really interesting and informative." *(What was interesting about it and what did you learn?)*

"Well done and planned. Results were 100 percent!" *(What do you mean by 100 percent results?)*

How to Get Blurbs

Don't despair if getting meaty, pertinent praise is beginning to seem like Mission Impossible. Here are half a dozen tricks that help you pull this business off.

Unsolicited letters. Although *unsolicited* means "something for which you haven't specifically asked," you can do better than simply sit by the mailbox and pray. When you give a speech, close with, "I'd love to hear from you after you have a chance to apply my ideas." When a customer calls to place an order, say, "Please let me know how the system performs for you." At the end of a column, invite readers to agree or disagree with you. When I recorded my audiotape, "Become a More Productive Writer," I ended with, "...and let me know what worked for you. You can reach me, Marcia Yudkin, at.... Until then, goodbye." Within two months of the tape's release on the Sounds True label, I received an excited letter from a listener that proved useful to me.

Feedback forms. You can provide clients postage-paid postcards to mail back to you with comments, or, at a seminar, ask participants to fill out an evaluation form before they go home. If you're trying to get quotable material, how you word the questions makes an enormous difference. Avoid rating scales like "poor-fair-good-excellent" or "1–10" in favor of evocative questions such as:

↝ What were the three most valuable things you learned today?

↝ How would you characterize the service you received at Mighty Motors?

↝ How does Dependable Diaper Deliveries compare with your other options?

↝ What changes happened in your life as a result of your membership in Live, Don't Diet?

↝ What would you say to someone considering becoming of member of Friends of the Earth, United?

↝ What kind of person would most benefit from working with Dr. Grandview?

Solicited letters. I've both called and written regular clients to ask if they would send me a couple of sentences about the specific results they've gotten from working on their writing with me. Almost everyone obliged. Claudyne Wilder, author of *The Presentations Kit*, says that you make the task much easier for people when you give them samples of good blurbs as models. "I like to have a range of quotes, so I might also suggest, for example, 'Would you say something about my teaching style?'" Wilder adds. A bit of flattery encourages cooperation. Wilder called a client for whom she'd done a lot of training and asked, "Would you be the quote person for my video?" implying that that would be an honor, not an obligation. Similarly, I asked a client if she'd like to be featured as one of my "success stories" on a future flyer. She took it as a compliment. Wilder warns, however, not to promise ahead of time that you'll use someone's endorsement. She did that once, received something that was embarrassingly unusable, and had the author of it call her up and ask why it wasn't on her flyer.

On-the-phone and conversational comments. If someone offers spontaneous praise, seize the moment and ask, "Can I quote you on that?" Immediately write down their words and get permission to use them. I agree with a framed piece of calligraphy I have that reads, "Writing abides. The spoken word takes wing and cannot be recalled."

Writing them yourself and getting them approved. Dan Poynter, author of *The Self-Publishing Manual*, says that he has written blurbs himself, called up organization presidents he's met, and said, "How does this sound?" It seems to me you have to be an awfully versatile writer to concoct your own blurbs without them all sounding alike. People writing their own blurbs have such different ways of expressing themselves that you'll get more real-sounding quotes when the words come out of the mouths of your clients. I've seen comments posted on Amazon.com in which readers express suspicion that all the praise from other reader reviewers was fake or came from the author's cronies. This tends to happen when quote after quote gushes in much the same style.

Facts that substitute for blurbs. Certain facts carry the clout or cachet of verbal testimonials. Here are some I've seen used:

- ❖ Ninety percent of Sam Speaker's speaking engagements represent repeat or referral business.
- ❖ Oprah wears them [a make and model of shoes].
- ❖ The official birdie of the North American Indoor Badminton Association.
- ❖ One of only seven people in the world to receive the designation, "Master Page Turner."

Without any specific words of praise, these imply endorsements and can come in handy in news releases and media kits. Don't forget to highlight your media mentions and any awards you've won as testimonial-like credentials. Even if it were only a one-sentence announcement, you can say "as featured in the *Dallas Morning News.*"

Let me add three don'ts to this list—three ways of getting blurbs that I have experienced but most definitely do not recommend. The first came in my e-mail from a man from whom I had bought something online. "I shipped your item today," he wrote. "And don't forget, when you're asked to rate my service, make sure that you give me five stars." Boy, did this rub me the wrong way. I hadn't even received my order yet, much less seen what kind of condition it was in, and he was asking me to give him five stars! It doesn't go over well when you assume your customer will be satisfied. He should have written,

"I shipped your item today, and if you're completely happy with it, I'd be grateful if you gave me five stars. If there's a problem, please let me know, and I'll try to straighten it out right away."

The second no-no involves asking someone to recommend a product sight unseen or a service not yet experienced. Even if you're best buddies with someone, you shouldn't expect anyone to put his or her reputation on the line without any evidence or with only a partial or preliminary sample. I would have thought this went without saying, but several times authors have sent me just five or 10 pages out of a full-length book and asked me to write an endorsement. This ignores the essential meaning of a testimonial—its basis in fact—as well as the point that someone could be held morally (if not legally) responsible for recommending something trashy or defective.

Third, if someone declines to write a blurb or offers criticism instead, don't react angrily. I've been berated for being a "heartless" or "stupid" person when I've begged off writing a testimonial because the product did not meet my standards. Once, when I couldn't bring myself to endorse a book that I felt had flimsy and questionable content, a peer not only heaped abuse on me but also threatened to ruin my reputation. On the other hand, a couple of people reacted with class and politeness when I turned down their request for a blurb. Perhaps they privately cursed me, but I think of them favorably and feel they handled an awkward situation well.

All of these do's and don'ts apply to getting valuable user comments posted at Amazon, eBay, and other such Websites. Studies have shown that these comments have a tremendous influence on shoppers. I've had the greatest success getting substantive raves at Amazon when I replied to an e-mail praising one of my books, "Thanks for your comments. Would you mind taking a couple of extra moments and posting what you wrote me on Amazon.com? Here's how." More than 80 percent of the time, my respondent then does so. Sending colleagues a review copy of a book and asking them to post comments on Amazon has succeeded less frequently.

The Ethics of Editing and Using Blurbs

"Nice guys finish last."

"War is hell."

"What's good for General Motors is good for the country."

Are you shocked to learn that none of these hallowed sayings were actually uttered exactly as we now quote them? In tracking down famous quotations for his book, *Nice Guys Finish Seventh: False Phrases, Spurious Sayings and Familiar Misquotations*, Ralph Keyes discovered that Leo Durocher, manager of the Brooklyn Dodgers, actually said, in talking about the New York Giants, "The nice guys are all over there. In seventh place." General Sherman in fact used a lot more than three short words: "There is many a boy here today who looks on war as all glory, but, boys, it is all hell." And the wimpier but authentic words of Secretary of Defense Charles E. Wilson were, "For years I thought that what was good for our country was good for General Motors and vice-versa." Reporters and speech-givers afterward molded interesting thoughts into electrifying ones. And the lesson that I draw from this is: So can you.

As long as your testimonial writers are alive, you should ask their concurrence with your snappier version of their words, and, indeed, with quoting them at all if the comments were unsolicited. Someone I know sent a copy of her book to a public figure, received a warm personal letter of thanks, and then went right ahead and excerpted the letter in all of her publicity. That doesn't sit right with me. Because the blurb derived from private correspondence rather than from public comments or from a context in which it was clear that the comments might become public, I think the well-known person deserved the right to say yes or no to being quoted. I understand that it's even against the law in some states to use people comments for commercial gain without their permission. The same goes for condensing and polishing remarks that the maker did know were for a quote. You don't want people who'd been saying nice things about you hollering, "Out of context!"

In addition to the four criteria I explained earlier in this chapter, when you edit blurbs, get rid of all unnecessary words and any repetitions. If the wording sounds stiff or unnatural, call the writer and ask him how he'd express that idea over a beer to a close friend or colleague. And insert enough context so that outsiders know what the testimonial is praising.

For example, I received an unsolicited letter from a woman in my magazine-writing workshop. Here it is, unedited:

→→ ←←

Dear Marcia,

You asked me if I can now respond, 'I'm a writer.' Well, I guess the answer is, yes.

While I already 'got my money back,' the more important thing is I do feel purposeful and productive in my identity of creating my own work (rather than being employed by another). Hopefully, that will pay off for the rest of my life.

I enjoyed your classes and hope to see you again sometime.

Kathi P. Geisler

→→ ←←

The first step in turning this thank-you letter into a testimonial is to decide which parts carry the most weight. To me, someone predicting that a 10-session workshop will pay off for the rest of her life is pretty strong. So I would make that the central idea of the blurb. Next, I would ask myself if Kathi left out anything that might help the reader appreciate her comments more. She didn't mention that she got several articles published that she'd brought to the workshop, so with her permission I would add that. Putting that together with the identity theme in two or three punchy sentences yields the following:

→→ ←←

"While attending your freelance writing workshop, I got my first paid articles published in newspapers. Not only can I now call myself a writer, but I also feel confident about being able to create my own work, rather than being employed by another. I think this will pay off for the rest of my life."–Kathi P. Geisler, Chelmsford, Massachusetts

→→ ←←

Note that I could just as well have put this paragraph in third person: "As a result of Marcia's freelance writing workshop..." Finally, I needed to call Kathi, explain my editing, and ask her approval for the edited blurb. (I did, and she agreed.)

Some people get hung up on getting a strong, concise, pertinent letter signed by the endorser on company letterhead. Although this does look great framed in a waiting room, it's unnecessary and even counterproductive for the media. Reporters would rather have a dozen testimonials bunched together on one or two pieces of paper than a dozen pages they have to spend time and energy flipping through. And once you've passed the gauntlet of your first few print interviews, you'll have less room in your media kit for individual endorsement letters.

OFFERING TESTIMONIALS YOURSELF

So far, in this chapter, I've discussed getting testimonials from others to produce a big boost in your credibility with the media and with the general public. However, you can also write testimonials for other business providers and get valuable free publicity as a result.

Keep in mind that many large and small organizations seeking publicity for themselves need to have customer success stories they can pull out of their files for news releases and interviews with reporters. If you send in your compliments and your results, you could find yourself part of an article about a company with which you do business. Establishments with walk-in traffic, such as car dealers and restaurants, often post the actual letters on the wall or in a window to influence people in the waiting room or passersby. Best of all is when an outfit for which you've written a testimonial posts your comments and your identity and Web address on its Website. That link could generate some serious traffic for you.

Joan Stewart, publisher of the newsletter *The Publicity Hound*, recommends that you volunteer a testimonial when you've gotten excellent results from paid advertising. "Call your advertising representative and offer a testimonial," she says. "Explain that you'd be happy to share with readers the results of your ad. And because you're smart, you'll even let them take your photo to run with the testimonial.

Several of my friends have done this quite successfully. Because the newspaper prints the ad with your testimonial over and over again, you can get thousands of dollars in free ad space for nothing but the time it takes you to write the testimonial and sit for the photo. The newspaper, of course, loves the idea because a third-party endorsement can pull in even more advertisers."

VIRAL MARKETING: THE ULTIMATE TESTIMONIAL

Throughout this book, I've offered ways to catch the attention of the media, which has value for you because it has the power to reach thousands or millions of readers, listeners, or viewers at a stroke. However, sometimes it's possible without the aid of traditional media to mobilize fans of your organization, product, or service to recommend you to friends and colleagues and thus rapidly spread your influence. During the dotcom boom, this marketing goal acquired the unfortunate name of "viral marketing." At bottom, this simply involves inspiring people to contact others about your offerings and providing a tool for them to do so.

Apart from the Internet, you can get viral marketing working for you by supplying customers and clients with nice-looking postcards featuring you that they can send to people they know. Hotels and motels have used this technique for decades. The same dynamic applies when you enclose not one but two business cards in business correspondence. Implicitly, the second card suggests that people pass it along to a friend.

Using the Internet, several techniques encourage people to share their enthusiasm for what you offer with others. First, there are numerous "send this to a friend" scripts available for your site that make it easy for someone to forward a Webpage or send someone a "take a look at this!" message. Second, if you publish an e-mail newsletter, be sure to remind readers to forward the newsletter, if they like it, to colleagues, friends, and relatives. I used to place this reminder in the subject line of my newsletter until a subscriber pointed out that people read the header before they've read the newsletter contents and therefore don't encounter that prompt when they're feeling most enthusiastic. I now place it near the bottom of each issue.

Although some companies have experienced fantastic results from rewarding people for referrals to their friends, I would caution you about a possible backlash from doing this. When you offer incentives for recommending your site, and more valuable incentives for recommending it to more people, you risk people giving you e-mail addresses whose owners may get extremely annoyed at being contacted with this message. This could bring on accusations that you are "spamming" and create bucketloads of trouble.

You're better off creating something that people like so much they share it in a spirit of fun or helpfulness rather than self-interest. Things that get forwarded a lot online usually have at least one of these three qualities: relevance—something that hits the spot of current needs exactly; humor—something that brightens one's day; or uniqueness—something that makes one think, admire, or feel moved. Generate something with one of those qualities, and people will pass it around even if you neglect to remind them to do so!

Chapter 20

How to Concoct Creative Angles, Images, and Exploits

So I've convinced you that you need an original idea to earn media coverage for your ordinary pick-your-own-apples apple orchard. But you're stumped. Your thoughts feel like sludge, the only possibilities you've come up with bore you, and disgust is growing by the minute.

Then it's time to go ahead and give up. Stop trying so hard! Stop trying, period. Creativity goes into hiding when willpower is out flexing its muscles. Let go of the problem completely and do something else. If that feels too undirected, just before you quit, send a message to your unconscious mind that some time in the next few days you'd like to have a brainstorm. Then answer your phone messages, eat lunch, go out to the floor and serve customers, or do whatever else needs to be done. Later on, when you're biting into a french fry or punching numbers into the cash register, a clever headline will probably whisper in your ear or flash onto your mental video monitor. If that age-old, proven method doesn't yield a "eureka" when you need it, don't worry. Use the creativity kindlers in this chapter to discover the spark that lights a fire under the media for you.

THE METAPHOR GAME

One of the easiest and most effective ways to make a same-old-anything sound fresh is to describe it using a metaphor, a figure of speech that compares something ordinary to something more surprising, funny, or exotic. The books *Guerrilla Dating Tactics*, *Guerrilla Marketing*, and *Guerrilla P.R.*, for example, each compare something that doesn't literally involve gunmen hiding in the hills for guerrilla warfare. I used a cooking metaphor in the following lead of a news release about an otherwise not-that-newsworthy conference:

> "Business for Boston, Massachusetts," a conference at Northeastern University on June 19 and 20, offers a compelling recipe for aiding the troubled regional economy: Take more than 40 of the largest New England purchasers, from Raytheon and Massport to Digital and ITT Sheraton. Add representatives of several hundred local companies capable of fulfilling their needs. Mix in an educational setting designed to maximize exchange of information about needs and procedures. Estimated yield: $40 million of new orders for participating small, minority and women-owned businesses based in the area.

Far from yawning, the *Boston Herald* sent both a reporter and a photographer and ran a big spread on the second day of the conference.

Taking off from a traditional parlor game, I've devised the following questions, which help you come up with numerous metaphor candidates. Some people get best results when they close their eyes after each question. From all the images and words that come up, choose and develop the metaphor that excites you most and suits your purposes. Feel free, of course, to scrap my list and make up your own— or just let yourself fantasize without any trigger questions.

1. If your product, service, or message were a vegetable, which one would it be?
2. If it were a job, which one would it be?
3. If it were a kind of weather, which kind would it be?
4. How about a tool?
5. A temperature?
6. An animal?
7. A smell?
8. A crime?
9. A toy?
10. Something to wear?
11. A country?

12. A spare-time activity?
13. A sound?
14. An exact time of day?
15. A department in the supermarket?

Turnaround Is Fair Play

List at least 20 clichés and see how many of them you can twist into an angle. Here are half a dozen tired phrases and sayings to get you started:

❖ "George Washington slept here."

❖ "You can never go home again."

❖ "A stitch in time saves nine."

❖ "Boys don't make passes at girls who wear glasses."

❖ "That's a bit of a sticky wicket."

❖ "It's not over until the fat lady sings." *(Aha! We could stage some sort of a closing ceremony with a plump soprano providing entertainment.)*

You can find a Website devoted to clichés and even order up a random serving of 10 clichés at *www.westegg.com/cliche.*

Borrow for the Morrow

Letting successful publicity inspire you is smart. Echo what someone else has done, but in a different key or on a different instrument.

1. Analyze the appeal of best-selling products or movies, especially those you and your target market like and respect. Any ideas about what you could do or say that, without copying, would borrow that appeal?

2. Read trade magazines for a business area that seems leagues away from yours. If you design fabric, who's making news in accounting, and why—and can you try something similar?

3. Pick up the newspaper and articulate why each story on the front page landed there. Then invent similar headlines and stories involving you. Examples:

"Microsoft and 2 Cable Giants Close to an Alliance." (*Oh, maybe I could form an alliance with someone everyone thinks is in a different business.*)

"Hidden Economy: Immigrants Underground." (*Hmm, what's the underside of the law? Fee-padding? Maybe I could explain the innovative steps we take to avoid overcharging clients.*)

"City Leaders Hold Line on Taxes in the City Budget." (*Let's see, suppose I held a line in price increases....*)

IMAGINE THAT!

Playing "what if" has paid off for innumerable inventors and authors. How about for you?

1. Suppose you could afford a famous spokesperson, alive or dead. Who would you choose?

2. Imagine a scenario in which your product saved the world, or, a little more modestly, in which it earned a presidential proclamation. How might it do that?

3. Pretend you're serving 10 additional audiences you don't particularly pay attention to now. What would they be, and which might have news value?

4. Suppose the only legal medium for publicity was a sandwich board on which you could paint one picture or up to five big words. What would you put there?

5. If you were doing what you do now in prehistoric times, what would that be like? How about in Bora-Bora? Or on the fourth moon of Jupiter?

6. Complete this story: "Once upon a time there was an enterprising young lass (or lad) named ＿＿＿ who had ＿＿＿ed and wanted the whole kingdom to know about it. So she (or he)...."

FUNNY STUFF

Laughter loosens the lid on creativity. Joel Goodman of The Humor Project calls this "the HAHA-AHA! connection."

1. What do you say to yourself or others about what you do that gets rueful, jovial, or side-splitting laughs?
2. If people were to poke good-natured fun at you in a spoof, how could they do it?
3. Imagine a humorous commercial featuring your organization. Might a toned-down version incorporated into a news release interest the public?
4. Suppose you had to act out what you do and what's so special about it according to the rules of charades. How would you do it?
5. Ask a kid who knows you what he or she imagines that you do all day. Or ask a whole carpoolful of kids how they would spend the day if they were running your organization.

EAR TO THE GROUND

Sometimes the very idea we need passes by us in disguise. If we pay careful attention, we're more likely to recognize it.

1. What are the stories you or patrons tell over and over again about yourself? What do these show? Is there a tantalizing thread running through them?
2. Take out last year's appointment calendar or annual report. Did you do something last year that deserved to be publicized?
3. What are the complaints you hear about competitors that no one hears about you?
4. Which emotions motivate your devotees: Fear? Pride? Impatience? Hope? Is there a story there?
5. Eavesdrop on your audience. Is there something you know about them that they don't seem to know?
6. What casual comments, worries, or compliments keep showing up in your e-mail?

IMPROMPTU PERFORMANCES

In my live creativity seminars, participants perform an improvisational exercise in pairs. While standing up, person A pretends to hand person B something, which person B pretends to take. Person A asks person B, who's now holding the object, a series of unscripted questions about the object; person B makes up the answers, whatever feels right in the moment. For example:

A: Hey, I read something about you today in this magazine here. (Hands it to B.)

B: (Takes the magazine.) Oh yeah?

A: Yeah, look on page 37.

B: (Turns pages.)

A: What does it say?

B: (Pretending to read.) It says I just got elected chairman of the Recycling Society.

A: Does it have a picture?

B: Yeah, it shows me together with a sculpture made out of crushed aluminum cans.

A: How did you get into the magazine?

And so on. So long as A keeps asking questions and B answers spontaneously, this becomes fun, easy, and revealing. After a few minutes A and B switch roles. A variation would be for A to say, "Hey, I saw you on TV today," and hand B the VCR remote for the tape.

If you can't find a friend to try that with, another of my seminar exercises works well for one. Sit down with a piece of drawing paper and crayons or colored markers. Using two different colors, draw any two shapes or lines. Then turn the paper upside down. You now have before you the beginnings of a picture of how you finagled free publicity. Pick up your crayons or markers and without thinking about it, complete the picture. Then give it a caption.

Both this and the improvisational exercise coax your unconscious mind to come out with its perspectives on how publicity might emerge naturally and comfortably for you. Whichever of these creativity kindlers you use, take note of any responses that make you laugh or send a chill down your spine. Those are the ones that, refined, hold the potential to strike home with the public.

Chapter 21

Becoming Findable Through Search Engines

When the World Wide Web was new, enthusiasts would "surf" for hours, clicking from site to site in an orgy of exploratory joy. They would also pounce on suggestions from the media or friends of new and interesting Web pages to visit. During those pioneer days of 1996, Canadian Edward Palonek had created FoundMoney.com, which helps people locate and recover unclaimed funds to which they're entitled. He received a life-changing phone call from a producer for Oprah Winfrey's show who had checked out his Website and invited him onto the show. Throughout the course of the next few months, his business exploded.

"Every phone we had would ring, day or night, for months," he reminisces. "It was a full-time chore just to keep the servers going to keep up with the demand. Oprah raised people's consciousness about the idea of unclaimed money being out there. Her show did a fabulous job of conveying how easy it could be to find this money, no strings attached. It was unusual then to have such a useful Website, and our continued popularity today undoubtedly has roots in that Oprah appearance."

Now that practically every business in the developed world has a Website, it's considerably more challenging to inspire excitement about your site, or indeed to have people find it. Rather than surfing aimlessly, journalists and producers—as does the general public—use Internet search engines to find companies and information on specific topics. If you make some small but significant adjustments in your publicity writing, you can greatly increase the odds that media people and potential customers, fans, or clients will find your Website. Even if you don't have a Website, you should be aware of these principles so that when your news releases wind up online from a newswire or distribution service, they rise toward the top of the listings when someone searches for information on what you sell or do.

How Search Engines "Think"

When considering the wording on Web pages that search engines are data-crunching, you need to know that search engines do not think human beings do, who classify and organize information in accordance with all the common sense they possess. Instead, search engines are dumb and extremely literal.

For instance, if you read a headline about a nursery having a sale, you immediately know several things right there. Without being specifically told, you know that trees, shrubs, and bulbs are undoubtedly on sale. Even though the word *nursery* also means a place where children are cared for, you also know that this is not an indication to call your attorney general to investigate baby selling. You know so deep in your bones that babies aren't normally put up for sale that that interpretation of the word probably wouldn't even occur to you. However, search engines don't know how to generalize, reason, apply common sense, or draw inferences. They simply use certain rules to index the text exactly according to the words used. Although the "artificial intelligence" resources of the search engines are improving year by year, they still do not classify and offer Websites based on words not used. For a search engine, a rose is a rose is a rose and not a color or a flower or a potential name for a new daughter.

This stark fact has profound implications for whether or not your publicity materials come to people's attention through search engines. If you don't include in your news release or on your Web page the precise word or phrase people typically type into a search engine, people searching for that nugget of information will not find that document or page. Furthermore, if you guess wrongly about which words and phrases people most commonly use in searches, you may lose out on search engine traffic altogether. Accordingly, you need to become conscious of your terminology and use language in some ways that may not jibe with best practices for writing intended for print.

Here are some insights and steps that follow from the nonthinking nature of search engines.

Use the words and phrases your target market uses. After I published the first edition of this book, one expert whose opinion I value commented that the term *press release* is outmoded and inaccurate, because "the press"—as in printing press—refers only to print media and leaves out broadcast and online media. I took his point to heart and revised most of the mentions of "press release" in this new edition of the book to read "news release." However, in anything to appearing online, I continue to use "press release." Why? Because according to Wordtracker, a service that tallies how many times people hunt online for words and phrases (see Chapter 24 for more on this), people search for "press release" 20 times more often than for "news release" and more than 50 times more often than for "media release."

Chicago-based marketer Reno Lovison found this factor extremely frustrating while working on the promotional copy for a treatment program called "Try for Dry," which helps children who wet their beds. "We decided when we began the program to downplay the term 'bedwetting' because the psychologist on our team felt that the term had a pejorative connotation," says Lovison. "Also, it is kind of a misnomer, because strictly speaking, the condition is 'sleep wetting,' as children wet when they are asleep, not necessarily when they are in bed. We prefer the word 'enuresis,' which is the professional term for wetting. Yet without the word 'bedwetting,' our site would appear in no search engines, forcing me to compromise our message and riddle our site with the term 'bedwetting.' This is an example of the tail wagging the dog."

A twist on this came up when a client of Greg Jarboe, former vice-president and chief marketing officer of Backbone Media, wanted to describe its business focus as "private media marketing solutions." Not only was that term completely unknown to its target audience and thus a complete dud for search engine traffic, the phrase *private media* was already in common use in the pornography industry, with a salacious meaning. Jarboe managed to persuade the client to use a more recognizable phrase for what the company did, *custom publishing,* in the subhead of a news release.

Sometimes, rather than a term that is preferred but not in common use, there are two alternate wordings for the same concept. In such a case, you'd do well to use both if you can. For instance, many practitioners in the legal field prefer to call themselves attorneys, but the word *lawyer* is in wider use. According to Wordtracker, more than three times as many people perform the online search "find a lawyer" as type in "find an attorney." Jarboe advises being mindful of differences between American and British English, and, when appropriate, conniving a way to include both spellings, such as in "search engine optimization—which our British cousins call 'search engine optimisation.'"

Include generic terms along with brand names or made-up phrases. Suppose you have a new car cleaning product called "Auto Self Shyne." Until this name becomes well-known, no one is going to search for that exact phrase. Instead, they'll type in phrases such as "car cleaner" or "home carwash product." It may take some thinking and market research to come up with the common classifications for your product—phrases you'd do well to include in the copy of news releases and text for your Website. Greg Jarboe says that an excellent formula for working in the generic term is to add it following the brand name, set off by commas: "Backbone Media, an Internet marketing company," or "Auto Self Shyne, a home carwash product."

Likewise, coming up with creative ways to describe aspects of your product, service, event, or cause penalizes you when it comes to search engine results. When I recently performed the exercise of taking a news release I'd originally sent out with a good response in 1995 and rewriting it for search engine pick-up now, I found myself deleting spunky verbiage such as *wordsmith* and *penster* in favor of more well-worn nouns such as *writer, copywriter,* and *editor.* Similarly, I reworded *business owners flummoxed by their marketing ineptitude* to *business owners in need of marketing help.* The release became a bit more boring to read so that it would attract search engine traffic.

Include general classificatory words and phrases. In the old days, a release about a special event at a nursery would implicitly be understood as relevant to those interested in landscaping and planting even if it did not use those words. When you'll be posting or distributing a release online, insert words for the broader concepts under which your news falls. For instance, a release about a child identification tool should include the words and phrases *child safety tool, anti-kidnapping,* and *parenting aids.* When such language doesn't come to mind, visit competitors' Websites or browse through their catalogs to jog your thinking.

Avoid jargon, specialized terminology, and nicknames when it's your terminology, not the customer's. For example, if you own a bed-and-breakfast in Truro, Massachusetts, which is part of Cape Cod, don't abbreviate it to a "B&B" rather than a "bed-and-breakfast" (Wordtracker indicates that the latter is searched for about nine times more often than the former), and don't lapse into "the Cape," as those already familiar with the area call it, rather than "Cape Cod." Indeed, because most tourists would be hunting for a place to stay on "Cape Cod" and not specifically in "Truro," you should use the former term more often than the latter. Because every organization and peer group develops in-group jargon, it's sometimes difficult to stay conscious of what customers and potential customers call things.

Keep in mind that the vast majority of marketers I've seen in action significantly overestimate the extent to which their target audience understands their jargon. I once came across a software Website that touted itself as something along the lines of "the foremost CRM solution for small businesses." When I went to a meeting of small business owners later that day, I polled them on how many knew the meaning of CRM. Just one in 10 did, and when I revealed that it stands for "customer relationship management," most were still mystified. Only when I translated that as "it helps you keep track of your customers, whether you're in touch with them by phone or e-mail or in person" did the light of understanding dawn on the rest. That software company needed to use phrases such as *customer contact, software integrating many points of contact,* and *customer loyalty tools* along with the buzzword CRM.

According to Greg Jarboe, acronyms (such as CRM) so often stand for different things to different groups of people that you're best off staying away from them for search engine purposes: "'AIM' stands for the 'Associated Industries of Massachusetts' as well as for 'AOL Instant Messenger.' Usually the full wording gets more searches than the initials anyway."

Insert examples of what you're talking about. The 1995 news release about my business editing or marketing rewriting service that I recently reexamined from the point of view of writing for search engines already itemized some of the documents I reworked for clients: "sales letter, press release, ad, or brochure." But if I hadn't included those specific instances of what I was talking about, I'd be wise to do so for search engine purposes. Include as many nouns as possible in your publicity copy if your clientele might search for particular items. Someone who's trying to find the closest place to buy plastic nails may well type in "plastic nails Park Slope" rather than "hardware store Park Slope."

Vary the parts of speech you use for key terms. I had a good chuckle when I searched on Google for both "optimizing a press release" and "press release optimization." The first six references that came up in the former search were instances of an article I had published on the topic of this chapter; in the latter search my work was nowhere to be found. Clearly I should have used "press release optimization" in my text as well as "optimizing a press release." As is the case with many of the other nuances I've outlined here for becoming findable through search engines, ensuring such variations is definitely not second nature to either skilled or beginning writers. Indeed, Cathy Platon, who does marketing communications for Proficient Networks, told me that she uses a checklist to ensure she includes common industry terms and variations for good search engine pickup. "As a result, our press releases on the newswires and sites that run newswire releases usually get much higher postings than our home page," she says.

Include keywords as text rather than as graphics. Sometimes a site has all the words and phrases it needs for good search engine results, except that the keywords are embedded within graphical files that search engines can't read. You may need to redesign the basic template of your Website so that the crucial language appears as text in some attractive font rather than in an image file. Or you can rewrite the page copy so that you add those words and phrases within the page text. Sometimes just changing your headline or adding subheads does the trick.

For local businesses, include geographical nouns in publicity pieces. If you offer in-person services and products mainly within a certain geographical radius, brainstorm a list of the place names potential clients or customers might use to find a landscaper or real-estate attorney or kids' clothing store in your service area. Use the geographical terms customers favor, including the names of larger cities or neighborhoods that you serve. For instance, if you were a roofer based in Goshen, Massachusetts, the town of 900 people where I live, you'd want copy such as this on your home page and in any news releases: "serving Springfield, Northampton, Amherst, Greenfield, the hilltowns, and the rest of the Pioneer Valley of Western Massachusetts."

Include URLs in news releases. This sounds obvious, but it's actually not well known that you should always insert your Web address someplace in the first paragraph of a release, and not only in the last paragraph or where your distribution service has an information slot for a URL. Often news sites display just the first paragraph of a release along with a link to read more. When your URL shows up in that first paragraph, readers can click to your site right away without the intermediate click to read the rest of the release. Faster access means higher click-throughs.

Remember that anything you do to get good rankings in search engines should be consistent with the business image you wish to maintain. For instance, normally you wouldn't want to tarnish your credibility by including ignorant misspellings of key words related to your business in a news release or other publicity copy, even if those misspellings were very popular. The value of trustworthiness in the eyes of educated readers, both customers and the media, is just too important.

GET FOUND FAST WHEN BIG NEWS BREAKS

Suppose you're the world's best-informed expert on Medicare fraud, but your low-profile Website doesn't seem to have been picked up by the search engines. Then news breaks that members of a colossal fraud ring have been arrested. Reporters all around the country are scrambling not only to pin down the facts but also to locate experts who can provide perspective. Here's how you can set yourself up for a whirlwind of media interviews, faster and cheaper than you could issue a news release: Set up a Google Adwords ad.

The Google Adwords program enables you to create a four-line pay-per-click ad that shows up whenever anyone searches Google for whatever keywords you specify. In the situation I've described, journalists will be flocking to Google, and your little ad can show up for their search in the #1 spot if you simply outbid everyone else for the phrase "Medicare fraud" for the next day or two. It won't take more than 20 minutes to set this up, and you pay only according to how many people click on your ad. Google lets you specify the maximum amount you'll pay per click and the maximum you're willing to spend per day, and you can start and stop the ad whenever you say. Your ad could go like this:

Medicare Fraud Expert

NIH-funded researcher has facts,

statistics, insights at fingertips.

www.professorgriffon.com/about.htm

For proof that journalists pay attention to Google ads and not only to the regular, unpaid search listings, consider the experience of Nancy Collamer, a career consultant who had published an e-book called *The Layoff Survival Guide*. She noticed that few ads came up when people searched for "unemployment" or "layoffs" and decided to try her luck with an ad for her publication. Among those who spotted her ad and clicked to her site was a reporter for the *Wall Street Journal*, who referenced her e-book in an article.

"It was just one line, but by nine o'clock that morning I had an e-mail from a vice-president at McGraw-Hill asking if I'd ever thought of going with a big publisher. Later that day a high-powered executive called for career counseling who said, 'I saw you in today's *Wall Street Journal*,'" says Collamer.

She credits Google directly or indirectly with appearing three times in the *Wall Street Journal* and once in the *Asian Wall Street Journal*. She later leveraged those media appearances into others in *Redbook*, *US News and World Report*, *Ladies Home Journal*, *Fortune*, *Newsweek*, *Time*, *Working Mother*, and *Money*. Advertising isn't supposed to influence the media, but Google puts you in the right place at the perfect time and can build your credibility if you play its game wisely.

Chapter 22

Making Time to Publicize

When Dwight D. Eisenhower became president, he decided he would fulfill his duties with the utmost efficiency. Top priority every day would be those matters that were both urgent and important. Eisenhower had to jettison his resolution, however, when he discovered that what was urgent rarely was important, and what was important rarely showed up as an urgent problem.

You'll probably find that Eisenhower's lesson applies to your experience in finding time to do publicity. Although publicity offers important benefits, it rarely presents itself as urgent. If you constantly concentrate on immediately pressing tasks, such as answering client calls, preparing UPS shipments, and arranging payroll, you may not get around to taking the steps that lead to valuable media publicity. No one system solves this problem for everyone. So as you read the suggestions in this chapter, notice those that appeal to you and begin taking advantage of them right away.

3 MODELS FOR GETTING AROUND TO PUBLICITY

Making time to publicize might mean making it your number-one priority for a brief time period or focusing on it regularly along with everything else you do. Here are the advantages and disadvantages of three different approaches.

1. Steady Drops of Water

Just as salespeople know they need to make a certain number of cold calls per day to find new customers, you may decide to put publicity-seeking on your agenda every day that you work. John Kremer, author of *1001 Ways to Market Your Books*, says he aims at doing five promotional things a day. "This might mean calling someone, writing a letter, mailing a review copy, asking someone for a blurb. Because I've made it a habit to be always thinking about publicity and always looking for opportunities, I get more ideas that aren't obvious." Spreading out publicity efforts within your regular routine may make it easier to spare the time. However, this method may preclude the big push that could accompany a grand opening, product release, or special event.

2. Waves

Instead of working on publicity every day or every week, you can set aside time a few times a year for intensive publicity efforts. This approach especially makes sense if your business or organization has seasonal activities, special events, or periodic new services or products. But it also works well if you're the planner type and set annual goals for results you'd like to see. For example, schedule Wave #1 at the end of February, Wave #2 in May, Wave #3 in August, and so on. If your business has a slow time of year (most of December for trainers, for instance, or the dead of winter for some retailers), use that time to write news releases, compile your media list, or do your newsworthy customer survey. However, by putting publicity out of mind when it's out of your schedule you might miss some opportunities, such as articles that provide a good pretext for a letter to an editor.

3. Tsunamis

Once every couple of years you might find the energy and stimulus to launch what Jeffrey Lant calls a tsunami: a tidal wave of publicity. Here you're so confident of your newsworthiness that you minimize your other activities and go all out. You make phone pitches, complete follow-up calls, and schedule interviews until you're teetering on exhaustion. The effort Norman George put out to reach 10 million people about his Edgar Allan Poe anniversary celebration was, for him, a once-in-a-very-long-while event. If you're releasing a book that you're determined to make a best-seller or mounting a demonstration that you hope will change minds and laws all over the country, a tsunami may be in order. Usually a tsunami creates ripple opportunities of which you'll want to take advantage, instead of just drying out afterward.

GETTING AND STAYING ORGANIZED

For publicity, my most important system is my way of catching and saving ideas. All of the possibilities that pop into my mind while reading or puttering around I write down in one place, a bound notebook. When I execute one of those ideas, I check it off. Once in a while I reread the list and see what jumps out at me as something I could get moving on now. Although this may seem a boringly simple system, I find it invaluable to have all the ideas gathered in one place rather than scattered to the winds on scraps of paper. If you're an inveterate scraps-of-paper type, I recommend at least designating a file or shoebox for storing them together.

Another thing to collect is other people's ideas. Clip articles about people in any field whose media coverage catches your eye or makes you marvel out loud. People in the advertising business call this a "swipe file." Of course, you don't steal and you don't copy exactly; you borrow and adapt—perfectly kosher and legal.

Third, create a place to collect and save information about periodicals, shows, and reporters that seem to be interested in your topic area. I've finally set up a computer file for this, having realized that keeping this information in seven different places (one of which is nowhere) only makes lots more work for me.

Fourth and finally, keep a file for copies of all the publicity materials you draft or send. In 1980, I dashed off a letter to *The New York Times* Education Supplement offering to write an article. Not only did the Education Editor call me the day he received the letter, but he also accepted and published the article I wrote, my first, which subsequently opened up countless other opportunities to me. Because this happened in the days before computers and I didn't bother with a trip to the copy shop before I dropped the letter in the mailbox, I don't have the text of what unexpectedly launched my second career (although I do recall my opening line). If your news release or public-service announcement leads to fame and fortune, wouldn't you want to have saved it? Remember: You never know.

CREATING A PUBLICITY PLAN

You can take a lot of the pain and bother out of the process of getting PR by creating a one-year, month-by-month publicity plan. Let's suppose, first, that you have an ongoing business for which you'd like to get some visibility and improved credibility. After getting clear on your goal and your target market, decide how often you'll contact the media. (Once a month is realistic and manageable for most businesses if you've done much of the creative thinking ahead of time.) The next step is brainstorming publicity angles. (Use the "10 Ways to be Timely" section in Chapter 2 as a tool for nudging ideas.) Also look at publicity various competitors and colleagues have achieved, both by reading the paper or watching the news attentively and by checking out the links in their online press rooms. Sometimes you can get coverage by fashioning a pitch that's the exact opposite of their image, and sometimes you can add a twist to what they've done. For instance, if other tree management companies in your area have a brawny "he-man" personality, you might decide to portray yours as kinder and gentler. If you see that an accountant across the country got ink by challenging the tax service's telephone advice, you could try going head to head with tax-preparation software programs.

Once you have at least as many publicity ideas as you need for your annual program, assign them to certain months, keeping in mind the seasonality of some angles and publications' lead times. For monthly magazines, you need to get releases or pitch letters to the media at least four or five months ahead of the cover date; for daily newspapers a week to 10 days' lead time is smart. Be mindful, too, of your own typically busy times of the year and plan accordingly. For instance, the accountant could keep to a once-a-month schedule more easily by writing the releases to be distributed in February, March, and April ahead of time.

Consider as well the best method to distribute your releases. If you're going to use a paid distribution service, add to the first month to-dos the task of researching and deciding which service to use. If you're going the do-it-yourself route, your task list early on should include visiting the library or visiting Websites to construct your own custom media list.

For the launch of a new business, product, or service, your publicity plan might be much more concentrated and intense for the initial period and less strenuous later in the year. But in the same way, begin by getting clear about your goal and target market, come up with angles, take lead times into account, and be specific in your plan about which publicity actions you will take when. Having it all written down and organized by month makes it more likely you'll follow through with the tasks in your plan.

PROBLEMS AND SOLUTIONS

Do you wait and wait and wait and wait because you want your release or phone pitch to be sensational? Then you need a way around perfectionism. If you've written something, set it aside overnight and proofread it carefully. Then, if you can't pinpoint any fixable flaws, tell yourself there aren't any, and send it out. Or put someone dependable in charge of quality control and have him or her declare the readiness of your stuff to go out. The same goes for an oral pitch: Practice, and then ask for a thumbs up/thumbs down assessment from someone you trust. If it's a go, stop practicing and do it.

Suppose you'd like to try a publicity wave but simply can't carve out time amidst your other responsibilities. Actually, some of the work involved in putting out, say, a news release, can be done while you're doing something else. Divide the steps into tasks that are creative and those that are routine. Apply yourself to the creative steps, such as thinking up an angle, while you're doing something that requires only partial attention, like scrubbing the deli counter, or mowing the lawn. As I explained in Chapter 20, inspiration may not come immediately, but even a half-brained stint of attention to the problem hastens a solution.

Does the whole process feel overwhelming? Then start out with the smallest, least time-consuming step. Or contact the placement office of a local college to find an intern with an interest in business, journalism, or communications. An intern works on a project part-time for you in exchange for experience to put on his or her resume, college credit, or both. Given a copy of this book, any reasonably intelligent and motivated college student should be able to execute a publicity campaign for you.

Are you an inveterate procrastinator? Try the buddy system: With a friend or colleague, set deadlines and keep each other on track with either encouraging or guilt-tripping phone calls—whichever works. Or promise yourself rewards just for getting mobilized (the publicity you receive after getting going will be a bonus). And then there's one of my favorite approaches. A fencing coach whose team wasn't doing their daily jogging got team members to promise simply to put on their running clothes once a day. Everyone found it easy to make and keep that promise. Then once they were dressed to run, it felt simple and natural for them to head on out and do three miles. You could adapt their success by resolving merely to take your list of publicity ideas out of the drawer once a day and look at it.

Ilise Benun, president of The Art of Self-Promotion in Hoboken, New Jersey, told me about a startling discovery she made when she began helping clients as a professional organizer. She says, "I would start going through piles of paper with someone, and inevitably at the bottom of the pile there would be some self-promotional thing that they could never bring themselves to do. For example, someone wrote to them asking for information and they just couldn't answer." Why? Her answer is worth thinking about if you say you want to launch publicity for yourself, take a step or two and never get around to following through: "Organizational disaster, I found, is usually a cover for fear of putting your work out into the world."

Reread Chapter 3 if Benun's words hit home.

PART V

KEEPING THE PUBLICITY
MOMENTUM GOING

Chapter 23

Capitalizing and Building on Your Free Publicity

A ndy Warhol, who received plenty of publicity during his life for both his art and his personality, once said, "In the future, everyone will be famous for 15 minutes." Once you receive your first 15 minutes, you'll probably want more, and like Warhol himself, you certainly do not have to remain content with that small portion. For a sustained, expanding media presence, commit yourself to a longterm effort and follow a few simple guidelines.

How to Stretch 15 Minutes of Fame to a Lifetime

Create and maintain a relationship with the media. Write thankyou notes to people who have written about you or put you on the air. Talk show host Al Parinello says that of the 2,500 guests he interviewed, only 10—less than 1 percent—wrote to thank him afterward. Send media contacts more information about what you're up to from time to time, whether a personal note with your next news release, a brief letter along with your new product brochure, or a postcard from Iceland, where you're participating in a trade show.

Among the people I interviewed for this book, I could tell the real pros at publicity because they asked for my address and phone number for their records, wanted to know more about the kind of writing I did, and sent follow-up materials promptly, whether or not I had asked for them. They also stated their willingness to serve as a resource on their specialization or industry. On the other hand, a few said they didn't have time to be interviewed. I'll have more to say about the latter group in a bit.

As with any important career contact, try to give and not just get. After Ethel Cook, a Bedford, Massachusetts, consultant on office management issues, got a write-up about her time-management ideas in *Entrepreneurial Woman,* she sent the editor who had made contact with her clippings about other interesting businesswomen from time to time. "It keeps my name in front of her," Cook explains, "and it gives me a chance to spread the wealth. I do think it will come back to me, but if not, that's okay, too." Similarly, Claudyne Wilder thinks that one of the reasons her book *The Presentations Kit* was featured in a nationally syndicated review column was her attitude when the columnist called her up. "I'm convinced most of us talk too much. I try to be gracious and listen and not just talk. I took the approach, 'Who are you, what do you need, and how can I help you?'" she says. "I suggested other books he might want to review."

Don't turn down publicity opportunities. Saying "I'm too busy" when someone from the media calls you makes about as much sense as saying "No, thanks" when someone says, "I'd like to give you a few thousand dollars of free advertising." Yet one nationally prominent consultant did essentially that when I requested a 20-minute phone interview for this book. First, she set up an appointment for three weeks later; the day before we were to talk, her assistant called to cancel (not reschedule), relaying this answer to my question of what the firm had done to get publicity: "I guess we've just been lucky." They'd be much, much luckier if they gave the press higher priority!

Compare the attitude of Steve Schiffman, who returns media calls even during the days he's on the road presenting seminars. "I tell people we have to take a break because I have to give some quotes to *Success* magazine, and they love it. I got the contract for my second book, *The Consultant's Handbook,* because my editor called and said someone else was supposed to do it but she was too busy. Why on earth would you turn down something like that? I'm always available when someone else pulls out of an interview, whether it's 9 p.m. or whatever." Similarly, Jeffrey Lant told me that, years ago, he put the word out that he'd be available at any time when someone else cancelled, and radio and TV producers did call to ask him to fill in. "Even if I was asleep or sick, I did it," he says.

I've thought a lot about this "no time for interviews" stance and concluded that it must come from fear, ignorance about the benefits of publicity, or an unthinking rigidity about fitting interviews around other obligations. Keep in mind that few magazine or newspaper reporters or book writers keep 9-to-5 hours. Are you sure you can't find 20 minutes in the evening instead of watching the news? One woman crunched away on her lunch while I interviewed her—fine with me. A man once instructed me to call him on Christmas day at his in-laws' house. I worried what his wife's parents would think, but I called. Others have asked me to call while they're driving. In this instance, I try to make sure they have a hands-free hookup. If you really do want the benefits of publicity outlined in Chapter 1, then make time when opportunities arise.

Even if the opportunity seems a small one, seize it. Both Janet Jordan of Keystone Communications and Ethel Cook were featured in *Entrepreneurial Woman* because of articles by or about them in the New England Women Business Owners newsletter, which circulated to just a few hundred people—including magazine editors on the other coast. Similarly, an obscure talk show can be rebroadcast elsewhere and, as social worker/author Merle Bombardieri says, "You never know when a producer or host will get a job with a bigger station and remember you. It happened to me."

Be gracious about snafus. Career journalists have long, long memories and extensive files. I was startled last year to receive an interview request from a reporter for *Investor's Business Daily* who said he'd interviewed me six years before on the same topic. "Just about everything comes around again eventually," he told me. The corollary of this is that complaining about being left out of a story or being uncooperative can sabotage your media chances years afterward. Always be positive when interacting with media representatives.

Keep a file of clippings. The surest, and most expensive, way to get copies of what people write about you is to subscribe to a clipping service, which usually charges a monthly fee plus a certain amount per clipping forwarded to you. (See Chapter 24 for companies that do this.) Until you're being quoted several times a week, you might as well try to track down the clips yourself. You can try asking the journalist who interviewed you to send you a copy of the completed piece, but they often can't or won't. Setting up a free Google news alert notifies you when your name or any other phrase you specify turns up in online news, but this doesn't help for print-only publicity mentions.

You can also ask when the piece is scheduled to appear and how you can order a copy of the publication. Usually newspaper reporters will give you the phone number of the "back copies" department, which charges you a dollar or so for a copy of the paper from a specific date. If you jot down the name and number of the reporter, you can call or e-mail after the date the article was to have appeared to confirm the date so you can order the copy on your own. If the publication that interviewed you is posted online, simply utilize its search box to find the article.

Once you have a copy of the published article, paste it up attractively, cutting it away from any surrounding advertisement, and arranging it concisely on as few pages as possible. Any good print shop knows how to copy newsprint without including type from the opposite side of the page or lines marking the edges of the article. Keep the original in a safe place! I used one clipping as a tip sheet and made copies of copies of copies so many times that it became unreadable. I eventually had to retypeset it to use it again. Although many people duplicate their press clippings on heavy glossy paper, regular copier paper does the job, too.

Most people paste up their press clippings with the masthead (the distinctively styled title from the top of the front page) of the publication and eliminate the publication date after a year or so has gone by. You can obliterate other inconvenient contents, too. From the feature article about him in *The Wall Street Journal*, Jeff Slutsky whited out the prices he was then charging and the name of his former business partner. Be aware that scanning the article as it appeared in print and posting the scanned clip at your Website might be considered a copyright violation. Links to the Web page containing the piece avoid this problem.

If you have a storefront or a waiting room, consider mounting and framing your clippings for the edification of customers or clients. When I'm scouting restaurants in unfamiliar territory and see a review posted in the window next to the menu, it makes a difference. One time, I was walking through midtown Manhattan and stopped to read an interesting article posted in the window of a Mailboxes, Etc. branch store. Because of what I read, I featured that operation in an issue of my Marketing Minute newsletter. Always include copies of your clippings in your media kit and send new ones with an attached personal note to potential clients and other reporters.

5. Let the world know about your publicity successes at your Website. Besides posting links to your coverage in the "News" area of your site, feel free to brag about a recent media hit on your home page. In fact, even when it's not so recent, you should let people know where you're being talked about. Even when the coverage appeared years ago, you can still trumpet on your site "As featured in *Redbook*" or "Praised by *Nebraska Networking News.*"

6. Keep a list of radio and TV shows in which you've participated. As this list grows, it becomes another valuable addition to your media kit. Recontact the producers periodically with new ideas to see if they'd like you to return to the show.

7. Consider creating tip sheets or other enticements so readers and listeners can get in touch with you. By telling a reporter or producer about something you'd like to offer for free, you may accomplish two things: You'll hear directly from people who might be excellent prospects for your products or services, and, when you hear from them, you'll know roughly when and where material about you appeared. With newspapers, particularly, an item might be written up originally for one paper and then, through syndication, show up later in many others. When syndicated business columnist Michael Pellecchia interviewed me about my work on creativity, he mentioned at the end of his article that anyone willing to fill out a two-page questionnaire about their creative process could send a self-addressed stamped envelope to me at my address, which he provided. I received more than 200 responses after his piece appeared in Fort Worth, Texas; Des Moines, Iowa; Newport News, Virginia; and Minneapolis, Minnesota. TV and radio shows often consent to mention your toll-free phone number or Web address. In the case of TV, they'll even flash it on the screen—if you ask. Although many radio and television people shrink from giving out contact information on the air, if you're offering something free to listeners, most stations agree to give out the details.

8. Recycle your publicity materials. I don't mean tossing your clippings into recycle bins, but constantly looking at everything you've done to see how you can get double or triple use out of them. If you've come up with a fresh, fascinating hook for a news release, can you turn it into a tip sheet or a seminar? If a topic for a lecture pulled an overflow crowd that couldn't stop asking questions, why not propose it for a radio call-in show? Letters to the editor can become news releases or op-ed pieces, whereas an appearance on a talk show becomes a pretext for a notice in your alumni magazine and local newspaper. Or how about digging articles you published years ago out of your files and pondering how you might update them for a book proposal?

9. Assess your successes. Try to analyze what went right and why, and use that knowledge for your next media campaign. If you build up a comfortable rapport with a reporter or producer, you can even ask what about your release made them contact you. Michael Pellecchia, the business columnist to which I previously referred, mentioned that he'd never heard of a creativity consultant who worked not with companies but with individuals. That hadn't even occurred to me as something noteworthy about what I was doing. If one news release gets a tremendous response and another nothing, mull over possible reasons and form hypotheses: a headline was weak, the timing was off, the angle wasn't distinctive enough.

10. Let me know what worked for you. Please send me copies of any news releases that worked, along with a note about your results, to Marcia Yudkin, P.O. Box 305, Goshen, MA 01032. In future editions of this book or other writings, I may want to share your success with others—which would mean more free publicity for you. And don't get too busy to celebrate any sort of publicity coup. The glow of passing the word to the public about you or something you believe in can be warm and sweet. Enjoy it.

Chapter 24

Resources for Your Publicity Campaigns

To find the most up-to-date references to online publicity resources, please visit the Resources page of my Website at *www.yudkin.com/ resources.htm*. I'm always happy to learn of new resources that should be added to this list, whether it's a publicity-related service of your company or something you've found useful. Please note that neither here nor on that page do I accept any compensation of any sort for recommending resources.

MEDIA DIRECTORIES AND OTHER REFERENCE WORKS

Just about every sizable library carries at least some of the following resources. Besides the public library in your hometown, investigate the holdings of nearby college and university libraries, whose reference facilities are often open to anyone who walks in. You should also know that if you have one quick reference question, such as "Who's the finance editor of *The Wall Street Journal*?" or "Is there a national organization of inventors?" most library reference departments will look up the answer for you on the phone. Call your library and ask for the reference department.

Bacon's Newspaper/Magazine Directory. Two volumes. *us.cision.com*; (866) 639-5087. The newspaper volume offers names, mail, e-mail, addresses, and phone and fax numbers of daily and weekly newspapers in the United States, Canada, Mexico, and the Caribbean, with names of section editors, as well as lists of columnists and news syndicates. Daily papers are also indexed by "Area of Dominant Influence" (ADI), so you can look up, say, Buffalo, New York, and find listed the newspapers that serve the greater Buffalo area, in descending order of circulation. It also includes office addresses and numbers of syndicated columnists. The magazine volume offers magazines, newsletters, and city/regional business tabloids indexed by subject classifications as well as alphabetically, with names of editors, mail, and e-mail addresses, and fax and phone numbers. Most useful of all, it reveals editors' contact preferences.

Bacon's Radio/TV/Cable Directory. Two volumes. *us.cision.com*; (866) 639-5087. Fewer libraries carry this set than the Newspaper/Magazine set. Contains names, addresses, phone and fax numbers, and profiles of all U.S. and Canadian radio and broadcast or cable TV stations, as well as hosts, producers, and broadcast times for specific programs. Like the Newspaper/Magazine volumes, this has "Area of Dominant Influence" index along with a subject index that allows you to look up, say, "business" or "health," and locate all the relevant shows.

Bowker's News Media Directory. Three volumes. *www.bowker.com*; (888) 269-5372. Volume 1 covers newspapers; Volume 2, magazines and newsletters; Volume 3, radio and TV stations.

Broadcasting and Cable Yearbook. *www.bowker.com*; (888) 269-5372. Geographical listings of all radio, TV, and cable stations in the United States and more than 1,000 in Canada; includes format, target audience, and name of programming director, but not individual hosts/producers. Useful as a starting point for pitch letters or phone pitches; call for names of peopleto whom to pitch.

Chase's Calendar of Events: The Day-by-Day Directory to Special Days, Weeks, and Months. *www.mhprofessional.com* (877) 833-5524. Contains thousands of special days, weeks, months, and anniversaries to which you can tie your publicity, indexed by date, title, and themes.

Directories in Print. *www.galegroup.com* (800) 877-4253. A great source of information about reference works in which you should plant free listings. If you're a consultant, for instance, more than half a dozen directories listed would probably give you free publicity. Includes special "buyers' guide" issues of magazines and membership directories of professional organizations.

Editor and Publisher International Year Book. *www.editorandpublisher.com* (800) 562-2706. Lists daily and weekly newspapers in North, Central and South America, the Caribbean, and Europe, including military, black, gay and lesbian, ethnic, religious, alternative, and college newspapers, all with circulation figures; mail and e-mail addresses; fax and phone numbers; and names of editors.

Encyclopedia of Associations. Three volumes. *www.galegroup.com* (800) 877-4253. Guide to more than 20,000 national organizations, professional societies, trade groups, and interest groups, from the Aaron Burr Association to the ZZ Top International Fan Club, most publishing a newsletter or magazine for members and many representing speaking opportunities; indexed alphabetically by topic, from aardvarks to Zionism.

Gale Directory of Publications and Broadcast Media. Five volumes. *www.galegroup.com*; (800) 877-4253. Geographic listings by state and city of weekly and daily newspapers, magazines, and radio and TV stations. Most periodical listings include editors' names and e-mail addresses; radio and TV entries are less useful, including the format (news, hit radio, country, and so forth) but not names of program hosts or producers.

Literary Market Place. *www.literarymarketplace.com.* Almost every library owns this. Includes listings of freelance editors, ghostwriters, publishing consultants, literary agents, lecture agents, and radio and TV programs that feature books, clipping bureaus, and writers' conferences. The corresponding site offers all the data in the printed volume for paid subscribers and a limited amount of that information for non-subscribers.

National PR Pitch Book. *www.infocomgroup.com* (800) 959-1059. Editions for business, politics, health, technology, food and travel, and financial PR. Each includes individual editors' and reporters' names (pronunciation, too), phones, beats, and e-mail addresses, along with best time to call, pet peeves, and story preferences.

Oxbridge Directory of Newsletters. *www.mediafinder.com* (800) 955-0231. Complete contact information for more than 14,000 U.S. and Canadian newsletters, from *Apartment Law Insider* to *Zen Notes.* States that newsletters constitute 30 percent of all publications.

Standard Periodical Directory. *www.mediafinder.com* (800) 955-0231. Very brief listings of more than 75,000 magazines, yearbooks, and directories published in the United States and Canada, with name of editor-in-chief and contact information. Because subject headings are extremely broad, you'd have to do a lot of searching and screening to use this for sending out news releases.

Standard Rate and Data Service. *www.srds.com*; (800) 851-7737. Two volumes of special interest to *6 Steps* readers: Business Publication Advertising Source and Consumer Magazine Advertising Source. Designed for advertising placements, but helpful for PR placements, too. The consumer volume includes categories such as bridal, crafts, sports, and youth, each with a brief profile, editor's name, circulation, and complete contact information. Most ad agencies subscribe to SRDS and may be happy to donate slightly outdated issues to you rather than the dumpster.

Ulrich's International Periodicals Directory. *www.ulrichsweb.com*; (866) 737-4257. Three hefty volumes. Helpful if you want to publish something professional or academic to be read by, say, actuaries or zoologists. Has international scope so you could send a release (if you should want to) to *Zhongguo Qiyejia* (Chinese Entrepreneurs) or *Saagverken* (Sawmills, published in Sweden). Start with the subject cross-index.

ONLINE MEDIA DIRECTORIES (NO COST)

Alternative Press Online Directory. *www.altpress.org.* Jump site for hundreds of leftist, feminist, and alternative-lifestyle publications.

Computer/Internet Media Directory. *www.online-pr.com/ prcmpmed.htm.* Links for computer, e-commerce, and Internet magazines.

Ecola. *www.ecola.com.* Jump site for more than 8,400 newspapers and magazines and 1,100 TV stations.

ERSys. *www.ersys.com.* Geographically organized directory that leads you to local newspapers, radio, and TV outlets.

Financial Media Directory. *www.online-pr.com/prfinmed.htm.* More than 100 sites that report on the world of finance.

Kidon Media-Link. *www.kidon.com/media-link/index.shtml.* Worldwide and multilingual directory for newspapers.

New Pages Guide to Alternative Periodicals. *www.newpages.com.* Find little-known magazines ranging from *Aboriginal Voices* to *Yoga International*.

Newsletter Access. *www.newsletteraccess.com.* Online directory of some 5,000 print newsletters.

Newslink. *www.newslink.org*. Find links here to thousands of newspapers, magazines, and radio and TV stations worldwide.

Talk Radio Directory. *www.radio-directory.com/fr_newstalk.cfm*. List of radio stations in the United States, Canada, and a few other countries with the news/talk format.

Trade Publications. *www.tradepub.com*. Find hundreds of specialized industry publications here, from *ABA Banking Journal* to *Wireless Week*.

World Wide Arts Resources. *wwar.com/categories/Publications*. Jumping-off page for publications in the visual, literary, and performing arts.

PURCHASABLE OR SUBSCRIPTION-ACCESS MEDIA DATABASES OR LISTS

Contacts on Tap. *www.cornerbarpr.com/cot/signup.cfm*. Online access to media contact information for a low annual fee.

Easy Media List. *www.easymedialist.com*. Quickly create your own custom media list for repeated use, by state, metropolitan area, or industry. Buy only the contacts you need.

Gebbie Press. *www.gebbieinc.com*. Bargain-basement printed media directory and more expensive access to an online media database.

Gordon's Radio List. *www.radiopublicity.net*. Reasonably priced list of more than 1,000 radio shows that interview authors and experts.

Media Contacts Pro. *www.mediacontactspro.com*. Downloadable databases for the U.S. or worldwide.

MediaFinder. *www.mediafinder.com*. Access to online information about magazines, newspapers, catalogs, journals, and newsletters, priced by the month or the year.

Mondo Times. *www.mondotimes.com/member/register.html*. Reasonably priced access to online media database for an annual fee.

Online Press Releases. *www.onlinepressreleases.com*. Combines software and a wide-ranging media database, enabling you to submit your news releases easily to your media targets.

News Release Distribution Services

Ascribe Newswire. *www.ascribe.org.* Low-cost distribution of media releases for nonprofit organizations.

Black PR. *www.blackpr.com.* Low-cost distribution of releases to African-American newspapers, magazines, and TV and radio stations.

Business Wire. *www.businesswire.com.* Efficient vehicle for distributing business-oriented news releases.

Canada NewsWire. *www.newswire.ca.* Use this distribution service for news specific to Canada.

Corporate News. *www.corporatenews.com.* Perfect for high-volume publicists, this service offers one-price, unlimited distribution for three, six, or 12 months.

eReleases. *www.ereleases.com.* Service that delivers your releases to general and targeted media contacts by e-mail.

Emailwire. *www.emailwire.com.* Offers a year's worth of online distribution of an unlimited number of releases for one annual fee.

HispanicPRWire. *www.hispanicprwire.com.* If you need to reach Hispanic media in the United States, use this service.

HotProductNews. *www.hotproductnews.com.* Releasing a new product? Submit your news release about it here, free.

Internet News Bureau. *www.internetnewsbureau.com.* E-mail news release distribution service for related material.

LivePressWire. *www.livepresswire.com.* Segments media circuits by country (United Kingdom, United States, 14 European countries) as well as by topic; you pay at the end of the month.

M2 PressWIRE. *www.presswire.net.* Europe's largest international news release distribution network; charges a flat annual fee rather than per release.

Medianet. *www.medianet.com.au.* Distribution of your news to Australian media.

Pressbox. *www.pressbox.co.uk.* Post your media releases here for free at this UK-based site.

Press Release Network. *www.pressreleasenetwork.com.* Offers a wide range of geographical and industry distribution circuits worldwide.

PR Newswire. *www.prnewswire.com.* Similar to BusinessWire, but geared to distributing releases on general (not business) topics.

EVENT PUBLICITY SERVICES

Craig's List. *www.craigslist.org.* List local events free here, in the subsite for your city or region.

EventCrazy. *www.eventcrazy.com.* After becoming a member of the site (it's free), list your events that are open to the public.

Eventful. *www.eventful.com.* Another listing site that lets you submit events for free.

Full Calendar. *www.fullcalendar.com.* For a small charge per event, this site submits your announcement to event calendars at newspapers, sites, radio stations, and relevant e-mail lists. Covers many but not all metropolitan areas.

Going. *www.going.com.* No-cost event listings at a site geared to the youngish crowd.

Women's Calendar. *www.womenscalendar.org.* Need to publicize an event for women? If you're a nonprofit organization, it's free here; otherwise, there's a fee.

Zvents. *www.zvents.com.* List workshops, concerts, exhibitions, art fairs, sporting events and other events for free, also getting exposure at numerous partner sites.

LEADS SERVICES

Help a Reporter. *www.helpareporter.com.* Free service sending you e-mails from reporters looking for interviewees.

PR Leads. *www.prleads.com.* Leads from reporters and producers, designed for individuals' use and popular with consultants, authors, and speakers.

ProfNet. *www.profnet.com.* Geared for organizations that have multiple experts on staff.

Travel Publicity Leads. *www.travelpublicityleads.com.* Exclusively for those in the travel industry.

EDITORIAL CALENDARS

Media Calendars. *www.mediacalendars.com*. Online access to editorial calendars from thousands of publications for an annual fee.

Wooden Horse Publishing. *www.woodenhorsepub.com*. Inexpensive access to an online database of hundreds of editorial calendars, designed for freelance writers but useful for PR purposes, too.

CLIPPING SERVICES

BurrellesLuce. *www.burrelles.com*; (800) 631-1160. One of the most established clipping services, in business since 1888.

Clip and Copy. *www.clipandcopy.com*; (206) 484-8561. Free clipping service with a scope of more than 300 publications.

Clip Genius. *www.clipgenius.com*. Online clipping service starting at just $17.95 a month.

CyberAlert. *www.cyberalert.com*; (800) 461-7353. National or worldwide clipping service for a monthly fee.

Google News Alerts. *www.google.com/alerts*. For free, get notified by e-mail whenever any phrase you select (such as your name or specialty topic) appears on news or blog sites.

Webclipping.com. *www.webclipping.com*; (212) 965-1900. Monitors sites, online discussion boards, and top online publications.

TELESEMINAR TOOLS

Free Conference Call. *www.freeconferencecall.com*. Use this company's free conference-call lines to present and record teleseminars for up to 96 participants. Yes, it costs nothing!

Seminar Announcer. *www.seminarannouncer.com*. Announce your free teleseminar here, to attract participants at no cost.

Simple Event. *www.simpleevent.com*. Free conference-call line for larger audiences that includes advanced features to better manage multiple presenters for up to 1,000 listeners.

Teleteach for Profit. *www.yudkin.com/teleteach.htm*. A comprehensive home-study course providing all you need-to-know to present teleseminars for publicity or as a profit center.

VoiceText Communications. *www.voicetext.com.* Besides providing bridge lines for rental, they'll record your teleseminar for you to duplicate and sell on CD.

RECOMMENDED BOOKS

Although a few of the older books are out of print, used copies are available at the major online bookstores. Check your local library, too.

ON GETTING MEDIA PUBLICITY

Borden, Kay. *Bulletproof News Releases: Help at Last for the Publicity Deficient,* second edition. Marietta, Ga. Franklin-Sarrett Publishers, 2002. This book is very useful if you're aiming at publicity in your local newspaper.

Brown, Lillian. *Your Public Best,* second edition. New York: Norton, 2003. From the former chief TV make-up artist for CBS News, this book is especially slanted to the needs of political figures, but it offers almost 60 pages of advice for anyone on dressing and making up for TV, along with tips on advanced challenges such as using a teleprompter and surviving a media stakeout at your house.

Kremer, John. *1001 Ways to Market Your Books,* sixth edition. Fairfield, Iowa: Open Horizons, 2006. For publishers and writers, includes plenty of ways to promote books, some offbeat. Revised and updated every few years.

O'Keefe, Steve. *Complete Guide to Internet Publicity: Creating and Launching Successful Online Campaigns.* Hoboken, N.J.: Wiley, 2002. Copious details on constructing online newsrooms, using discussion groups for publicity, creating online contests, and running chat tours, especially for authors.

Parinello, Al. *On the Air: How to Get on Radio and TV Talk Shows and What to Do When You Get There.* Franklin Lakes, N.J.: Career Press, 1991. Delightful guide to doing your best on radio and TV talk shows by the co-host of a syndicated radio show. Most valuable features: translations of studio hand signals and a list of professions of which producers are wary for guests.

Rein, Irving, Philip Kotler, Michael Hamlin, and Martin Stoller. *High Visibility: Transforming Your Personal and Professional Brand*, third edition. New York: Mc-Graw-Hill, 2005. An eye-opening quasi-academic study of the process of making and maintaining celebrityhood, in entertainment, sports, politics, the professions, and other realms, including the role of coaches, managers, and the media, as well as the person aspiring to fame and his or her audience.

Ryan, Charlotte. *Prime Time Activism.* Boston: South End Press, 1991. A fascinating treatise on the politics of newsworthiness. Highly recommended if you're trying to get publicity for a cause.

Schmertz, Herb, with William Novak. *Goodbye to the Low Profile: The Art of Creative Confrontation.* Boston: Little, Brown and Co., 1986. If *60 Minutes* calls you, hold them off until you run to the library and borrow this book. Excellent advice for dealing with hostile media, from a vice president for public affairs at Mobil Oil.

Scott, David Meerman. *The New Rules of Marketing and PR: How to Use News Releases, Blogs, Podcasting, Viral Marketing and Online Media to Reach Buyers Directly.* Hoboken, N.J.: Wiley, 2007. Very good overview of the possibilities of social media and online marketing to supplement or bypass the traditional media.

Vitale, Joe, and Jeffrey Gitomer. *There's a Customer Born Every Minute: P.T. Barnum's Amazing 10 "Rings of Power" for Creating Fame, Fortune, and a Business Empire Today, Guaranteed!* Hoboken, N.J.: Wiley, 2006. Highly entertaining and illuminating account of the legendary show promoter P.T. Barnum's methods of attracting attention, many of which are still applicable today.

Yale, David R., and Andrew J. Carothers. *The Publicity Handbook, New Edition: The Inside Scoop from More than 100 Journalists and PR Pros on How to Get Great Publicity Coverage.* New York: McGraw-Hill, 2001. Recommended for nonprofit organizations, this book includes guidelines for press conferences, choosing and training spokespeople, handling crisis situations, and useful checklists for all the basic strategies.

ON GETTING PUBLISHED

Bennett, Hal Zina, with Michael Larsen. *How to Write With a Collaborator.* New York: BackinPrint.com, 2004. If I've convinced you that getting your work into print makes sense but you know you lack the time or skill to write yourself, consult this book on the collaboration option. Contains sample collaboration agreements and a comprehensive overview of the benefits and pitfalls of cowriting.

Guide to Literary Agents. Cincinnati, Ohio: Writer's Digest Books. Annual directory of literary agents who can place a book manuscript with a publisher, divided into those who charge up-front fees and those who charge only commissions, and indexed by the kind of material they are willing to consider. Available in most bookstores that have a writing or publishing section.

Herman, Jeff. *Jeff Herman's Guide to Book Publishers, Editors, and Literary Agents.* Stockbridge, Mass.: Three Dog Press. Annually updated. Along with the Writer's Digest volume just listed, another terrific resource for finding a literary agent or a publisher. Includes personal data about book publishing personnel so that you can match interests and backgrounds with the subject matter of your book project.

Poynter, Dan. *Dan Poynter's Self-Publishing Manual: How to Write, Print and Sell Your Own Book 16th edition.* Santa Barbara, Calif.: Para Publishing, 2007. With a computer and page-layout software, it's easier than ever to turn your ideas into a credibility-enhancing book. Poynter takes you through all the steps from generating the contents of the book to getting it printed, promoting it, and then coping with being a published author.

Writer's Market. Cincinnati, Ohio: Writer's Digest Books. Annually updated. Indispensable resource if you want to write for magazines. Lists thousands of consumer and trade magazines, with contact information, pay rates, kinds of material each publication seeks, in subject areas ranging from advertising to women's magazines. Its list of book publishers is too spotty to be of much help. Widely available in bookstores and libraries; list price for the 2008 edition was just $29.99, with the same price for the online edition, available at *www.writersmarket.com.*

Yudkin, Marcia. *Freelance Writing for Magazines and Newspapers: Breaking In Without Selling Out.* New York: HarperCollins, 1988. "Anyone who buys Ms. Yudkin's book can count on a huge return on his or her investment. I don't think I've ever read a dissection of my profession that was as thorough, as fair-minded and as full of genuinely helpful information." —C. Michael Curtis, Senior Editor, *Atlantic Monthly.*

ON WRITING

Goldstein, Norm, editor. *The Associated Press Stylebook and Briefing on Media Law.* New York: Basic Books, 2007. Alphabetical directory to standardized spelling, usage, punctuation, and so on, with special chapters on avoiding libel, respecting copyright, and using the Freedom of Information Act.

Levine, Rick, Christopher Locke, Doc Searls, and David Weinberger. *The Cluetrain Manifesto: The End of Business as Usual.* New York: Basic Books, 2001. If your boss expects you to write publicity materials that sound like a bureaucrat, read this book for impassioned arguments on why that's a foolish approach.

Venolia, Jan. *Rewrite Right! How to Revise Your Way to Better Writing.* Berkeley, Calif.: Ten Speed Press, 2000. Highly recommended handbook for editing your own news releases, tip sheets, and articles. Advice on cutting out jargon, clichés, and sexist language and on putting in the commas, apostrophes, and capital letters that the media expects.

ON SPEAKING

Schloff, Laurie, and Marcia Yudkin. *Smart Speaking.* New York: Plume, 1991. A problem-solving guide to communicating effectively in more than 100 situations, from calling people you don't know to speaking to an audience to coping with poor listeners.

Walters, Dottie, and Lillet Walters. *Speak And Grow Rich,* revised edition. New York: Prentice-Hall, 1997. Solid overview of the speaking industry by the longtime owner of a speaking bureau.

Weiss, Alan. *Money Talks: How to Make a Million as a Speaker.* New York: McGraw-Hill, 1998. Opinionated yet practical advice on getting speaking gigs and turning them into a revenue stream, from someone with the Ferrari and testimonials that prove his success.

RECOMMENDED PUBLICATIONS

Book Marketing Update. *www.bookmarketingupdate.com*; (484) 477-4220, Ext. 106. If you're an author or publisher, this newsletter gives you insider tips, creative ideas, success stories, and contact information for getting on major talk shows and publicizing books in other ways.

Free Publicity. *www.publicityinsider.com*. Substantive tips on getting media coverage without spending a fortune, from PR veteran Bill Stoller.

Publicity Hound. *www.publicityhound.com*; (262) 284-7451. Useful and engaging free weekly newsletter from Joan Stewart, containing tips, resources and a "Help this Publicity Hound" feature.

Media Relations Report. *www.ragan.com*; (800) 878-5331. Geared toward PR practitioners for medium to large organizations, contains features on pitching and media trends.

PUBLICITY RESOURCES

ABC Pictures
1867 E. Florida St.
Springfield, MO 65803
www.abcpictures.com
(888) 526-5336

A wholesale source of inexpensive glossy lithographed photos appropriate for inclusion in media kits. In 2008, for example, 500 8 × 10 black-and-white head shots cost just $90.

RADIO-TV INTERVIEW REPORT

Bradley Communications Corp.
390 Reed Road
Broomall, PA 19008
www.rtir.com
(484) 477-4220

Virtually everyone I know who's been listed here felt they more than got their money's worth of radio interviews. Fee includes help coming up with an angle that makes sense for radio/TV. Most of those listed are book authors; suggest that your publisher pay.

PROFESSIONAL ORGANIZATIONS

International Women's Writing Guild
Caller Box 810
Gracie Station
New York, NY 10028
www.iwwg.com
(212) 737-7536

Newsletter and conferences that help women connect with a collaborator or ghostwriter, freelance writers, or someone willing to coach you to the professional exposure you want.

National Speakers Association
1500 S. Priest Drive
Tempe, AZ 85281
www.nsaspeaker.org
(480) 968-2552

Professional education, networking; more than 30 local chapters throughout the United States and Canada.

National Writers Union
113 University Place, 6th Floor
New York, NY 10003
www.nwu.org
(212) 254-0279

Agitates for better working conditions for writers, represents writers in grievances against publishers; professional education and networking.

Public Relations Society of America
33 Maiden Lance, 11ᵗʰ Floor
New York, NY 10003
www.prsa.org
(212) 460-1400
Organization for professional PR people, with more than 100 local chapters.

Toastmasters International
P.O. Box 9052
Mission Viejo, CA 92690
www.toastmasters.org
(949) 858-8255
Structured program of mutual aid in becoming better speakers; speaking contests and awards. 8,500 local chapters throughout the world.

Association for Women in Communications
3337 Duke St.
Alexandria, VA 22314
www.womcom.org
(703) 370-7436
Professional organization for women in journalism, PR, marketing, graphic design, and related fields.

RECOMMENDED MEDIA COACHES

1) **Susan Harrow**
   Harrow Communications
   4200 Park Blvd, #333 W
   Oakland CA 94602
   (888) 839-4190
   www.prsecrets.com
   harrowcom@prsecrets.com

2) **Laurie Schloff**

The Speech Improvement Company

1614 Beacon Street

Brookline, MA 02446

(617) 739-3330

www.speechimprovement.com

laurie@speechimprovement.com

3) **Rebecca Shafir**

Mindful Communication

61 Turkey Hill Road

West Newbury, MA 01985

(978) 255-1817

www.mindfulcommunication.com

rebeccashafir@att.net

4) **Cynthia White**

IndependentActor NYC

11 Maiden Lane, #8C

New York, NY 10038

(212) 587-7756

www.independentactor.com/mediacoaching.html

cwhite@independentactor.com

RESOURCES ON SEARCH ENGINES

Keyword Suggestion Tool. *inventory.overture.com.* Type in a word or phrase and see how often people searched for it in the previous month.

Search Engine Watch. *www.searchenginewatch.com.* Stay up to date or catch up on the latest changes in the world of search engines.

SEO Tools. *tools.seobook.com.* Free tools for researching keyword popularity, checking your Google rank and more, along with free search engine optimization tutorials.

Wordtracker. *www.wordtracker.com.* Click on "free trial" to research and compare how many searches are performed on particular keywords and phrases.

OTHER RECOMMENDED ONLINE RESOURCES

All About Public Relations. *aboutpublicrelations.net.* Excellent collection of articles on various aspects of online and offline PR.

Article Directories. *www.arcanaweb.com/resources/article-directories.html.* Frequently updated directory of general and topical article banks to which you can submit articles to increase your traffic.

Buzzkiller. *www.buzzkiller.net.* Learn which trendy phrases journalists hate and why.

Contact Any Celebrity. *www.contactanycelebrity.com.* For a small fee, find addresses for political, literary, or entertainment figures to seek endorsements or blurbs.

Industry Portals. *www.virtualpet.com/industry/mfg/mfg.htm.* Industry by industry, sites you'll want to check out when trying to reach a narrow audience.

Naming and Branding Articles. *www.namedatlast.com/namingarticles.htm.* Learn how and why to give your offering a newsworthy name and clever tag line.

Publicity Resources. *www.yudkin.com/resources.htm.* My most up-to-date list of recommended PR and marketing resources on the Web.

Sample Campaigns and Documents. *www.patronsaintpr.com/samples.html.* Sample publicity materials from online publicity pioneer Steve O'Keefe.

Index

About the Author

Since her first appearance in print in the Sunday *New York Times* in 1981, Marcia Yudkin has built a global reputation as an author, publicity and marketing consultant, and speaker.

Her 11 books include *Web Site Marketing Makeover* (Top Floor Publishing) and *Internet Marketing for Less than $500/Year* (Maximum Press). Her articles have appeared in hundreds of magazines, including *The New York Times Magazine*, *TWA Ambassador*, *USAir Magazine*, and *Business 2.0*. She has been featured in *Success Magazine*, *Entrepreneur*, *Business96*, *Business99*, *Home Office Computing*, *Working Woman*, dozens of newspapers throughout the world, and four times in the Sunday *Boston Globe*.

Her "Marketing Minute" segment ran weekly for more than a year on WABU TV throughout New England, and she has written and delivered numerous commentaries on WBUR, the National Public Radio station in Boston, as well as on NPR's national "Marketplace" program. Her free weekly newsletter on creative marketing and publicity reaches many thousands of loyal subscribers from all around the world.

Marcia Yudkin's consulting clients include small- to medium-sized businesses and professional firms, from Internet entrepreneurs, software manufacturers, and publishers, to attorneys, physicians, financial planners, videographers, writers, and consultants. She has spoken on how to get publicity for national conferences and regional trade associations.

To reach Marcia, visit her Websites at *www.yudkin.com* or *www.pressreleasehelp.com* or e-mail her at marcia@yudkin.com.